HOW TO DO

AIRCRAFT SHEETMETAL WORK

How to Do

Aircraft Sheetmetal Work

BY

CARL NORCROSS

Managing Editor, "Aviation" Magazine; Author of "Getting a Job in Aviation"; Coauthor of "The Aviation Mechanic"

AND

JAMES D. QUINN, JR.

Lieut. (jg), U.S.N.R.; Officer in Charge, Ground School, U.S. Naval Air Station, New York; Formerly in Charge of the Aviation Trades Center, National Defense Training Program, New York City; Coauthor of "The Aviation Mechanic"

McGRAW-HILL BOOK COMPANY, INC.

NEW YORK AND LONDON

How to Do Aircraft Sheet Metal Work

by Carl Norcross
and James D. Quinn Jr

Originally published by
McGraw-Hill Book Company Inc
New York

Reprinted by
Lindsay Publications Inc
Bradley IL 60915

ISBN 1-55918-189-3

2 3 4 5 6 7 8 9 0

1997

PREFACE

The largest single group of men in most aircraft plants consists of those who handle sheetmetal. They do a wide variety of work, but regardless of whether they cut or file, form or rivet, finish or assemble aircraft parts, they are of more value to the factory, and to the nation as well, if they have a basic understanding of aircraft sheetmetal work.

It is the aim of this book to present the fundamentals of airplane sheetmetal processes and to do this in clear, simple language. The technical language and complex formulas of the aeronautical engineer are not needed here and, consequently, are not to be found in this book. Clearness, accuracy, and brevity are constantly emphasized.

This is primarily a how-to-do-it book. The text has been organized logically from a teaching viewpoint, beginning with the simplest processes and leading on step by step to the more difficult jobs. It is believed that students learn most quickly if they know why they are required to learn a particular process. Consequently there is considerable motivation in the chapters that follow. Learning is also more rapid if there are clear, well-selected photographs and drawings. The authors studied hundreds of photographs and believe that those that were chosen add considerably to the value to the book.

The subject matter of the book is based on several sources of information. The authors have visited nearly all the aircraft factories in the United States since they began work on this book. They have talked with personnel directors, factory superintendents, shop foremen, army and navy inspectors, and with mechanics on the job. By utilizing all this experience, the book attempts to train men for aircraft work in a way that has been specified by military air services and by the aircraft industry.

The authors have analyzed courses of study of many of the leading private and public aviation schools and have benefited by this experience in choosing and arranging the subject matter. Likewise, the book benefits from the many years of experience that one of the authors had in a large aviation high school and in the United States Navy. The authors also have had the good fortune to be able to study the many manuscripts that come in each month to *Aviation* magazine from production engineers and factory superintendents in all parts of the country. This has been a means of keeping up to date on changing processes.

Each chapter of the book is followed by 10 or more questions. Ability to answer these questions is a good indication that the student has mastered the subject matter of the book.

The five projects of Chap. 15 require all the basic sheetmetal skills and the use of the common sheetmetal tools. To complete these projects in a satisfactory manner requires from 160 to 175 hours of shopwork. Additional projects for shopwork may be developed from the blueprints of Chap. 1. The authors have concluded, after visiting many public and private schools, that most schools prefer to use their own projects for the practice of riveting, drilling, and other work where the same job must be repeated many times. However, a close study of the projects of Chap. 15 will convince the instructor that a surprisingly wide variety of skills is necessary to complete the work. In addition, two of the projects become useful tools for the sheetmetal mechanic to add to his toolbox.

Preparing a book is always a joint undertaking. Many people and aviation firms have been helpful in providing material and photographs. Most of the photographs were sent to *Aviation* magazine by airplane companies, and the sources of individual pictures have been acknowledged in the captions. A number of photographs were taken especially for this book by Gerald Moran and Hans Basken of the McGraw-Hill Publishing Company. Drawings were made under the supervision of Henry Groll. Their help is appreciated. Blueprints were received from several firms whose names are listed on the drawings.

Appreciation is due to Elliott V. Noska, Principal of the Manhattan High School for Aviation Trades. Thanks are especially due to John Walden who has made many helpful suggestions, and to the following other aircraft sheetmetal instructors: Francis Newcomb, John Wirth, Santo Frontario, and Capt. C. L. Youmans. Miss Phyllis Brock was of great assistance in reading proofs of the book and her help is greatly appreciated.

C. N.,

NEW YORK CITY. J. D. Q., JR.

CONTENTS

HOW TO DO AIRCRAFT SHEETMETAL WORK

CHAPTER 1

SIMPLE BLUEPRINT READING

Blueprints are the language of the engineer. They convey the ideas and directions of the engineer to the man in the shop who is either making or assembling parts. Blueprints contain in brief form as much information as could be written out in a number of pages of directions. If a sheetmetal mechanic is to make progress in his work, he must understand the engineer's language and directions.

A few years ago, when airplane plants were relatively small and when every mechanic was able to do a variety of work, it was essential that all shopmen know how to read blueprints. Today aircraft factories have grown to tremendous size, and an era of specialization has begun. In most aircraft plants it is not necessary that every worker know how to read prints. In fact, many workers in a sheetmetal department are not given an opportunity to work from blueprints. They work under the close direction of a crew chief, or leadman, who handles all the required prints. A mechanic may work from a pattern or operate a simple machine and make the same part time after time. He receives his instruction from a leadman or from a subforeman and can turn out satisfactory work without being able to follow directions on a print. The same is true in assembly departments.

Blueprint reading, however, is a necessary qualification if a man is to gain promotion. When aircraft factories are in a period of rapid expansion, it is often possible for a new employee to become a leadman in fairly short time, especially if he has had a thorough training. Blueprint reading is one of the first essentials for advancement.

In most aircraft plants a knowledge of blueprint reading is also a great advantage to a man applying for a job. Even though he may be assigned to a department where he will not handle prints, his chances for getting a job are much better if he is familiar with the rudiments of reading engineering drawings.

In a book of this size it is impossible to discuss all phases of blueprint reading. A book of 100 pages or more devoted solely to blueprints would be needed to cover all phases of aeronautical prints and the variations that exist in different factories. However, a beginning sheetmetal man is not required to handle complicated assembly drawings or interpret difficult prints. In this brief chapter only basic but essential data on blueprint reading are included. The information given here is sufficient to help you to get your first job and to understand simple blueprints.

Scale of Drawings.—Parts shown on blueprints are drawn in several different scales, and the scale is marked on the print. Scales are full size, double size, one-half, or one-quarter, that is, in relation to the actual size of the part to be made. Measurements must always be determined from the dimension sizes given on the prints. Never use a ruler or a pair of dividers to take measurements directly from blueprints. When the print was made, the paper may have shrunk slightly; and if you measure the print, your dimensions will probably be incorrect. Prints vary in size from small sheets that would fit into your notebook to prints 12 ft. or more in length.

Classes of Prints.—There are three principal classes of blueprints: detail drawings, assembly drawings, and installation drawings.

Detail drawings are of a single part. These are the easiest to understand, as they are less complicated than other classes of prints. They show the fabrication of the individual part, including such operations as cutting, drilling, filing, and forming.

Assembly drawings show how two or more parts are secured together. They show the location of each part and describe the bolts, rivets, welds, or screws that hold the parts together. When an assembly print shows a relatively large part of an airplane, such as a wing section, it is called a *major assembly print*.

Installation drawings describe how an auxiliary unit or a system is installed in the airplane. Thus drawings showing how machine guns are mounted in the wings or the installing of the electrical system would be called *installation prints*.

Title Block.—When you study a blueprint, the first thing that you should look at is the title block. This is drawn in a box, usually in the lower right-hand corner, but sometimes it extends along the entire lower margin of the print. It tells you even more than the name of the part, the assembly, or the installation, as it gives the name of the company for whom the print is drawn, the materials used, the airplane model, how many parts per ship are needed, the scale of the drawing, the tolerances required, the finish necessary, the number and date of the print, and often considerable other information. Do not depend on your memory or ability to recognize drawings at a glance. You may choose the wrong part or select the wrong material to make it. Always study the title block.

Figure 1 is a reproduction of a blueprint from the Douglas Aircraft Co. The *title block* is in the lower right corner, and the *change block* is at the lower left. First note the number. The first figure in a blueprint number *usually* denotes the size of paper on which the print is made, although all firms do not follow this practice. This is for easy identification of prints when a search is being made in a file. The numeral 1 denotes a print 8½ by 11 in., which is the smallest standard size. A numeral 2 denotes a print 11 by 17 in.; 3 indicates a print 11 by 34 in.; 4 is a 17 by 22 in. print; and 5 is any size larger than 4. In some factories the letters "A" to "E" are used instead to denote these five classifications, and others use a numbering system from 1 to 9, or 1 to 13, or have developed their own system.

On the bottom line look for the name of the part. The most important word is put first in the title, and the rest of the title describes the part. The scale is full size. Considerable information is given as to the material from which this support is to be made. Under "Material" you will see that the print calls for aluminum-alloy sheet that is 0.051 in. in thickness. The description also specifies that the sheet be of 24S-O Alclad, which is Alclad sheet in the annealed state that must later be heat-treated. Both Army and Navy specifications for this material are indicated by number (AC11067 Type I; Navy 47-A-8 Cond. A), details of which are given in Army and Navy books. (The AC signifies Air Corps). As far as the mechanic is concerned, the kind and the thickness of the material used are of chief importance.

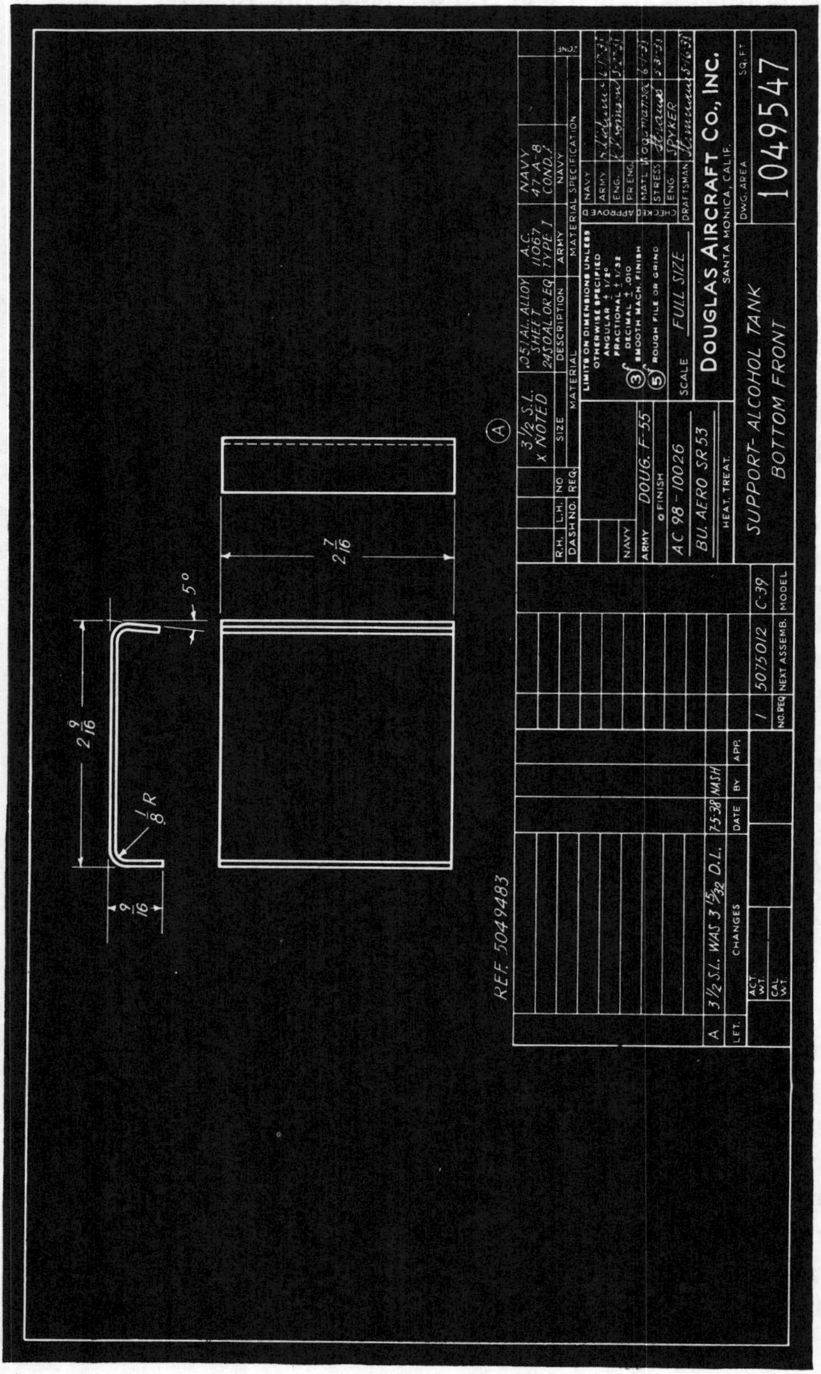

FIG. 1.—A detail drawing from the Douglas Aircraft Co.

The size of the sheet from which the part is made is given as $3\frac{1}{2}$S.L. The letters signify *stock length.* Dimensions are always given in inches. The letter "A" in a circle just above the size means a change. If you look at the lower left-hand corner of the print, you will see a letter "A" followed by a statement that formerly $3\frac{1}{2}$S.L. (stock length) had been $3\frac{15}{32}$ D.L. (D.L. is developed length). Stock width is noted on the drawing.

The date and the name of the person making the change is given. If another change had been made on this print, the letter "B" would be on the line above, and a "B" in a circle on the print would indicate the place of the change. The third change would be lettered "C," and so on. Every line of the change block should be closely scrutinized.

In the column labeled "No. Req." you will see that one support only is needed for each airplane (see bottom line); after the part is made, details of how it is assembled to the ship are shown on print 5075012, as is indicated in the "Next Assem." column. Note also that the part is for model C-39 (which is a Douglas transport built for the Army Air Corps).

Title blocks usually show how a part is to be finished. This part must be finished according to Air Corps specification 98-10026, which is the same as the Bureau of Aeronautics (Navy) specification SR53. This information is found in Army and Navy specification books for guidance. Often different parts of a detail part are finished in different ways. This is shown on a print by a small circle next to the appropriate part with a letter "f" joined to the right-hand side, as shown in the center of this title block. The figure in the circle denotes the finish, as follows:

1. Buff.
2. Hand finish.
3. Smooth machine finish.
4. Rough machine finish.
5. File or grind.
6. Sand blast.

A number of firms have different finish numbers.

Tolerances, or possible variations in dimensions, are usually included in title blocks. Occasionally this is not done, as an aircraft firm has standard tolerances that are understood to apply unless mention is made to the contrary. On the title block that we are discussing, the tolerances are stated for *angular, fractional,* and *decimal* measurements. The fractional tolerances are given as plus or minus $\frac{1}{32}$ in. This means that a measurement of $2\frac{7}{16}$ in., for example, is still acceptable if it is $\frac{1}{32}$ in. over or $\frac{1}{32}$ in. under that amount. The angle of 5 deg. shown on the print may actually be at any point between $4\frac{1}{2}$ and $5\frac{1}{2}$ deg. to be acceptable, as the tolerance allowance is $\frac{1}{2}$ deg.

At the right of this title block are the initials of the draftsmen and engineers who drew or approved the print, with the dates on which they signed their initials. You will also observe that although this is a small and relatively insignificant part, the Army inspector also approved the drawing.

Most aviation schools have a number of aircraft prints of all sizes. The student should take every opportunity to study title blocks so as to note the variations among prints and among different aircraft concerns.

Numbering Systems.—As mentioned previously, the first figure in the blueprint number usually denotes the size of the paper on which the print is made. The rest of the number is assigned to that particular print for identification. This number is for filing and reference.

Dash Numbers.—Many pairs of airplane parts are identical except that one part is made for the left side of the plane and the other part for the right side. In such cases much time is saved in drawing prints if both parts can be made from the same print. It is customary to show the drawing for the left-hand part. Above the title block is printed the number, such as:

45678 L. H. shown.
45678-1 R. H. opposite.

This means that the right-hand part is a mirror duplication of the left-hand part shown in the drawing. The left wing of a plane, for example, will not fit the right side. Yet if the left wing is held before a large mirror, the image in the glass would seem to fit on the right side. You can prove this to yourself by holding your left hand so the back of it is toward a mirror. It looks like a right hand. The figure "-1" is usually reserved for the right-hand part.

All plants do not follow this rule. At the Glenn L. Martin Co. a drawing that covers both a left and a right part is given two numbers, an uneven number for the left side and the next higher number for the right side. Other firms have their own numbering systems.

When several parts are shown in one print, each part has a different dash number, which is often enclosed in a small circle. The circle is placed near the part that it identifies, and a straight line with an arrow points to the part, or the line connects with the border of the part.

It is of utmost importance that you determine in advance whether the print calls for a left- or a right-hand part; otherwise the part made may be useless, and the material and time may be wasted.

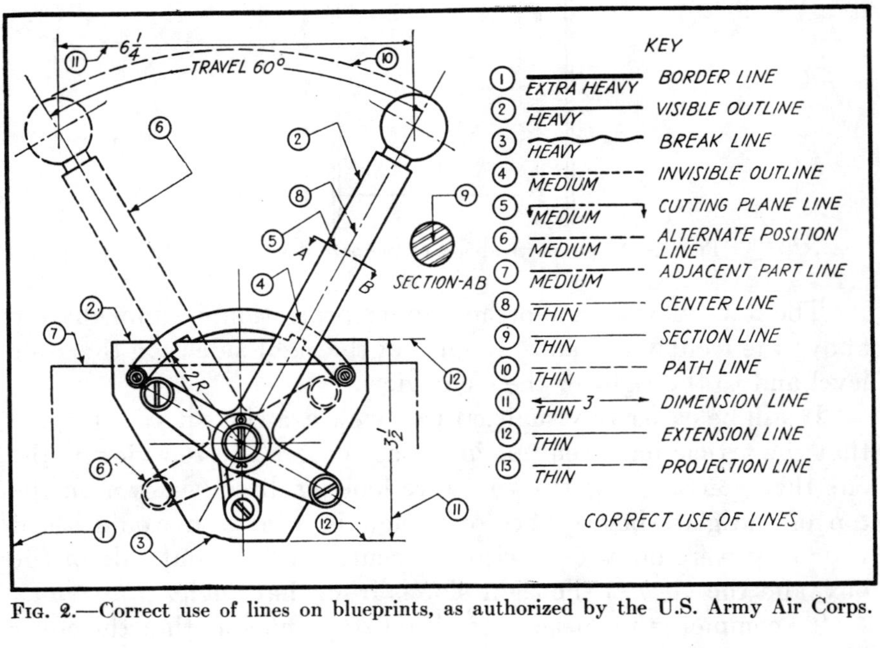

FIG. 2.—Correct use of lines on blueprints, as authorized by the U.S. Army Air Corps.

Alphabet of Lines.—If you have studied blueprints, you have noticed that various kinds of lines are used in the drawings. Each line has significance. The correct use of lines, as approved by the Air Corps, is shown in Fig. 2.

Orthographic Projection.—Blueprints are drawn to what is called *orthographic projection*. This means that all projecting lines lie at right angles to the plane of projection. It is most common to show three views: a top view, a front view, and a side view. Sometimes only one or two views are shown when a part is made from a flat sheet or when it is easy to understand a part with less than three views.

The tank support of Fig. 1 is shown in Fig. 3 in a perspective drawing.

When you see the drawing in perspective, you immediately recognize its shape because you are used to seeing sketches made in this way. At first three-view drawings will seem strange to you, but in a short time they will become as familiar as perspective drawings now are.

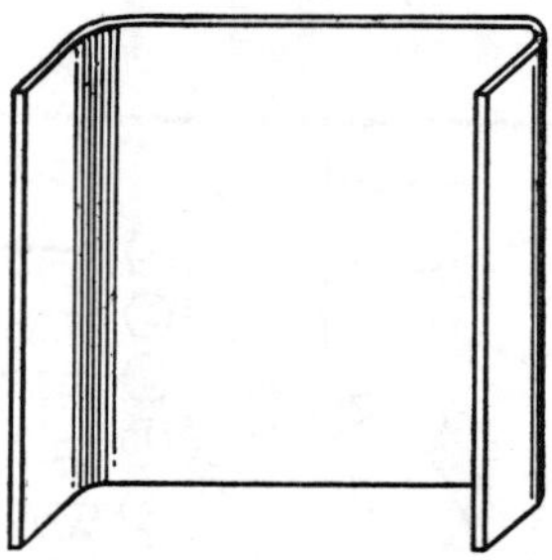

FIG. 3.—A perspective view of the part shown in Fig. 1.

The top view of an orthographic projection is immediately above the front view, and the view of the right side is on the same level and to the right of the front view.

It will be easier to visualize three-view drawings if you imagine that the article has been put in a glass box. The top view is the one that you would get if you were looking directly down on the top of the glass box. The front view is what you would see if your eyes were on a level with the center of the front side of the box, and the view of the right side is from that angle.

To complete this method of visualizing, imagine that the cover of the box is swung up and lies on the same plane as the front view. Imagine also that the right side is hinged at the front and swung around to be parallel with the front. The result is the way that blueprint drawings appear. This is shown graphically in Fig. 4.

Note that in the front view there are two vertical lines at the left and three at the right. The two at the left show the thickness of the metal sheet. At the right edge you see the thickness of the sheet; and as that side is bent in at a 5 deg. angle, you also see the rear corner. The view of the right side contains a dash line, denoting the thickness of the sheet. The dimensions given in Fig. 1 are self-explanatory except for the ⅛R, which signifies ⅛ in. radius for the bend.

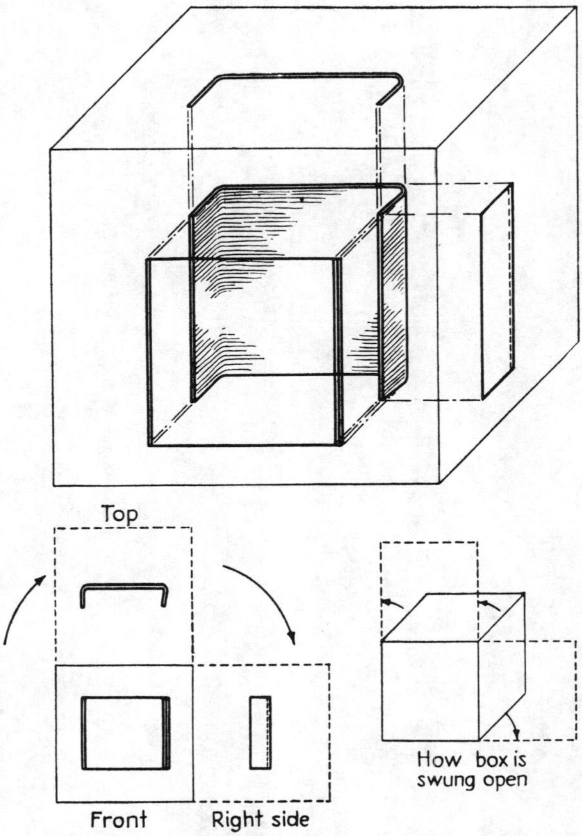

FIG. 4.—How to visualize orthographic drawings.

Figure 5 shows three bulkhead angles used in a Grumman G-23. The entire print is given, but concentrate at first on visualizing the parts shown. When you study the top view of the fitting on the left, it does not tell you very much. But add the front view just below it, and you begin to get a picture of the fitting. However, when you study these two views with that of the right view, you conclude that the part looks like the drawing on the left in Fig. 6.

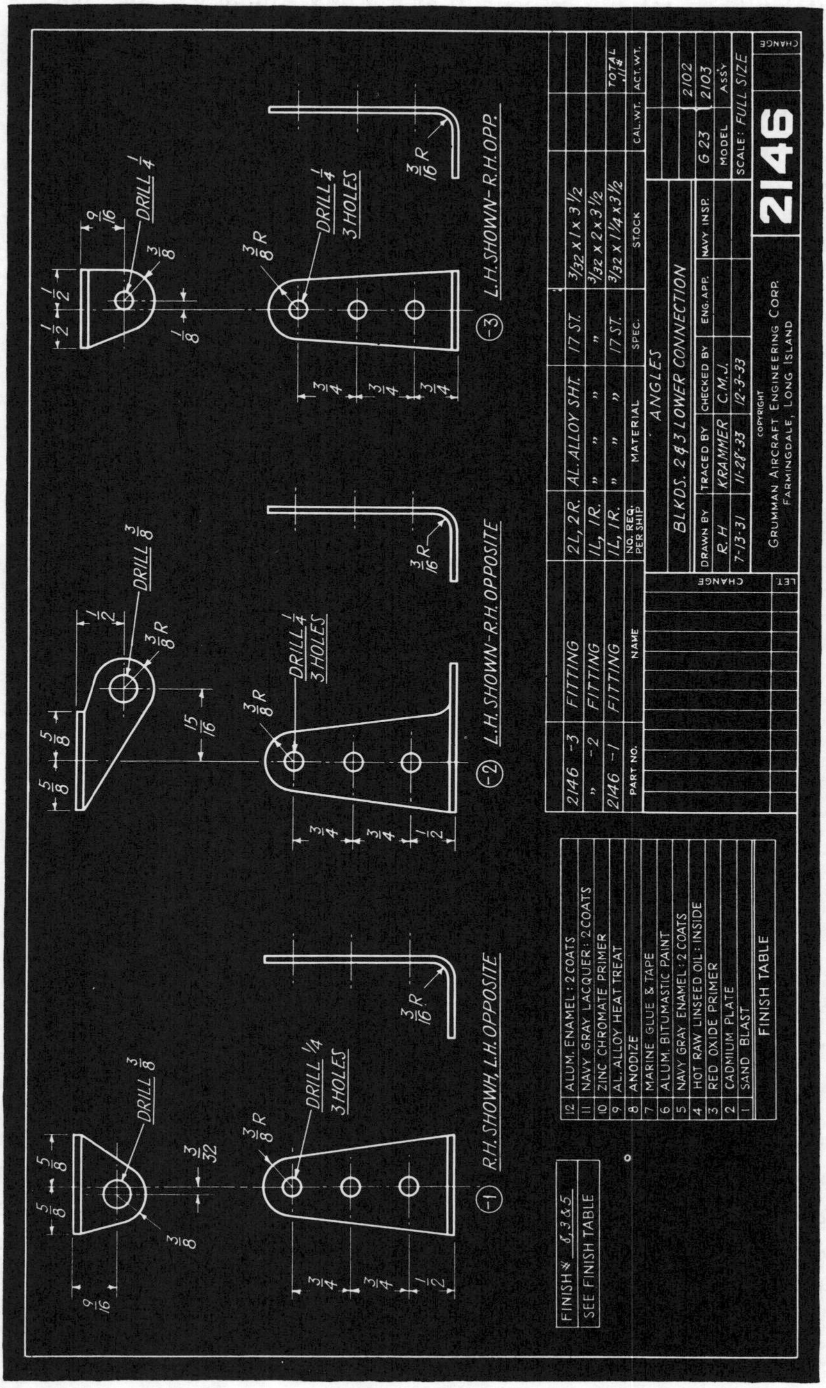

FIG. 5.—Drawing of bulkhead angles for a Grumman airplane.

The center drawing in Fig. 5 is a little more difficult to visualize. Study the drawing, and you will see that the fitting is much the same as that on the left except that the bend at the bottom is at a different angle, as at the right in Fig. 6. The fitting at the right in Fig. 5 is a variation of these two.

There are several points about the print shown in Fig. 5 that you should study. As three parts are shown on the one drawing, notice that each part has a separate number. That shown on the

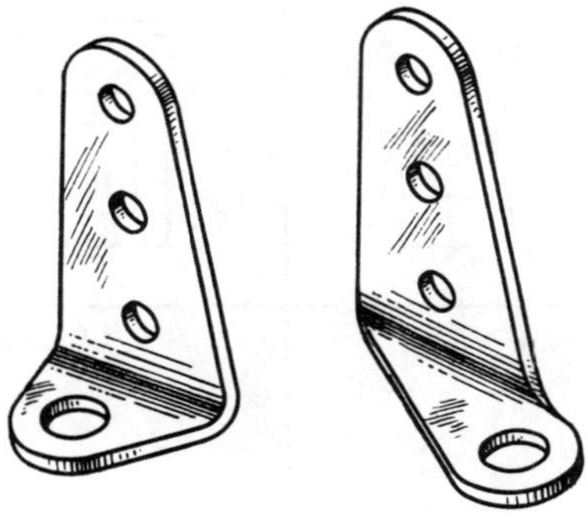

FIG. 6.—Perspective drawings for detail parts of Fig. 5.

left is 2146-1. It is a *right-hand* part, and the left-hand part is opposite. Note that the drawing calls for one such left-hand part and one right-hand part.

The drawing in the center is 2146-2 and is a left-hand part. One left-hand and one right-hand part are called for. The drawing on the right is 2146-3 and is a left-hand part, for which the print calls for two left-hand and two right-hand parts.

Study the material from which these angles are made, the specifications, and the stock sizes listed in the title block. Also note that the Grumman finish table, stamped at the left of the title block, is different from that given previously. The fittings shown must be finished to 8, 3, and 5 specifications, which call for anodizing, red oxide primer, and two coats of Navy gray enamel.

In order to provide additional practice in quickly visualizing blueprints, ten parts are shown in Fig. 7 on page 12. In each case two of the three views are shown, but one is missing. Study the two views, and then with a pencil sketch the view that is missing.

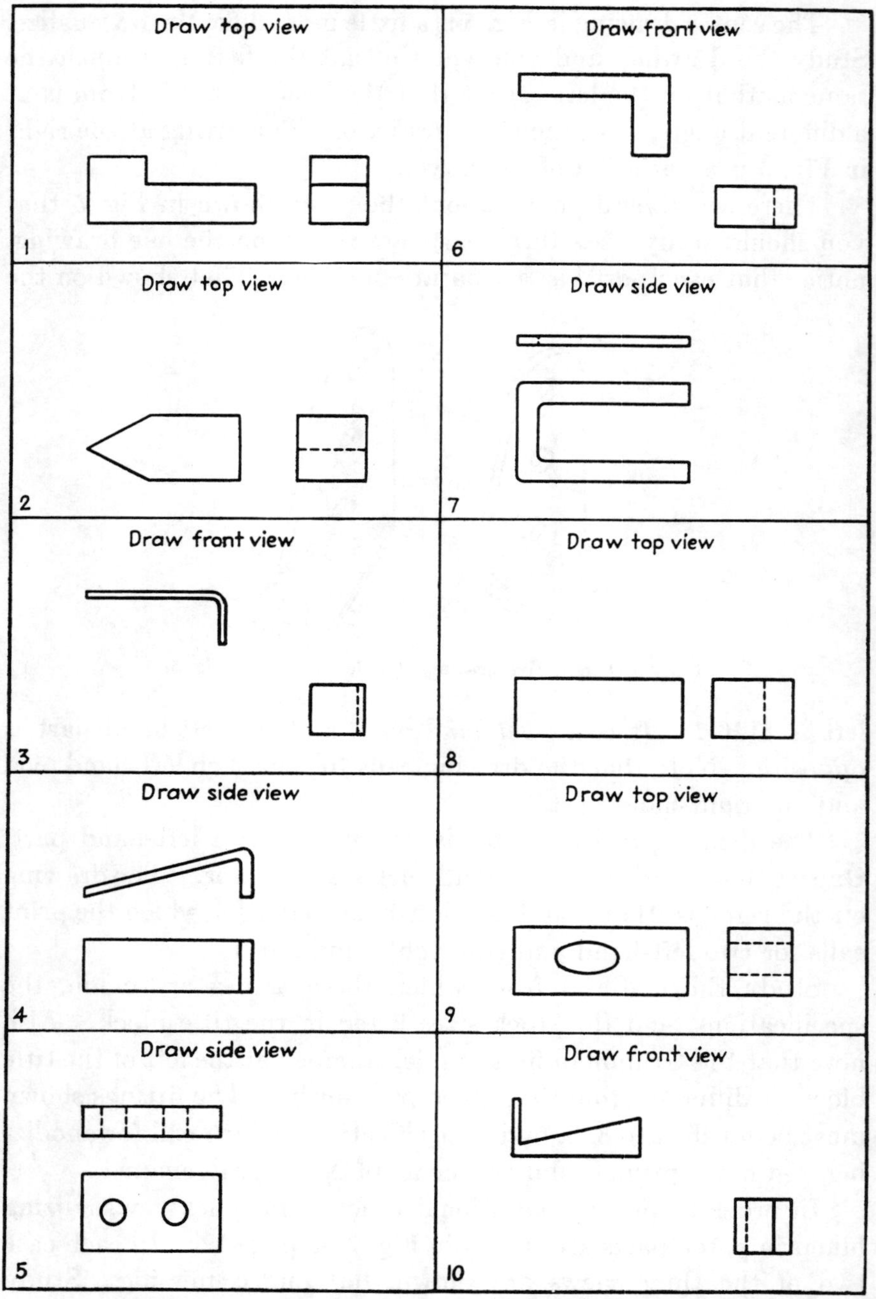

FIG. 7.—Fill in the third or missing view of each of the above parts.

Abbreviations.—Blueprints are often filled with abbreviations, which save a considerable amount of the draftsmen's time as well as much space on the print. A number of aircraft plants use abbreviations peculiar to that factory. The following are those in general use. Many of these abbreviations are also found on templates, as explained in Chap. 5.

ABBREVIATIONS IN COMMON USE

A.C., Air Corps
Adj., adjustable
Adt., apply drill template
Aft., after, often a view toward the rear of the airplane
Ail., aileron
Alc., Alclad
Alum., aluminum alloy
AN, Army-Navy
Assem., assemble or assembly
A.T.D.T., apply trim and drill template
A.W.G., American wire gage

B.A., bend allowance
B. Dn., bend down
B.H., bending hole
B.L., bend line
Blkd., bulkhead
Braz., brazier
Brkt., bracket
B. & S., Brown & Sharpe
B. Up., bend up
B.W.G., Birmingham wire gage

C.A.A., Civil Aeronautics Administration
C.A.B., Civil Aeronautics Board
Cap., capacity
C.Bore., counterbore
C.C., center to center
C.Drill., counter drill
C.F.M., cubic feet per minute
Chk., check
Chng., change
℄, center line
Cl., close, or closed angle
Corr., corrugated
C.P., center of pressure
C.P.S. cycles per second
Csk., countersink
C.T., contour template

Db., decibel
D.C., direct current
Dia., diameter
Dim., dimension
D.L., developed length
Dn., down
Drwg., drawing
Dups., duplicates
Dural., duralumin
D.W., developed width

Elev., elevator
Emp., empennage (tail group)
Ext., extrusion

Fair., fairing
F.H., flat head
Fig., figure
Fil., fillet
Fin., finish
Flg., flange
Fr., front
Fus., fuselage
Fwd., forward, a view toward the front of the airplane

G., gravity
Ga., gage

Hex., hexagonal
Hg, mercury
Horiz., horizontal
H.P., horsepower
H.T., heat-treat

I.B., or Inbd., inboard, toward the fuselage from the wing tip
I.D., inside diameter
In., inch
Install., installation

Jog., joggle

K.C., Kcs., kilocycles
K.P.H., kilometers per hour

L., left
Ldg. Gr., landing gear
L.E., leading edge
Leng. length
L.H., left hand
Long., longeron
Ltg. H., lightening hole

Matl., material
Max., maximum
Max. L., maximum loose fit
Max. T., maximum tight fit
Min., minimum
Min. L., minimum loose fit
Min. T., minimum tight fit
ML., mold line
MM., millimeters
M.P.H., miles per hour
M.S., machine screw

Nac., nacelle
N.A.C.A., National Advisory Committee for Aeronautics
N.A.F., Naval Aircraft Factory
N.C., National coarse thread
N.F., or N.F. Thrd., national fine thread
No., number
N.P.T., National pipe thread

O.B., or Out Bd., outboard
O.C., on center: dimension between centers of holes
O.D., outside diameter
Op., open or open angle
Opp., opposite
OS. Up., other side up

PH., pinhole
Prelim., preliminary
Prep., prepared
P.S.I., pounds per square inch
P.T., pipe thread

R., radius
Rd., round
Ref., reference
Reinf., reinforce, reinforcement
Req., required
R.F., radio frequency
R.H., right hand
Riv., rivet
RL., reference line
R.P.M., revolutions per minute
RR., rear
Rud., rudder

S.A.E., Society of Automotive Engineers
S.F.B., steel forming block
Sh., sheet
Shn., shown
S.L., stock length
S.L.T., steel layout template
S.O., dural in dead soft condition (Wrought annealed)
Spec., specification
S.R.T, heat-treated dural which is then rolled
S.T., heat-treated dural (Wrought tempered)
Sta., station
Stab., stabilizer
Std., standard
Stiff., stiffener
Sup., support
S.W., stock width
Sym., symmetrical

T.E., trailing edge
Temp., templet or template
Thd., thread
TS. Up., this side up

U.S.S., United States Standard

V., volts
Vert., vertical

W. & M. Ga., Washburn and Moen gage
W.D., War Department

Symbols Used on Drawings.—A number of symbols are found repeatedly on drawings. All cannot be given here, but the most common are shown in Fig. 8. It must be emphasized that there are many variations. All these symbols are not standardized, and markings used in one plant are not necessarily used elsewhere.

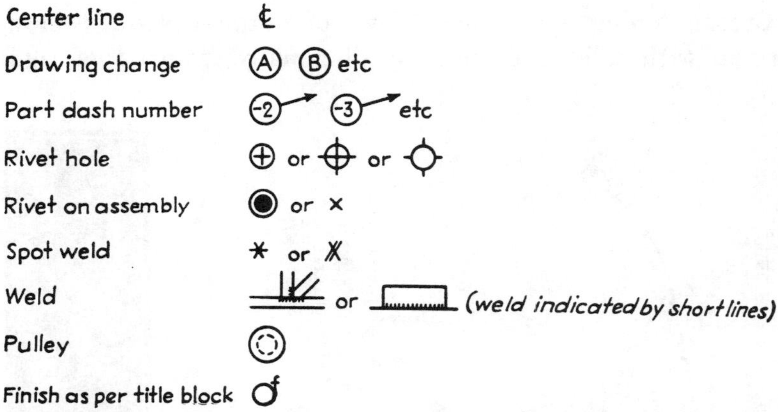

FIG. 8.—Except for the symbols showing a center line and welding, the student cannot be assured of finding these symbols to have the meanings indicated. There is considerable variation between aircraft firms, especially as to rivet symbols. The asterisk signifies spot weld in some firms, and prick punch in others.

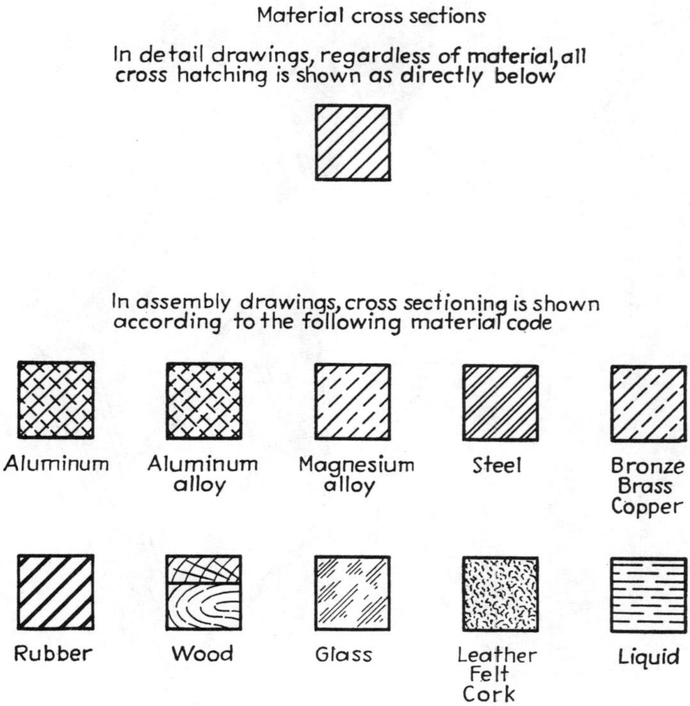

FIG. 9.—Material cross sections.

Part dash numbers, for example, are not put in circles by all engineering departments.

Crosshatching.—Sectional views of detail drawings show all material with solid lines running diagonally from upper right to

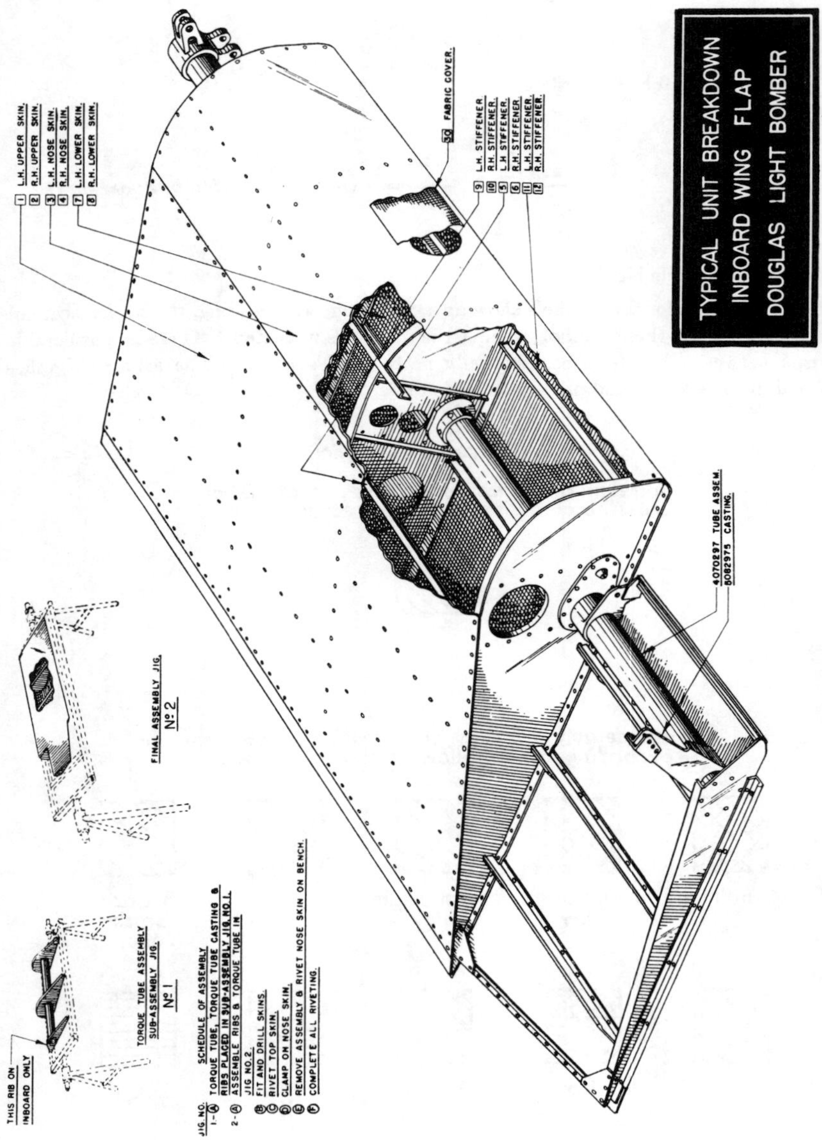

FIG. 10.—A perspective drawing used by the Douglas Aircraft Co.

lower left. In assembly drawings, cross sections are identified by different kinds of crosshatching, depending upon the material.

Crosshatching as approved by the Air Corps is shown in Fig. 9.

Perspective Drawings Used in Plants.—Because of the large number of new workers employed by aircraft factories, production engineers have found that in addition to the regular blueprints it is helpful if perspective sketches are also furnished to sheetmetal men. The Douglas Aircraft Co. has been one of the leaders in this movement.

A typical Douglas perspective sketch, or "cutaway" drawing, is shown in Fig. 10. The beginning sheetmetal mechanic can see readily that such a sketch would help him to visualize the detail parts involved as well as the entire assembly.

It must be emphasized, however, that such drawings are an aid to the mechanic only in helping him to visualize the part. Specific details are still found only on the blueprints.

Army-Navy Standards.—Specifications for many airplane parts have been written by the Army or the Navy. These are called *AN standards* or *specifications.* Nuts, bolts, rivets, cables and fittings, screws, and many other parts have been standardized and given numbers. When these parts are called for on blueprints, the AN number is printed on the drawing.

The Army Air Corps has some specifications entirely its own, and these are marked AC. Likewise, the Naval Aircraft Factory has set some standards, and these are abbreviated NAF.

It is enough in this chapter to know that details of all AN standards can be found in manuals. A more complete discussion of the different codes and how to use them is given in Chap. 3.

DETAIL DRAWINGS

There are three general kinds of drawings, as mentioned earlier: detail, assembly, and installation. Detail drawings are the simplest because they show one part. As in Fig. 5, there may be several details on one print, although it is more common to show only one part to a print in a detail drawing.

In the following drawings, study each section of the print carefully, and then answer the questions relating to that print given at the end of this chapter.

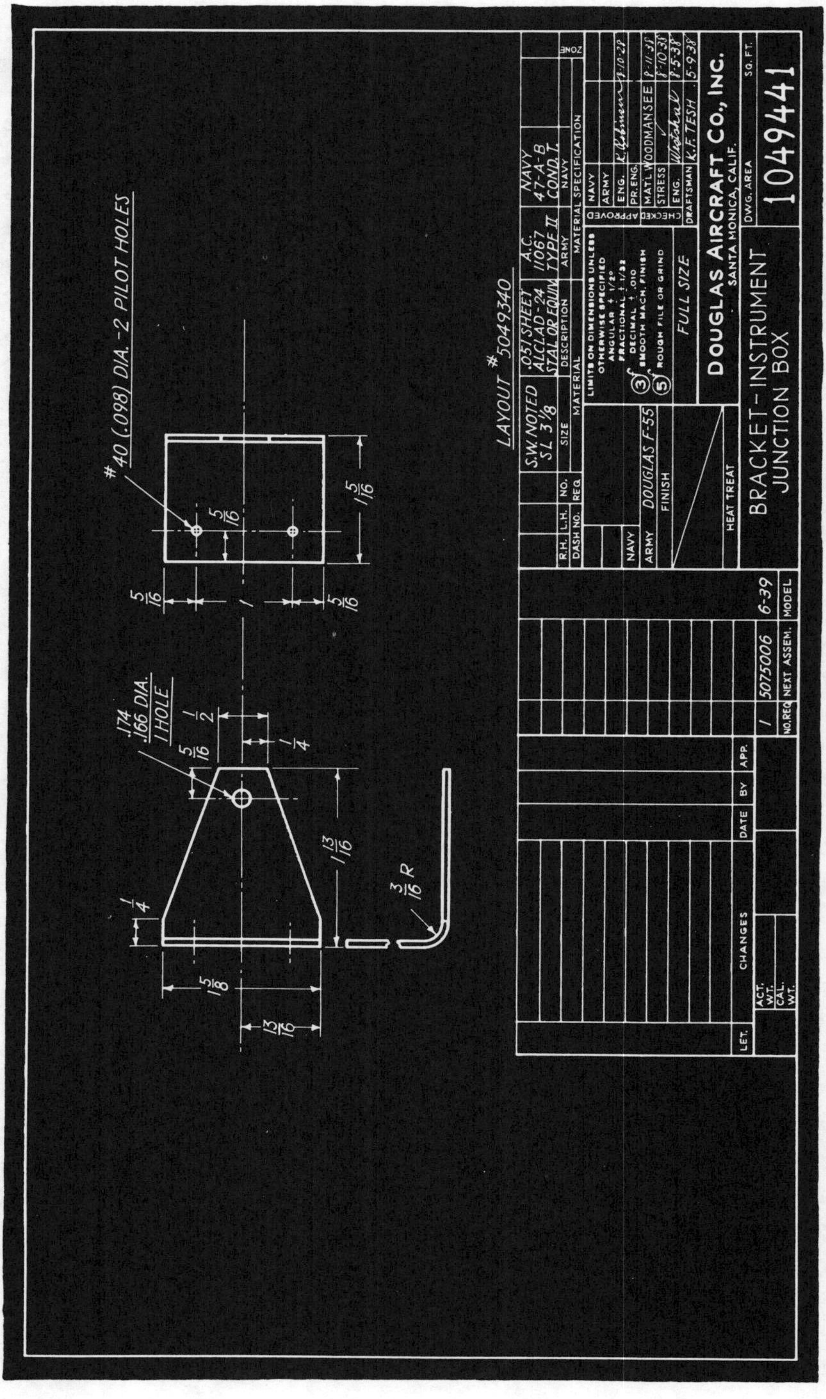
#40 (.098) DIA.-2 PILOT HOLES
.174 .166 DIA. 1 HOLE
3/16 R
LAYOUT #5049340
S.W. NOTED SL 3 1/8
.051 SHEET ALCLAD-24 STAL OR EQUIV.
A.C. 11067 TYPE II
NAVY 47-A-B COND. I
DOUGLAS F-55
FINISH
HEAT TREAT
FULL SIZE
DOUGLAS AIRCRAFT CO., INC.
SANTA MONICA, CALIF.
BRACKET-INSTRUMENT JUNCTION BOX
1049441
1 5075006 6-39
NO. REQ NEXT ASSEM. MODEL
CHANGES

FIG. 11.

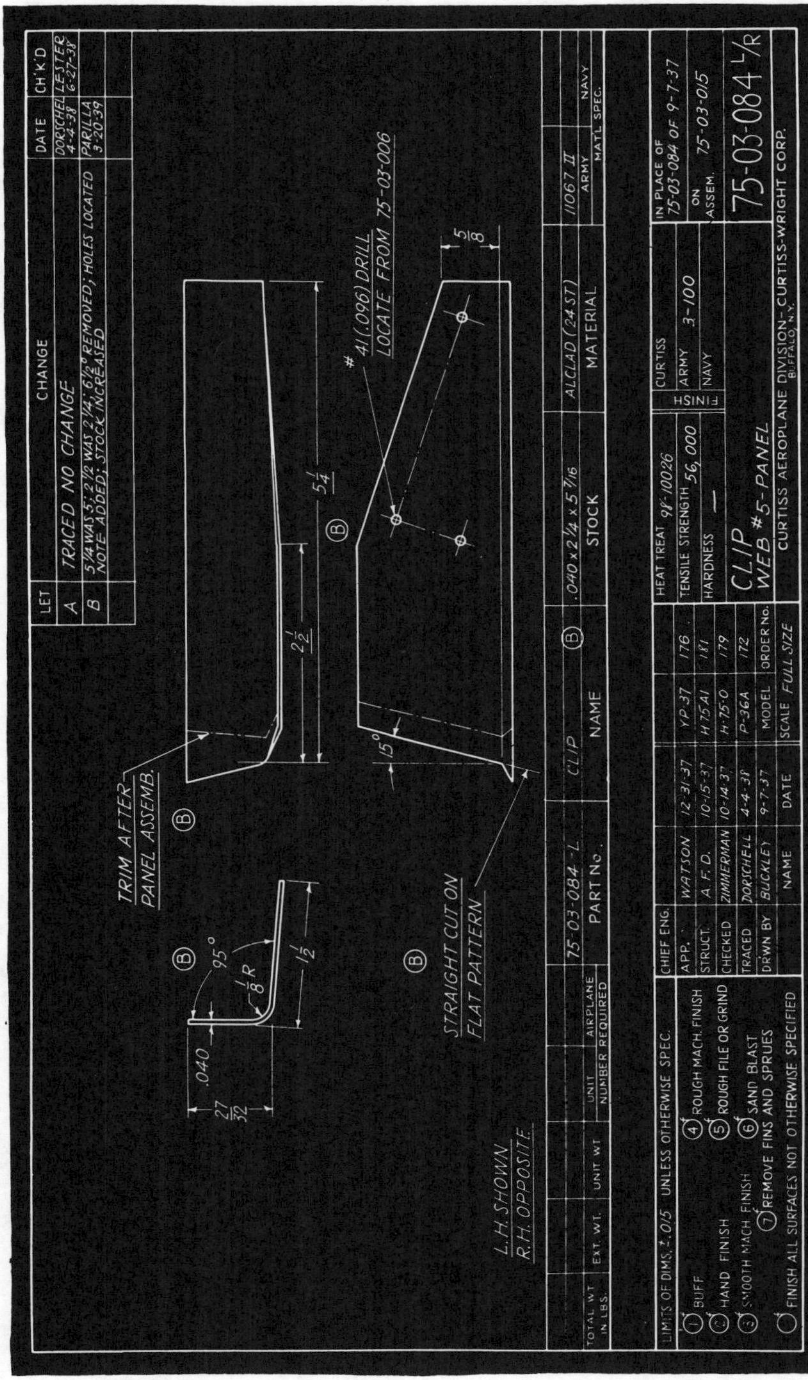
LET
CHANGE
DATE
CH'K'D
A
TRACED NO CHANGE
DORSCHEL 4-4-38
LESTER 6-27-38
B
5 1/4 WAS 5; 2 1/2 WAS 2 1/4; 6 1/2° REMOVED; HOLES LOCATED
NOTE ADDED; STOCK INCREASED
PARILLA 3-20-39
TRIM AFTER PANEL ASSEMB.
B
.040
27/32
95°
1/8 R
1 1/2
2 1/2
5 1/4
15°
5/8
#41(.096) DRILL
LOCATE FROM 75-03-006
STRAIGHT CUT ON FLAT PATTERN
L.H. SHOWN
R.H. OPPOSITE
75-03-084-L
CLIP
.040 x 2 1/4 x 5 7/16
ALCLAD (24 ST)
11067 II
TOTAL WT IN LBS.
EXT. WT.
UNIT WT
UNIT NUMBER
AIRPLANE REQUIRED
PART No.
NAME
STOCK
MATERIAL
ARMY
NAVY
MATL SPEC.
LIMITS OF DIMS ±.015 UNLESS OTHERWISE SPEC.
1 BUFF
2 HAND FINISH
3 SMOOTH MACH FINISH
4 ROUGH MACH. FINISH
5 ROUGH FILE OR GRIND
6 SAND BLAST
7 REMOVE FINS AND SPRUES
FINISH ALL SURFACES NOT OTHERWISE SPECIFIED
CHIEF ENG.
APP. WATSON 12-31-37 YP-37 176
STRUCT. A.F.D. 10-15-37 H75A1 181
CHECKED ZIMMERMAN 10-14-37 H-75-0 179
TRACED DORSCHELL 4-4-38 P-36A 172
DRAWN BY BUCKLEY 9-7-37
NAME
DATE
MODEL
ORDER No.
SCALE FULL SIZE
HEAT TREAT 98-10026
TENSILE STRENGTH 56,000
HARDNESS —
FINISH
CURTISS
ARMY 3-100
NAVY
IN PLACE OF 75-03-084 OF 9-7-37
ON ASSEM. 75-03-015
CLIP
WEB #5-PANEL
75-03-084 L/R
CURTISS AEROPLANE DIVISION-CURTISS-WRIGHT CORP.
BUFFALO, N.Y.

FIG. 12.

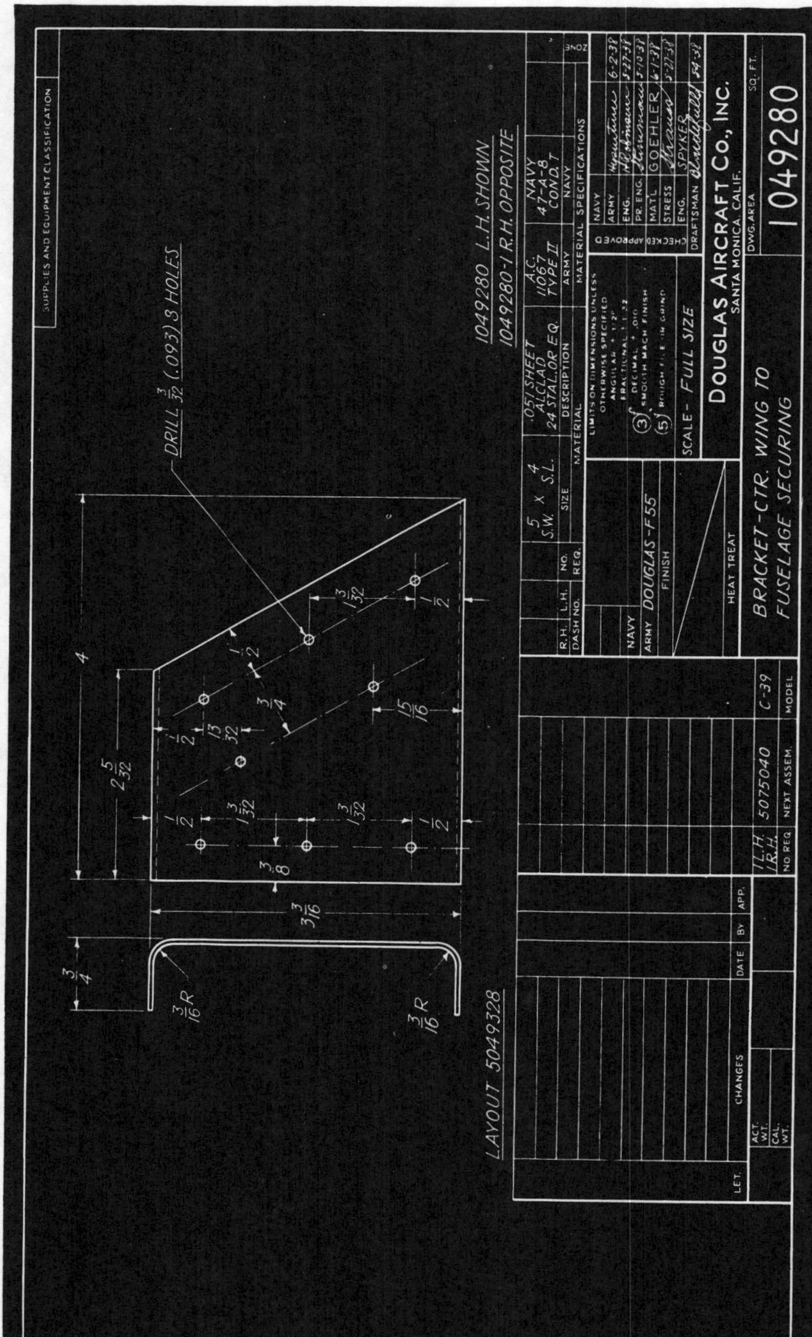
SUPPLIES AND EQUIPMENT CLASSIFICATION
DRILL 3/32 (.093) 8 HOLES
1049280 L.H. SHOWN
1049280-1 R.H. OPPOSITE
LAYOUT 5049328
.051 SHEET ALCLAD 24 STAL. OR EQ.
A.C. 11067 TYPE II
NAVY 47-A-8 COND. T
DESCRIPTION
ARMY
NAVY
MATERIAL SPECIFICATIONS
MATERIAL
5 x 4 S.W. S.L.
SIZE
R.H. L.H. DASH NO.
NO. REQ.
NAVY
ARMY DOUGLAS-F55
FINISH
HEAT TREAT
SCALE - FULL SIZE
DOUGLAS AIRCRAFT Co., INC.
SANTA MONICA, CALIF.
BRACKET-CTR. WING TO FUSELAGE SECURING
DWG. AREA
SQ. FT.
1049280
GOEHLER
SPYKER
DRAFTSMAN
CHECKED
APPROVED
ZONE
1 L.H. 1 R.H.
5075040
C-39
NO. REQ.
NEXT ASSEM.
MODEL
LET.
CHANGES
DATE
BY
APP.
ACT. WT.
CAL. WT.

FIG. 13.

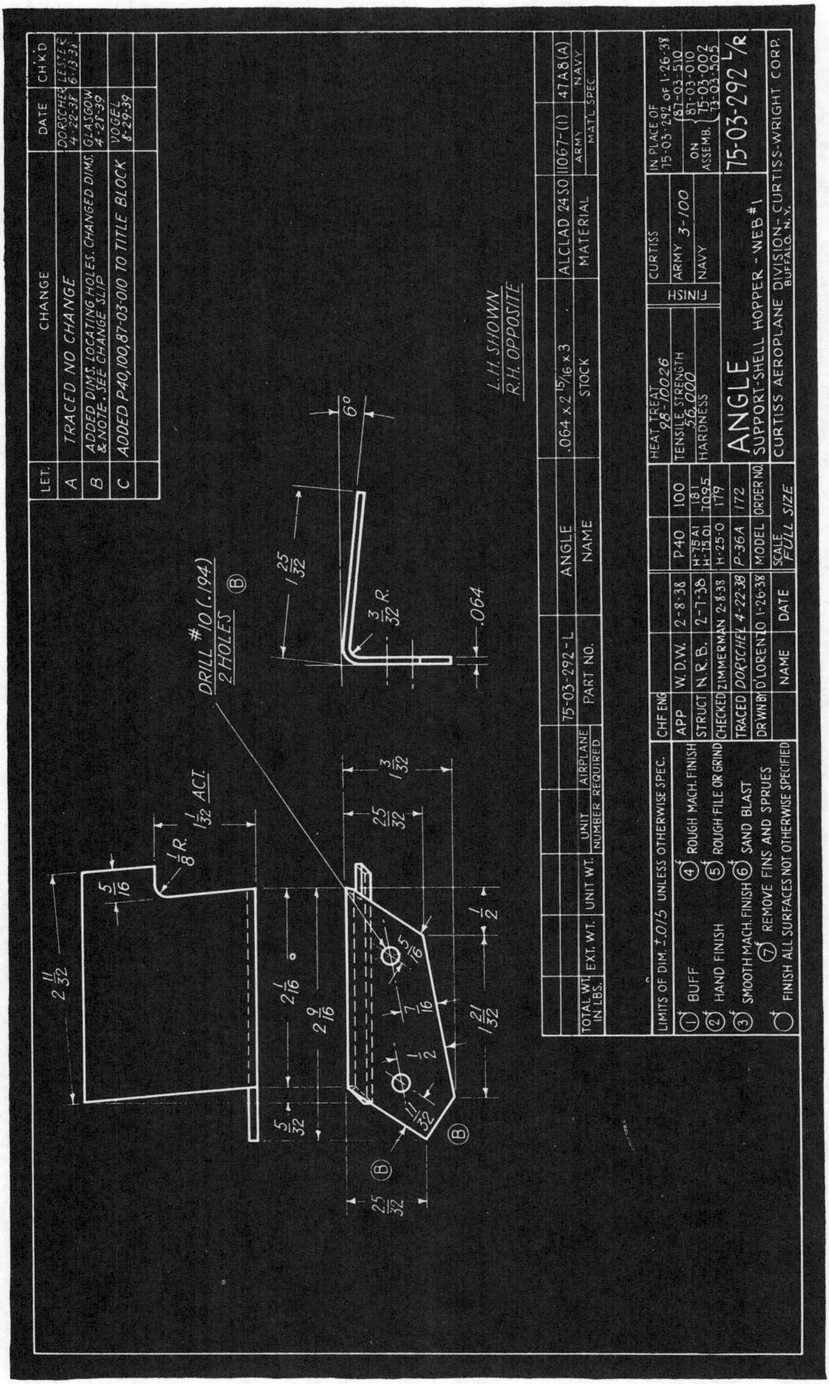
LET.
CHANGE
DATE
CHK'D
A TRACED NO CHANGE
DORSCHER 4-22-38
LESTER 6-13-38
B ADDED DIMS. LOCATING HOLES. CHANGED DIMS. & NOTE. SEE CHANGE SLIP
GLASGOW 4-28-39
C ADDED P40,100,87-03-010 TO TITLE BLOCK
VOGEL 8-29-39
DRILL #10 (.194) 2 HOLES
L.H. SHOWN
R.H. OPPOSITE
.064
6°
1/8 R.
3/32 R.
1 1/32 ACT.
75-03-292-L
ANGLE
.064 x 2 15/16 x 3
ALCLAD 24SO
11067-(1)
47A8(A)
PART NO.
NAME
STOCK
MATERIAL
ARMY
NAVY
MAT'L SPEC.
TOTAL WT. IN LBS.
EXT. WT.
UNIT WT.
UNIT
AIRPLANE
NUMBER REQUIRED
LIMITS OF DIM. ±.015 UNLESS OTHERWISE SPEC.
BUFF
ROUGH MACH. FINISH
HAND FINISH
ROUGH FILE OR GRIND
SMOOTH MACH. FINISH
SAND BLAST
REMOVE FINS AND SPRUES
FINISH ALL SURFACES NOT OTHERWISE SPECIFIED
CHF ENG
APP W.D.W. 2-8-38
STRUCT N.R.B. 2-7-38
CHECKED ZIMMERMAN 2-8-38
TRACED DORSCHER 4-22-38
DRWN BY D'LORENZO 1-26-38
NAME
DATE
P40 100
H-75 A1 H-75 O1 181 7095
H-25-O 179
P-36A 172
MODEL
ORDER NO.
SCALE FULL SIZE
HEAT TREAT 98-10026
TENSILE STRENGTH 56,000
HARDNESS
FINISH
CURTISS
ARMY 3-100
NAVY
IN PLACE OF 75-03-292 of 1-26-38
ON ASSEMB. 87-03-510 81-03-010 75-03-002 73-03-505
ANGLE
SUPPORT-SHELL HOPPER - WEB #1
75-03-292 L/R
CURTISS AEROPLANE DIVISION - CURTISS-WRIGHT CORP.
BUFFALO, N.Y.

FIG. 14.

ASSEMBLY DRAWINGS

Assembly drawings (in some plants called *class 2 prints*, in contrast with class 1 prints, which are detail or part drawings) show how two or more parts are assembled together. They are parts that can be assembled together in one department. Each part of the assembly is assigned a separate number, which refers back to the number on the detail print of that part. This part number often appears in a heavy circle on the assembly print, with an arrow pointing to the part.

Different aircraft factories have different systems for numbering parts on an assembly print. Usually a drawing covering a number of parts is given a full number (without a dash), and dash numbers that refer back to the part drawings are assigned for the individual parts. Thus an assembly print number may be 123456, and parts on the print are designated -2, -3, -4, -5, and so on. Figure 15 is a drawing of this type. The drawing number is 2112880, and there are three dash-numbered parts.

Part numbers do not need to be dash numbers, and assembly print 123456 may refer to any blueprint part number. Sometimes letters or combinations of figures and letters are used.

The two drawings shown in Figs. 16 and 17 illustrate how one company numbers assembly drawings. Print 5-16322 (Fig. 17, inside back cover) is an assembly drawing, showing the trailing edge of a wing rib. On this drawing are given numerous parts from which the assembly is made. At the top, left, appear two gussets. These are marked 5-16331-1 and 5-16331-2 and refer to drawing 5-16331, shown on page 24. It will also be noted that on the latter drawing, showing how the parts are to be made, on the lower left of the title block it is mentioned that the four gussets are used on assembly number 5-16322. The assembly drawing gives several other detail numbers.

An important part of an assembly drawing is the bill of materials. On drawing 5-16322 some 74 parts, including rivets, must be collected together before the assembly can be completed. Considerable information is given as to the stock size, material, specification, finish, and weights. Study this print carefully.

Cross-sectional Views.—In assembly drawings it is sometimes helpful if the mechanics can secure an idea of the cross-sectional

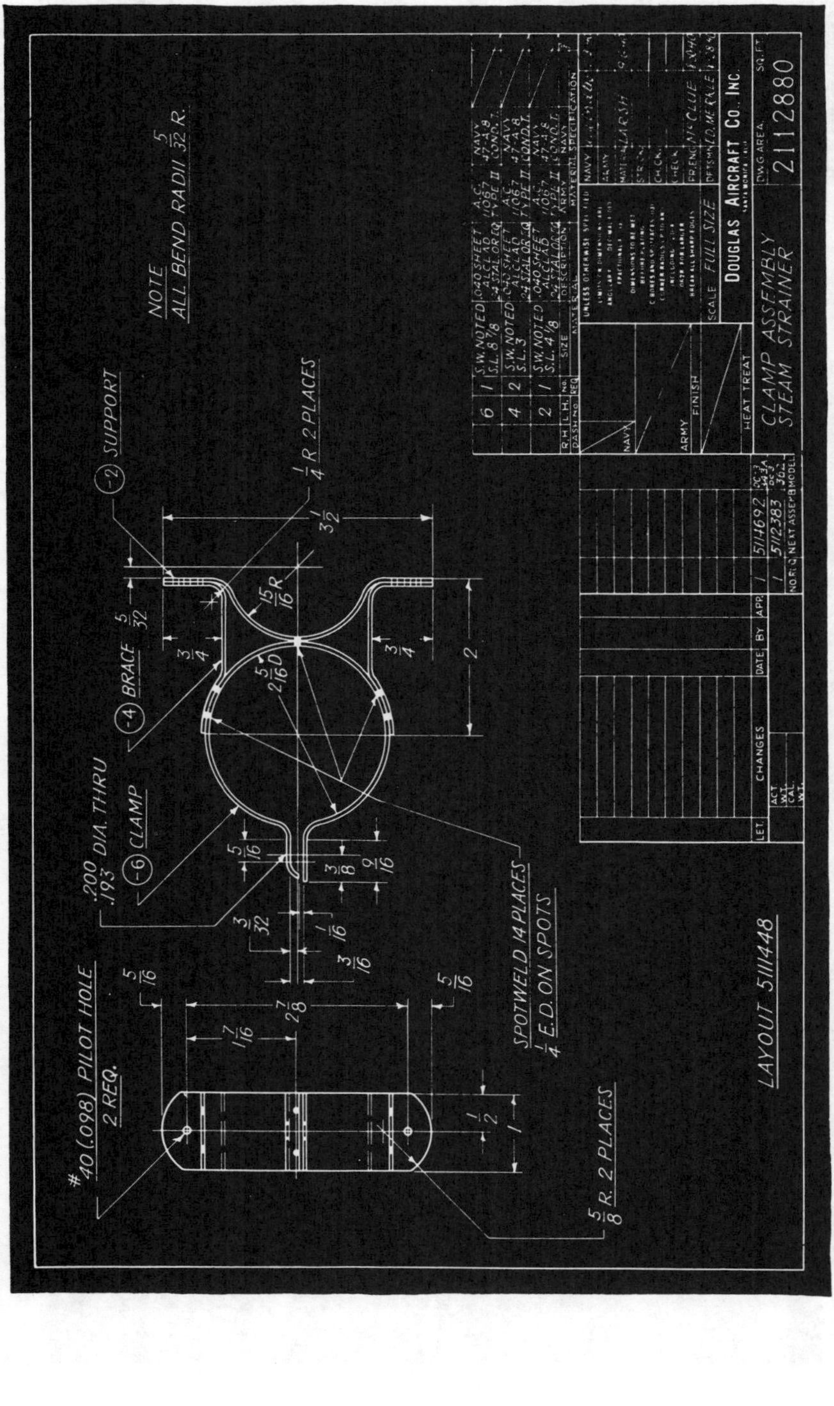
NOTE
ALL BEND RADII 5/32 R.
-2 SUPPORT
-4 BRACE
-6 CLAMP
SPOTWELD 14 PLACES
1/4 E.D. ON SPOTS
LAYOUT 5111448
DOUGLAS AIRCRAFT CO. INC.
CLAMP ASSEMBLY
STEAM STRAINER
SCALE FULL SIZE
2112880

FIG. 15.

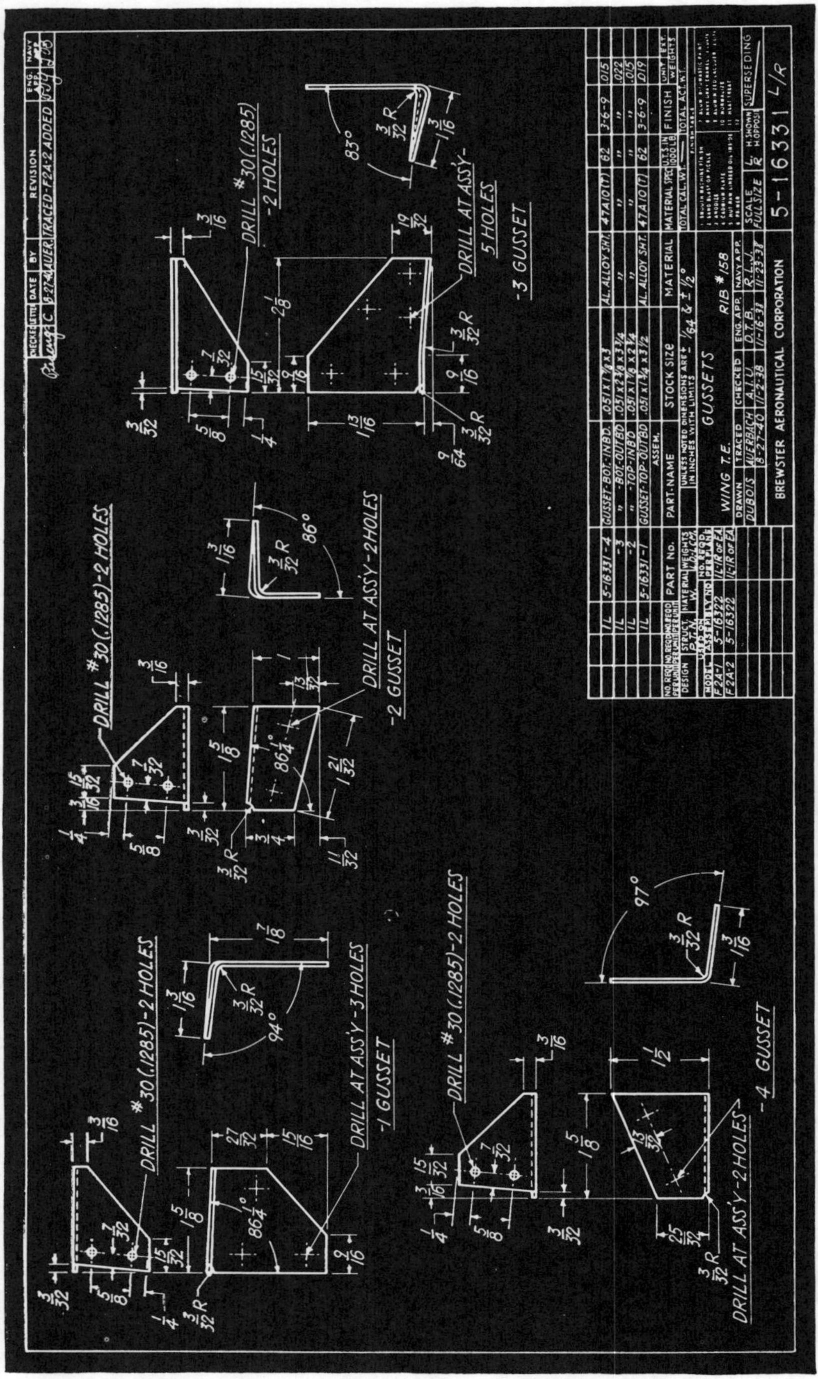

Fig. 16.—Detail parts which are shown assembled in Fig. 17.

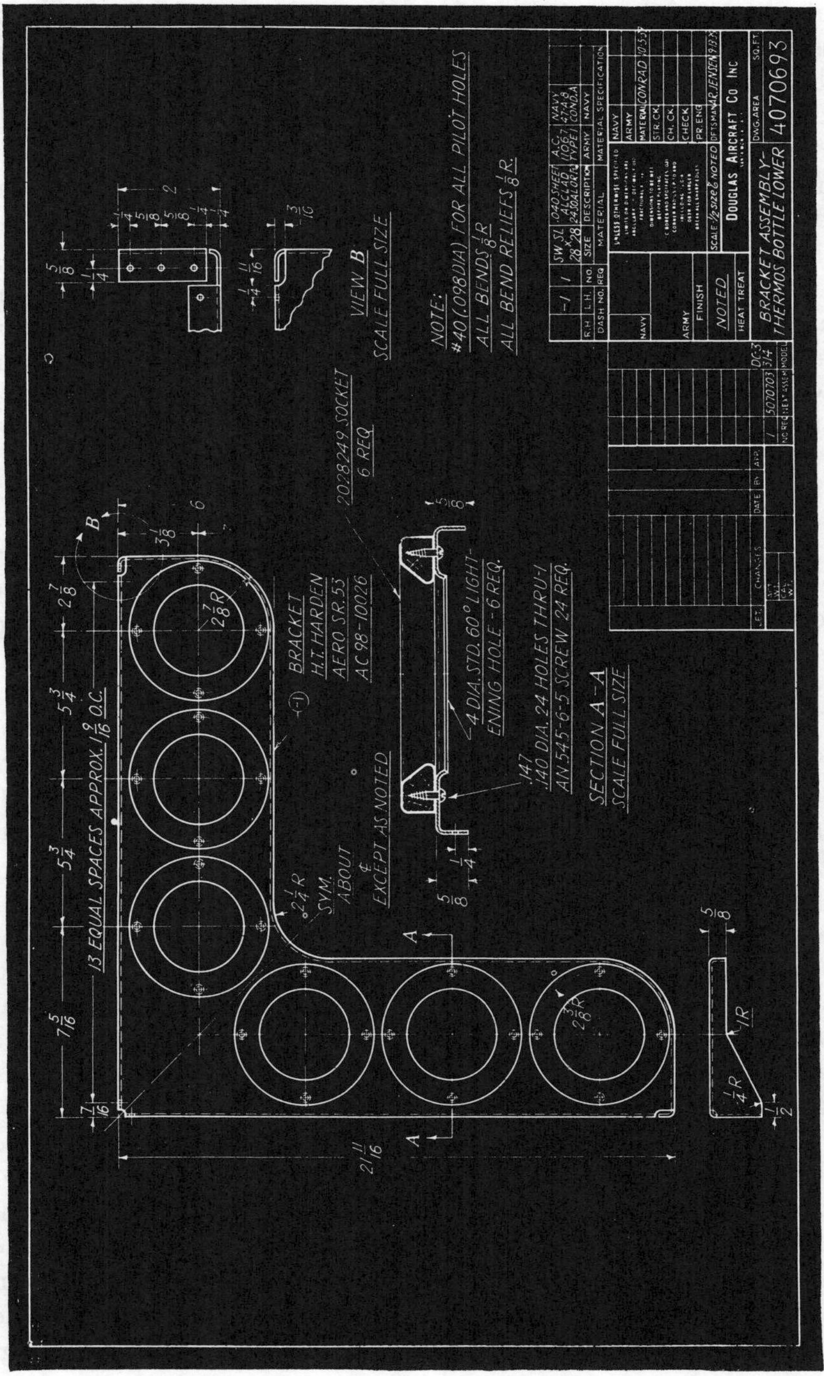
13 EQUAL SPACES APPROX. 1 9/16 O.C.
SYM. ABOUT ℄ EXCEPT AS NOTED
-1 BRACKET H.T. HARDEN AERO SR.53 AC98-10026
2028249 SOCKET 6 REQ.
4 DIA. STD. 60° LIGHTENING HOLE - 6 REQ.
.147 .140 DIA. 24 HOLES THRU-1 AN545-6-5 SCREW 24 REQ.
SECTION A-A SCALE FULL SIZE
VIEW B SCALE FULL SIZE
NOTE: #40 (.098 DIA) FOR ALL PILOT HOLES
ALL BENDS 1/8 R
ALL BEND RELIEFS 1/8 R.
DOUGLAS AIRCRAFT CO INC
BRACKET ASSEMBLY-THERMOS BOTTLE LOWER
4070693

FIG. 18.

appearance of the part that they are assembling. To fill this need, assembly drawings often show a plane passed through a section. This is shown in the Brewster drawing facing page 24. At the extreme left is a part of the drawing marked "Section A-A." This is how the cross section of that assembly would look at the point on the large drawing marked "AA." The arrows point to the direction in which you would see the cross section. Large assemblies may have a number of such cross-sectional views.

A cross section is also shown in Fig. 18. Imagine the bracket has been cut through at point "A-A." The view of "Section A-A" shows a cut through a round, wood bracket on which a thermos bottle rests. This print involves many points worthy of careful study.

INSTALLATION PRINTS

Installation prints show how subassemblies or assemblies are secured to the airplane. There is no sharp line of distinction between assembly drawings and installation drawings. In some factories blueprints are classified as subassembly, assembly, and installation prints. Elsewhere drawings are divided into class 1, 2, and 3 prints, with class 3 being installation drawings.

As a rule, installation drawings contain the number of the subassembly (or assembly) drawings but do not refer to the numbers of the detail parts. The beginning sheetmetal worker is not expected to be able to read complex installation drawings. In fact, he may seldom see such prints, as they are handled only by experienced workers or leadmen. Figure 19 is a reproduction of such a print. It shows the stick-control installation for a Grumman fighter. Note that the installation mechanic is referred back to several part drawings in case he wishes additional information. Also note the number of Army-Navy standard parts that are specified and located by arrows. The bill of materials contains many items, and it should be studied.

Other types of installation prints show the conduit system, the electrical system, how control cables are installed, piping for carrying gasoline and oil, engine and instrument installation, and so on. *Schematic* diagrams are often drawn to show such features as the plumbing system or the control system of an airplane. Often an isometric, or perspective, sketch of the airplane is made, and the particular system being discussed is superimposed on such a drawing.

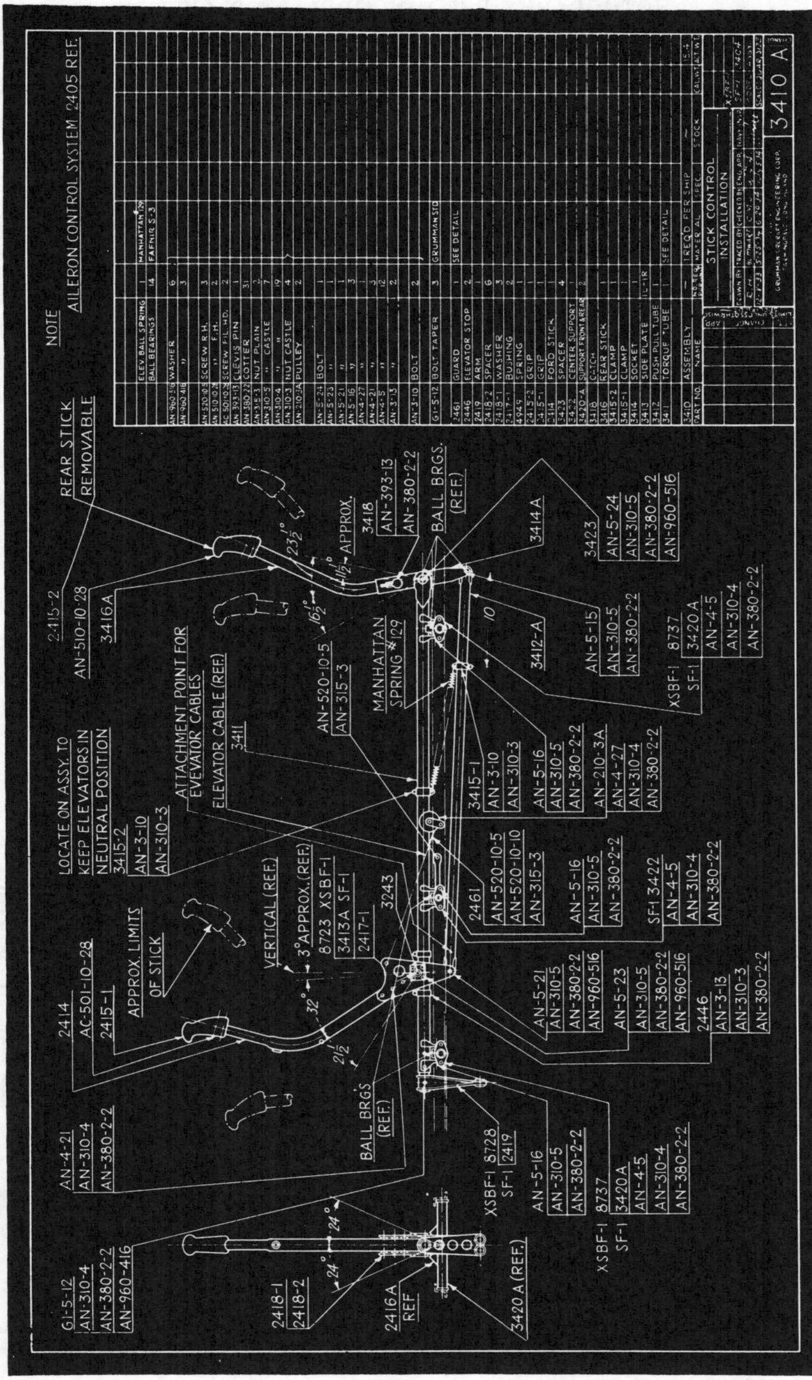

FIG. 19.—An installation drawing.

PHOTOGRAPHY USED IN AIRPLANE PLANTS

A photographic process that has been developed for use in airplane factories will be described briefly, as sheetmetal men may be called upon to work in plants using this process. Photographs are made of engineering drawings, and these can be printed directly on any kind of surface, including sheets of aluminum alloy, wood, cloth, or paper. In a busy plant, such as the Glenn L. Martin factory where the basic idea was developed, thousands of hours a year of draftsmen's time is saved and production work is speeded. A giant camera is used, and copies as large as 5 by 10 ft. can be made.

The method is used for several purposes. In experimental planes or in models to be used in wind tunnels or in towing basins, copies of full-scale drawings are reproduced directly on the sheet-metal or wood used in the airplane or the model. Then men in the shop cut and form the parts without having to lay them out from blueprints.

Reduced-size copies can also be made. The camera may take pictures of full-size drawings and then reproduce them to one-half, one-quarter, or some other fractional size. Similarly, reduced-size drawings may be "blown up" to full size for use in production.

Most airplane factories have a lofting floor, where full-scale layouts of the airplane are made. In some plants these drawings are made on heavy paper fastened to the floor. Other plants use dural sheets coated white on the top side, and drawings are made in pencil. When the photographic process is used, these sheets are photographed and copies are made for various departments. This saves much time, as it is not necessary to redraw the parts. Patterns (or templates) and jigs are also made through photographic uses. This is explained in Chap. 5. Lockheed and Consolidated are among other factories that use photographic methods to speed up their work.

Questions Relating to Blueprints in This Chapter

FIG. 1, page 4

1. By which airplane company was this drawing made?
2. What is the name of the part?
3. What is the scale of the drawing?
4. From what material is the part made?

5. What are the dimensions of the stock?
6. What are the dimensions of the finished part?
7. What tolerances are permitted?
8. In the top view, what do $\frac{1}{8}$R and 5 deg. signify?
9. What finishes are called for?
10. What does the letter "A" in a circle signify?
11. For what Douglas model is this part to be used?
12. How many such parts are required per airplane?
13. What is the next assembly number?
14. When was this drawing made?

FIG. 5, page 10

1. For what airplane were these parts designed?
2. What are the names of the parts?
3. What material is to be used?
4. Which are right-hand and which are left-hand parts?
5. What do the dash numbers in the circles signify?
6. What are the radii of the holes in the top views?
7. What is the stock length for 2146-3?
8. How many of each angle are required per airplane?
9. What are the over-all dimensions of -1?
10. How are the angles to be finished?
11. Have any changes been made since the original drawing was made?

FIG. 11, page 18

1. What is the name of this part?
2. For what model was it drawn?
3. What stock is needed?
4. What size sheet is called for?
5. What does "S. W. Noted" signify?
6. Make a rough perspective drawing of this bracket.
7. What is the radius of the bend?
8. What size pilot holes are made in the vertical section?
9. What tolerances are specified in the title block?
10. What tolerance is permitted in the hole shown in the top view?

FIG. 12, page 19

1. Is this a left-hand or a right-hand part?
2. How thick is the sheet stock?
3. What views are shown?
4. What other print is called for to complete this work?
5. Describe the change noted.
6. What do the encircled letters "B" signify?
7. Is heat-treating called for?
8. Make a rough isometric sketch of this part.

9. What is the meaning of No. 41 (0.096) drill?
10. See if you can trace a flat layout of this fitting.

FIG. 13, page 20

1. Are the flanges of this fitting bent at 90 deg. to the web?
2. What is the radius over which the flanges are bent?
3. What is the difference in length between the two flanged sides?
4. Are all drilled holes the same size?
5. Are the indicated radii of the sheet greater than the thickness of the material?
6. What is the meaning of "CTR" on the title?
7. What is the Air Corps reference number as to material?
8. If you had to assemble this part, what is the next drawing that you would need?
9. What is the number of the right-hand drawing of this fitting?
10. How can the width between the flanges be checked besides using the $3\frac{3}{16}$ dimension that is shown?

FIG. 14, page 21

1. What are the name and the number of this part?
2. To what use is this angle put?
3. Where on the airplane is this angle located?
4. Can this part be used on more than one Curtiss airplane?
5. What is the scale?
6. Is this a right-hand or a left-hand part?
7. What gage and what type of material is used?
8. Is heat-treating necessary?
9. How many drilled holes are required, and of what size?
10. What is indicated by the dashed lines?
11. Describe the changes indicated in the change block.
12. What is the next drawing that you would require for assembly of this part?

FIG. 15, page 23

1. What is the name of this part, and for what airplane was it designed?
2. Is sufficient information given on this drawing to make the parts as well as to assemble them?
3. Of how many parts is this assembly composed?
4. What is the method of fastening the parts together?
5. At how many points is the assembly fastened together?
6. Are all parts made of the same material?
7. What bend radii are indicated?
8. Is this assembly used for more than one model?
9. What size drill is used for pilot holes?
10. What is the radius at the ends of the -2 support?
11. Point out the two parts that are identical.
12. What size was the original blueprint?

FIG. 16, page 24

1. List each individual part number on this drawing.
2. How many bends are shown in the three views of -1, and at what angle?
3. Which of the two angles indicated in -1 is the bending angle?
4. What is the edge distance of the two No. 30 rivet holes?
5. Of the five holes indicated in -1, how many should be drilled at the time the fitting is made?
6. What radius is given for the relief opening in -2?
7. Will the fitting in -2 form an open or a closed angle?
8. How many of each part should be made?
9. What gage and kind of material is used?
10. What number blueprint shows the assembly of these gussets?

FIG. 17, inside back cover

1. What type of drawing is this?
2. How does it differ from the detail drawings shown previously?
3. Give the name and the location of this assembly.
4. Locate the four gussets (-1, -2, -3, -4) shown in the preceding print.
5. How are these gussets secured to the rib?
6. Describe the rivets used. (See page 58 for rivet code.)
7. Give the radii of the lightening holes in the opposite ends of the web of the rib.
8. What does "Section A-A" at the far left indicate?
9. Explain the bill of materials needed for this assembly.
10. How many round-headed, 17S rivets of 1/8 in. diameter are needed?

FIG. 18, page 25

1. Name the part and the material used.
2. How many lightening holes are required?
3. How is the drawing labeled "Section A-A" related to the larger drawing?
4. How does "View B" relate to the large drawing?
5. Indicate where differences in scale occur.
6. What material other than aluminum alloy is used in this assembly?
7. How many screws are required to hold sockets over the lightening holes?
8. What is the depth of the flange on the outside edge of the bracket?
9. What radius is given for all bend reliefs?
10. What size drill is used for pilot holes?
11. Is the center line of the lightening holes the center line of the bracket?
12. What does the abbreviation "O.C." at the top left of the drawing indicate?

Review Questions

1. Name three different classes of blueprints and briefly describe each class.
2. Give at least six kinds of information found in a title block.
3. Why is the number of a blueprint important?
4. What is a "dash number"?

5. Name six kinds of lines used in an aircraft drawing.

6. What is the difference between orthographic projection and isometric projection?

7. What is a finish table?

8. In a typical three-view drawing, which views are shown?

9. When left- and right-hand matching parts are required, which is shown on the drawing?

10. What is an AN standard? Name a few examples.

11. What is a class 2 print?

12. Of what value is a cross-sectional view? How is such a view identified?

13. In what kind of drawing would you find a schematic diagram?

14. How is photography used in airplane factories?

15. What variations might be found in blueprints in different aircraft plants?

CHAPTER 2

SHOP MATHEMATICS

To do his job properly and to advance to a job with higher pay, a sheetmetal man must have a working knowledge of shop mathematics. In connection with his work he must make certain mathematical calculations to determine the correct sizes of tools and materials. He must be able to add and subtract fractions, for example, to read blueprints, and to do layout work. These basic mathematical operations are simple and are not difficult to learn.

The purpose of this brief section is not to make mathematicians, but to review the fundamentals. Many of these points will have been studied previously by sheetmetal students, but many of them will also have been forgotten. Unless a man is constantly using fractions, for instance, he may have forgotten how to add quickly $3/16$ and $7/64$, how to determine rapidly which is larger, $21/64$ or $3/8$, or how to divide $3/16$ by $1/8$.

It is emphasized that this material is elementary. For students who have just taken any high-school mathematics course or for men who have had jobs in which they have had to use mathematics, this chapter is not needed and should be skipped. *Students who can quickly solve all problems at the end of the chapter do not need this review.*

Four fundamental processes underlie all arithmetical work: addition, subtraction, multiplication, and division.

The plus sign (+) is an indication of addition and when placed between two numbers signifies that they are to be added.

The minus sign (−) indicates subtraction, and when placed between two numbers means that the second is to be subtracted from the first.

The multiplication sign (×) signifies that the numbers are to be multiplied.

The division sign (÷) means that the first number is to be divided by the second.

The equal sign (=) means that all the numbers on one side equal all the numbers on the other side. The whole combination of numbers is called an *equation*.

ADDITION

Addition is the act of finding the sum of two or more numbers. *Example:* Find the sum of 687, 942, 1312, and 25.

```
 687
 942
1312
  25
----
2966 (sum, or answer)
```

SUBTRACTION

Subtraction is the process of finding the difference between two numbers. Suppose that you have a large sheet of metal from which you are to make two parts: a stabilizer and a fin. If the sheet is 120 in. in length, and one part will require 77 in., how much material will be left?

```
  120 (minuend)
–  77 (subtrahend)
-----
   43 (difference, or answer)
```

MULTIPLICATION

This is the process of multiplying two numbers together. *Example:* The area of a piece of sheetmetal is 64 sq. in., and 13 such pieces are needed. What is the total area required?

```
 64 (multiplicand)
 13 (multiplier)
---
192
64
---
832 (product, or answer)
```

DIVISION

Division is the act of finding how many times one number is contained in another. *Example:* You have a sheet of dural 120 in. in length and 48 in. wide. Your problem is to find how many rectangles 4 by 48 in. could be cut from the sheet.

$$120 \div 4 = ?$$

```
   30
4)120
```

This is called *short division.*

If you were dividing 9689 by 42:

```
                 230.69 (quotient or answer)
(divisor) 42 )9689 (dividend)
              84
              128
              126
                290
                252
                 380
                 378
                   2 (remainder)
```

This is called *long division.* Instead of carrying the answer out to two decimal places, you might have stopped after subtracting 126 from 128 and bringing down the 9. As 42 does not go into 29, the answer would have been 230 and $\frac{29}{42}$.

FRACTIONS

Fractions are used frequently in aviation sheetmetal work, and all mechanics should be familiar with their use. A fraction is one or more equal parts into which a whole is divided. A proper fraction is less than 1, such as $\frac{5}{8}$. An improper fraction is 1 or more, such as $\frac{8}{8}$ or $\frac{15}{8}$. The number above the line is the *numerator*, and the number below the line is the *denominator.* The word *terms* refers to both parts of the fraction.

Fractions may be reduced to lower terms or changed to higher terms. The fraction $\frac{8}{16}$ can be reduced to $\frac{4}{8}$ or still further reduced to $\frac{1}{2}$. Or $\frac{8}{16}$ can be changed to higher terms such as $\frac{16}{32}$, $\frac{24}{48}$, or $\frac{32}{64}$. Reducing fractions is done by dividing both the numerator and the denominator by the same amount. A fundamental rule is as follows: The value of a fraction is not changed if both numerator and denominator are either multiplied or divided by the same amount.

It is customary to reduce fractions to the lowest possible terms. The fraction $\frac{16}{64}$ in a measurement or size would be reduced to $\frac{1}{4}$, and $\frac{12}{16}$ would be reduced to $\frac{3}{4}$.

Adding Fractions.—In shopwork it is often essential to add a number of fractions. *Example:* $\frac{1}{2} + \frac{5}{16} + \frac{7}{8}$. To do this it is necessary to find the least common denominator, which is abbreviated L.C.D. The L.C.D. is the lowest number into which the denominators of the fractions will go evenly. In this case it is 16, since 2, 8, and 16 will all go into 16.

The fractions must all be reduced to sixteenths. To do this, divide 16 by the denominator and multiply the numerator by the

FIG. 20.—Side by side, down the final assembly line, go these Douglas bombers for both the British and our own Air Corps. Thousands of man hours have gone into the making of each airplane. If all subassemblies are to flow smoothly to form the completed ship, each mechanic must be depended upon to carry out his specific job.

result. In the fraction $1/2$, $16 \div 2 = 8$. $1 \times 8 = 8$. Thus $1/2 = 8/16$. To reduce $7/8$ to sixteenths, divide 16 by 8 (which is 2) and multiply by 7 (which is 14). Thus $7/8 = 14/16$. So we have:

$$1/2 = 8/16$$
$$5/16 = 5/16$$
$$7/8 = 14/16$$

The numerators added together equal 27, so the answer is $27/16$. This improper fraction equals $1\,11/16$. (See the blueprint on page 24 for an example of fractions that must be added to get over-all dimensions.)

Often it is necessary to add whole numbers, improper fractions, and proper fractions. This is done in the same way as in the preceding problem.

$$3 + \frac{7}{32} + \frac{1}{2} + \frac{3}{64} = ?$$

The lowest common denominator into which all the denominators will go is 64. If the whole number 1 $= \frac{64}{64}$, then the whole number 3 $= \frac{192}{64}$.

$$\frac{7}{32} = \frac{14}{64}$$
$$\frac{1}{2} = \frac{32}{64}$$
$$\frac{3}{64} = \frac{3}{64}$$

Adding the numerators, we get 241, and $\frac{241}{64} = 3\frac{49}{64}$. The last result is obtained by dividing 241 by 64.

In actual shop practice the whole number 3 would not be converted to sixty-fourths. The three fractions would be converted to sixty-fourths (which equals $\frac{49}{64}$) and added to 3.

In the addition $2\frac{5}{8} + 1\frac{3}{4} + 2\frac{5}{16}$, it is easiest to add the fractions separately and then add the result to the whole numbers.

$$\frac{5}{8} = \frac{10}{16}$$
$$\frac{3}{4} = \frac{12}{16}$$
$$\frac{5}{16} = \frac{5}{16}$$
$$\frac{27}{16} = 1\frac{11}{16}$$

The 1 is added to $2 + 1 + 2 = 6$. So the answer is $6\frac{11}{16}$.

Subtracting Fractions.—It is as necessary to be able to subtract fractions rapidly as it is to add them. Fractions should be reduced to common terms, and the smaller numerator taken from the larger.

Examples: $\frac{11}{32} - \frac{3}{16} = ?$

$$\frac{11}{32} = \frac{11}{32}$$
$$\frac{3}{16} = \frac{6}{32}$$
$$\frac{11}{32} - \frac{6}{32} = \frac{5}{32} \text{ (answer)}$$

Subtract $\frac{19}{64}$ from 3.

$$3 = 2\frac{64}{64} \text{ (from this subtract } \frac{19}{64}\text{)}$$
$$-\ \frac{19}{64}$$
$$2\frac{45}{64} \text{ (answer)}$$

Subtract $^{11}/_{16}$ from $4\frac{1}{2}$.

$$4\tfrac{1}{2} = 4\tfrac{8}{16} = 3\tfrac{24}{16}$$
$$-\ \tfrac{11}{16}$$
$$3\tfrac{13}{16} \text{ (answer)}$$

In this case it was necessary to change $4\frac{8}{16}$ to $3\frac{24}{16}$ because $^{11}/_{16}$ could not be subtracted from $^{8}/_{16}$.

Multiplying Fractions.—It is often necessary for a mechanic to multiply a fraction by a whole number. If a unit is $^{7}/_{16}$ in. wide,

FIG. 21.—Bell P-39 single seater fighters on the line at Selfridge Field, Michigan. These are the kinds of pilots who may be flying the airplanes you help to build. In many aircraft plants there are signs that read, "A concealed mistake may cost a brave man's life." You should always remember this in carrying out your work.

how much material is needed for 15 units? Multiply 15 by the numerator, which equals 105, so the answer is $^{105}/_{16}$, or $6\frac{9}{16}$ in.

Multiply $2\frac{1}{2} \times \frac{7}{8}$.

Reduce the mixed number to a fraction: $2\frac{1}{2} = \frac{5}{2}$.

$$\tfrac{5}{2} \times \tfrac{7}{8} = \tfrac{35}{16} = 2\tfrac{3}{16} \text{ (answer)}$$

This was accomplished by multiplying the numerators together and the denominators together.

Multiply $^{25}/_{64} \times \frac{4}{5}$.

A problem such as this can be simplified by dividing both a numerator and a denominator by the same number. This is called *cancellation.*

$$\frac{\overset{5}{\cancel{25}}}{\underset{16}{\cancel{64}}} \times \frac{\overset{1}{\cancel{4}}}{\underset{1}{\cancel{5}}} \qquad \frac{5}{16} \times \frac{1}{1} = \frac{5}{16} \text{ (answer)}$$

In the preceding problem the 25 in the first numerator and the 5 in the second denominator were divided by 5. The first denominator (64) and the second numerator (4) were divided by 4. In each case the new number was written next to the old number.

To divide fractions, invert the divisor and multiply.

$$3\tfrac{5}{8} \div 2\tfrac{1}{2} = ?$$
$$\tfrac{29}{8} \div \tfrac{5}{2} =$$
$$\tfrac{29}{8} \times \tfrac{2}{5} = \tfrac{58}{40} = 1\tfrac{18}{40}, \text{ or } 1\tfrac{9}{20} \text{ (answer)}$$

DECIMALS

Measurements are often given in decimals in aircraft work. To one who is not used to working in decimals, 0.0003 may seem confusing, but a mechanic using decimals soon feels at home with such figures if he understands the fundamentals.

The decimal system is a short form of writing fractions.

.6 = 6/10 = 6 tenths
.06 = 6/100 = 6 hundredths
.006 = 6/1,000 = 6 thousandths
.0006 = 6/10,000 = 6 ten-thousandths

It may help to think of decimals in terms of dollars and cents. $1.21 means one dollar and $\tfrac{21}{100}$ part of another dollar. If you saw a price that was marked $0.21, you would have no trouble figuring the 21 cents. You would not think of the 0.21 as $\tfrac{21}{100}$, although that is what it is. In prices, 0.08 means 8 cents, but in decimals it signifies $\tfrac{8}{100}$.

When you see decimals written, you can tell the amount by counting to the right from the decimal point: tenths, hundreths, thousandths, ten-thousandths, one-hundred-thousandths, millionths.

In reading a decimal the number indicating the numerator is read first as though it were a whole number, and then the denominator is stated. For example, 0.453 is read "four hundred and fifty-three thousandths." If it were 0.0453, it would be read "four hundred and fifty-three ten-thousandths."

In writing decimals the number indicating the numerator is written first, and then the decimal point is located.

Adding and subtracting decimals is the same as adding and subtracting money values. No student has difficulty subtracting $1.21 from $6.79. The decimal points are kept under each other.

Example: Add

$$\begin{array}{r} 7.74 \\ 19.07 \\ 221.0005 \\ 247.8205 \\ \hline \end{array}$$

In this example, it is assumed that two zeros follow the first two numbers. Zeros added to the last figure on the right side of the decimal point have no significance. Thus 7.74 is the same as 7.7400000.

In subtraction, zeros are also added as in addition.

$$\begin{array}{r} 45.3 \\ -\ 23.091 \\ \hline \end{array}$$

Here it is assumed that the 45.3 is 45.300.

$$\begin{array}{r} 45.300 \\ -\ 23.091 \\ \hline 22.209 \end{array}$$

Multiplying and dividing are the same as with dollars and cents. The chief necessity is to keep the decimal point in the right place.

In multiplying, forget the decimal points until you have completed the work, then point off as many places as you have figures to the right of the decimal points in both sets of figures. Thus 22.16 × 96.07 should be worked the same as 2,216 × 9,607. Point off four decimal places in your answer.

In dividing, write down the figures as though they were all whole numbers, then move the decimal point to the right in the divisor until the divisor becomes a whole number. Move the decimal point the same number of places in the dividend.

Example:

$$98.0514 \div 17.486$$

$$17.486\overline{)98.0514}$$

Move the decimal three places to the right in each number, and then the decimal in the answer is directly above the decimal between the 1 and 4 in the dividend.

$$\begin{array}{r} . \\ 17{,}486\overline{)98{,}051.4} \end{array}$$

DECIMAL EQUIVALENTS

It is necessary to know how to translate fractions to decimals and decimals to fractions. Both kinds of figures are used in aviation. The thickness of sheet is measured in thousandths; tolerances and clearances are also measured in thousandths usually; and bolts, rivets, and many measurements are in fractions such as eighths, sixteenths, thirty-secondths, or sixty-fourths.

The following table is published by courtesy of the Air Corps Technical School. The mechanic who learns a number of these figures will save himself a considerable amount of time later on. Tables of decimal equivalents are published by several of the tool

DECIMAL EQUIVALENTS

½	¼	⅛	1/16	1/32	1/64	Decimal	½	¼	⅛	1/16	1/32	1/64	Decimal
					1	0.015625						33	0.515625
				1	2	0.03125					17	34	0.53125
					3	0.046875						35	0.546875
			1	2	4	0.0625				9	18	36	0.5625
					5	0.078125						37	0.578125
				3	6	0.09375					19	38	0.59375
					7	0.109375						39	0.609375
		1	2	4	8	0.125			5	10	20	40	0.625
					9	0.140625						41	0.640625
				5	10	0.15625					21	42	0.65625
					11	0.171875						43	0.671875
			3	6	12	0.1875				11	22	44	0.6875
					13	0.203125						45	0.703125
				7	14	0.21875					23	46	0.71875
					15	0.234375						47	0.734375
	1	2	4	8	16	0.250		3	6	12	24	48	0.750
					17	0.265625						49	0.765625
				9	18	0.28125					25	50	0.78125
					19	0.296875						51	0.796875
			5	10	20	0.3125				13	26	52	0.8125
					21	0.328125						53	0.828125
				11	22	0.34375					27	54	0.84375
					23	0.359375						55	0.859375
		3	6	12	24	0.375			7	14	28	56	0.875
					25	0.390625						57	0.890625
				13	26	0.40625					29	58	0.90625
					27	0.421875						59	0.921875
			7	14	28	0.4375				15	30	60	0.9375
					29	0.453125						61	0.953125
				15	30	0.46875					31	62	0.96875
					31	0.484375						63	0.984375
1	2	4	8	16	32	0.500	2	4	8	16	32	64	1.000

companies in small pocket form, and many shops have large copies hanging on their walls.

In using the table, look first for the fraction along the top. If you are looking for the decimal equivalent of $\frac{3}{8}$, for example, look under $\frac{1}{8}$ at the top, and then look down that column to 3—which signifies $\frac{3}{8}$. At the right, in the column headed "Decimal" you will see the figure 0.375.

To find $\frac{15}{16}$, look under $\frac{1}{16}$ and then (on the right-hand half of the page) for 15; the decimal equivalent is 0.9375. Note that fractions over $\frac{1}{2}$ are on the right side of the page.

From this table you will also get a visual appreciation of fractions that are equal. For example, halfway down the table, on the left, you will see that $\frac{1}{4}$, $\frac{2}{8}$, $\frac{4}{16}$, $\frac{8}{32}$, and $\frac{16}{64}$ are in the same horizontal row. All are equal and have a decimal equivalent of 0.250.

The table can also be used to reduce fractions to their lowest terms. The fraction $\frac{41}{64}$ has no figure to its left and cannot be reduced to lower terms. The fraction $\frac{42}{64}$ is equal to $\frac{21}{32}$ but cannot be reduced lower. However, $\frac{48}{64}$ can be reduced to $\frac{24}{32}$, $\frac{12}{16}$, $\frac{6}{8}$, or $\frac{3}{4}$.

Review Problems

1. How many square inches of sheetmetal are required for a part with these dimensions: S.L., 43; S.W., 79?

2. If the above part were cut from a sheet 4 by 8 ft., how many square inches of material would remain?

3. You are given a piece of sheetmetal that is 48 by 72 in. From this sheet how many parts could you cut whose over-all dimensions were 18 by 24 in.?

4. If you were cutting small parts that were 6 by 4 in., how many could you cut from a sheet containing 4,608 sq. in.?

5. If a sheet contains 4,608 sq. in. and is 4 ft. wide, how long is it?

6. If a section of a wing is 425 in. in length, how many feet long is it?

7. Add these numbers:

$12\frac{3}{4}$	$39\frac{1}{2}$	$7\frac{3}{64}$	$14\frac{3}{4}$
$23\frac{1}{2}$	$46\frac{7}{8}$	$12\frac{1}{4}$	$9\frac{15}{16}$
$17\frac{5}{8}$	$54\frac{5}{16}$	$19\frac{7}{8}$	$73\frac{11}{64}$

8. Subtract:

$12\frac{7}{8}$	$17\frac{11}{64}$	$7\frac{1}{4}$	$21\frac{9}{16}$
$9\frac{1}{2}$	$5\frac{3}{8}$	$3\frac{7}{16}$	$17\frac{5}{64}$

9. How many rivets would be placed along a strip of sheet that is 167 in. in length, if the first rivet were $\frac{1}{4}$ in. from the end and rivets were $\frac{5}{8}$ in. apart?

10. Multiply these numbers:

$1\frac{3}{4} \times 3\frac{5}{16}$
$\frac{7}{8} \times 2\frac{1}{4}$
$1\frac{3}{64} \times \frac{9}{32}$
$5\frac{1}{2} \times 7\frac{19}{64}$

11. Read these numbers:

1.21
19.09
5.9
31.57
0.001
5.010
1.009
13.021
7.0005
3.0015

12. Add these figures: 7.23; 0.54; 0.001; 5.0010; 16.25; 31.125.

13. Multiply:

14.21×0.014
7.85×3.001
0.001×4.167

14. Give the decimal equivalent of these fractions: $\frac{1}{8}$; $\frac{1}{16}$; $\frac{1}{64}$; $\frac{5}{32}$; $\frac{7}{16}$; $1\frac{6}{32}$; $4\frac{7}{64}$; $\frac{3}{4}$; $3\frac{5}{64}$.

15. Give the fractional equivalents of these decimals: 0.21875; 0.375; 0.3125; 0.625; 0.750; 0.125; 0.250; 0.875.

CHAPTER 3

WORKING PROPERTIES AND STANDARDS OF AIRCRAFT MATERIALS

Although a sheetmetal mechanic working in an airplane factory spends most of his time handling the aluminum-alloy sheet that is furnished him from the company stock room, about the identification of which he need not concern himself, it is a great advantage for him to know something about the working properties and standards of the various metals used in airplanes. If he is helping to set up material for a hydraulic press, for example, he must know why aluminum-alloy sheet marked "24ST" is not satisfactory for certain types of work and why sheet in the "O" classification is better. To understand why Alclad sheet must not be scratched, he must know something about the composition of this material. Although he has studied blueprint reading, he cannot fully appreciate the rivet and bolt identifications until he has learned the basic AN specifications.

Properties of Metals.—Each kind of metal has several qualities, some of which are desirable for a certain use and some undesirable. Metallurgists have spent much time improving metals for airplane use by building up desirable qualities and toning down undesirable qualities.

Ductility is the property of metal that permits it to be drawn or stretched, compressed, bent, or twisted without fracture. It is this property which is taken advantage of when metals are drawn out into wire.

Malleability is the property that permits a metal to be rolled, bumped, or hammered. It is especially desirable in metals that are to be worked into such parts as cowlings, leading edges, wing tips, and other parts of the airplane where considerable curvature is necessary.

Elasticity means stretch. It is the quality in a metal that permits it to return to its original form after having been subjected to a stress. A certain amount of elasticity is desirable in many aircraft parts.

Hardness is the property of metals that enables them to resist penetration, wear and abrasion, or cutting action. Metal is tested for hardness in such instruments as Brinell or Rockwell machines.

Toughness is a desirable characteristic in all metals used in aircraft parts. Metal that is tough will not tear or shear readily and will stretch under tension without breaking. It is the opposite of brittleness. Ordinary window glass is hard but not tough, as it will break easily.

Fatigue resistance in a metal enables it to withstand repeated loads or reversals of loads. It is important in aircraft metals because when a ship is in the air it is subject to repeated vibrations. "Metal fatigue" is sometimes given as the reason for an airplane accident. Metal of some critical part has failed owing to fatigue, due perhaps to the continuous stress put upon that part.

Strength is a property that sums up many of the desirable qualities of metals. In aviation, metals are often compared on a strength-weight ratio, because these are two of the most important elements in the choice of materials. When a part has been scientifically designed so that it resists the loading that is applied, it is said to have strength.

In a discussion of metal properties, *stress* and *strain* should be mentioned. Stress is a force put upon a body and is usually measured in pounds per square inch, abbreviated p.s.i. This may be in the form of compression, tension, torsion, bending or shearing loads, or a combination of these. All airplane parts are subjected to stresses. When a part fails to return to its original form after being stressed, it is said to be *strained.* Consequently, a strain is a deformation. It is necessary that metals be deformed in the processes of manufacture such as bending and stamping. Once the part is in its finished form in the airplane, an additional deformation from being overly stressed will result in strain and a probable failure.

Stresses Acting on the Airplane.—As mentioned just above, various stresses are acting on the parts of an airplane while it is in flight. They have an important bearing on the metals used.

Tension is a force that pulls materials apart. A weight hanging at the end of a steel cable puts a tension force on the strands of the cable. The ultimate tensile strength of a cable or a piece of metal is the greatest tensile strength that it will develop.

Compression is a crushing or squeezing force. When an airplane lands, the shock-absorbing unit and most landing-gear parts are put under a compression force. When a giant hydraulic press forms sheetmetal parts, the force is compression.

Shear is a force that slides molecules over adjacent molecules. Rivets are sheared off when undue pressure is put on the plates or sheets being held together. Shearing strength is the resistance of a body to being cut in two by a pair of knife edges.

Bending is the force to which a part is subjected when it curves under a load. When a wing spar is bent down, the upper side of the spar is under tension, since it is being stretched. The lower side is compressed. Along the center line, or neutral axis, shear is developed.

Torsion is a twisting force. It may occur when one end of a member is held securely and the other end is twisted.

The foregoing forces seldom act one at a time. A combination of them is often at work, especially when the airplane is being buffeted about by gusty weather.

FORMS IN WHICH METALS ARE SUPPLIED TO AIRPLANE FACTORIES

Although a sheetmetal worker deals primarily with metal that is provided in sheet form, he should know at least the names of the other commonly used forms. They will be described briefly.

FIG. 22.—Sheetmetal reaches the airplane factory in large rectangular sheets. They must always be handled carefully as they are not acceptable if scratched. This shows special handling racks at the Glenn L. Martin factory.

Sheet Stock.—Both aluminum alloy and steel come from the rolling mills in flat and corrugated sheet. Flat sheet is used for a great variety of purposes. Corrugated sheet is used principally under the skin for reinforcing highly stressed wing sections.

The thickness of sheetmetal may be classified according to the Brown & Sharpe system of sheetmetal gages, although the mechanic usually refers to the thickness in thousandths of an inch or in fractional parts of an inch. Thus aluminum-alloy sheet may be called for that is 0.032 in. in thickness. Sheet steel for a fitting may be 0.065 in. in thickness.

Extrusions.—Extruded shapes are produced hydraulically by forcing metal through an orifice having the desired cross section. When you force tooth paste from a tube, you are extruding it. The aluminum-alloy longitudinal stringers used in fuselage construction are an example of extrusions.

Tubing.—Seamless tubing is produced in a variety of alloys and sizes. It is furnished in round, square, rectangular, oval, and streamlined shapes. Tubing is used for a variety of airplane parts. It is measured by both its outside diameter and its wall thickness in thousandths of an inch.

Rod and Bar Stock.—Most rod and bar stock in an aircraft plant goes to the machine shop. It is furnished in a number of cross-sectional shapes.

Forgings.—Forgings may be made by pouring molten metal alloys into dies that serve as molds. The metal is then pounded by heavy drop hammers which compress the molecules to form parts having great strength. Forgings are also made from preheated bar or rod stock which is given repeated blows of a hammer to force the material to conform to the contour of a steel forming die. Forgings are used for such parts as propellers, pistons, and fittings. They are usually made outside the airplane plant and machined and finished by the aircraft manufacturer or one of his subcontractors.

Castings.—The majority of castings used in aircraft construction are of aluminum alloy. Castings are made by pouring molten alloy in sand molds or in permanent molds or by forcing it under pressure into molds on die-casting machines. Permanent metal molds produce a casting of smoother finish and more exact measurement than sand molds. Die casting has many advantages, as this form has superior strength, accuracy, and finish. Castings are not usually so strong as forgings.

ALUMINUM ALLOYS

The principal material used by aircraft sheetmetal workers is aluminum alloy. It is different from any other kind of sheetmetal. Although it is much stronger than sheetmetal used in building construction, it is also much more delicate. Aluminum-alloy sheetmetal is like a prize-winning race horse which is strong enough to win races and yet is so sensitive that it will catch cold in slight drafts. When kept in proper condition, aluminum alloy will perform miracles, but if scratched or marred it may later develop cracks or become weakened through corrosion. Thus the first lesson to be learned is to handle the material carefully.

Aluminum alloy is used in airplane construction because, considering its light weight, it is unsurpassed by other metals in strength, working qualities, and other desirable characteristics. It weighs only one-third as much as the steel that would be necessary to accomplish the same structural purpose. It has the three most important attributes needed in aircraft metals: lightness, strength, and easy workability. This last characteristic means that it is easy to handle in the factory, as it can be riveted, welded, machined, and shaped with standard tools and machinery.

Several different grades or alloys of aluminum are used in building airplanes, and it will be well to describe them briefly so that you understand why different grades are specified for different purposes. "Commercially pure" aluminum contains less than 1 per cent of other alloying elements, chiefly iron and silicon. This is known in airplane factories as *aluminum*, and it is used in nonstructural parts where great strength is unnecessary. It is not so strong as aluminum alloy but is used where intricate forming is a requirement.

When the foregoing grade of aluminum has added to it more than 1 per cent of other metals, the result is called *aluminum alloy*. By the addition of small amounts of other metals, aluminum becomes a great deal stronger than the commercially pure metal. The metals most commonly used for this purpose are copper, silicon, manganese, magnesium, chromium, iron, zinc, and nickel. These metals may be added singly or in combinations. If the alloy is made in wrought forms, such as rolling, extruding, drawing, or forging, the alloying metals seldom total more than 6 or 7 per cent. Castings, however, may have a higher proportion of alloying metals.

There are several different grades of alloys in common use; and although two sheets may have the same thickness and appearance, they may have very different working properties. Sheets are stamped with symbols, such as 24S-T, so that the mechanic can identify them, but he should understand what the different symbols mean.*

Wrought alloys of aluminum are designated by the letter "S," which follows a number identifying the chemical composition, such as 17S. Wrought alloys are produced by rolling, extruding, drawing, and forging.

In one group of alloys, hardness and strength are produced by definite amounts of cold working after the final annealing, or softening, process. In these unheat-treatable alloys, fully annealed, or soft, material is designated by the letter "O"; fully hardened material is designated by "H," for example, 52S-O and 52S-H. Intermediate degrees of hardness are denoted by fractions, such as 52S-½H. These unheat-treatable alloys combine moderate strength with good workability. They are used principally for parts that must be bent or formed at considerable angles but where great strength is not needed.

In a second group of alloys, final hardness and strength are produced primarily by heat-treatment. Maximum physical properties or greatest strengths are obtained by a heat-treating process followed by aging. The annealed (soft) condition before heat-treating is designated by "O," but the same material is designated by "T" after the heat-treating and aging process. Thus 17S-O becomes 17S-T after heat-treating. The intermediate temper of these alloys, after solution heat-treatment and before

* In this book aluminum-alloy symbols, such as 24S-T, are written according to the code published by the Aluminum Company of America, since that company originates the codes. It will be noted that elsewhere this alloy is written 24ST or 24 ST. Any of these forms is correct as long as it is consistently followed.

aging, is designated by "W," for example, 53S-W. The letter "R" indicates strain-hardening by cold rolling after heat-treatment, as in 17S-RT.

This may seem a bit confusing to the beginning mechanic, but he will soon find that most of his sheetmetal work is done with S-O metals (signifying soft material) or with S-T material (which is fully hardened).

Designations of the various aluminum alloys and information about them are given in the table on page 52.

Alclad.—This is a trade name of the Aluminum Company of America. It signifies a sheet of aluminum alloy that has been covered on both sides with a thin, protective coating of pure alumimum. The first syllable of the word, *Al*, means aluminum, and second syllable, *clad*, means covered. The pure aluminum on the outside of the sheet retards corrosion as long as it is not scratched. If your hand is scratched, and the skin broken, the wound is open to possible infection. When the aluminum coating on Alclad is scratched, the exposed alloy is open to corrosion, which may set in with surprising rapidity.

Alclad is used to a great extent on all-metal airplanes. Usually the sheets forming the fuselage and the wings are of Alclad. Sheets are easily identified because they are stamped "ALC" preceding the identification of the metal, for example, ALC24S-T.

Anodizing.—Most military airplanes are camouflaged with paint for combat work. Because of its shiny, smooth surface, aluminum alloy is not a good base for paint, and it is customary to anodize the metal. Anodizing is the production of an artificial coating of aluminum oxide on the surface of aluminum alloys by electrochemical means. Parts are attached to an anode rod, then immersed in a chromic acid solution through which a direct electric current is passed. The immersion lasts only ½ hr. or more until the part becomes insulated. The effect is oxidation, or artificial corrosion, begun and arrested. The integral oxide coating thus formed not only serves as a basic protection to the aluminum alloy but serves as an excellent base for any paint put on afterward. The anodic film, being an insulator, also helps to prevent electrolytic action among dissimilar metals. However, like Alclad, anodized parts are subject to corrosion when the protective film is scratched.

FIG. 23.—Thousands of parts are anodized daily in a large aircraft plant. These racks are in the El Segundo plant of Douglas Aircraft Co. A crane will pick up the entire rack and move it to the anodizing tanks.

Heat-treating.—The great airplanes of today are possible because of strength given to metals through alloying and by means of the heat-treating process. In heat-treating, metals are heated to predetermined temperatures, held there for a specified period, and then either gradually cooled to room temperature or quickly cooled by contact with cold water. Metallurgists working in the laboratories of such firms as the Aluminum Company of America and in our technical laboratories have accomplished miracles in improving the properties of metals through heat-treating.

As the table on page 52 indicates, the tensile strength of grade 2S-O aluminum is 13,000 lb. per square inch. By slight changes in the alloying elements and by heat-treatment, the tensile strength of 24S-RT is brought up to 68,000 lb. per square inch. The difference between the same alloy not heat-treated and one that has been put through heat-treatment, in the case of 24S-O, is the difference between 26,000 and 68,000 lb. per square inch.

STRENGTH AND USES OF ALUMINUM ALLOYS*

Alloy	Tensile strength, lb. per sq. in.	Shearing strength, lb. per sq. in.	Use
2S-O	13,000	9,500	Nonstructural parts, deep curvatures formed by presses and drop hammers. Can be welded
2S-½H	17,000	11,000	Use is the same as for 2S-O, but this alloy is stronger and harder
2S-H	24,000	13,000	Still stronger and harder than the two above. General use the same
3S-O	16,000	11,000	Stronger and stiffer than 2S-O, but slightly harder to work. Often used for tanks and for parts formed in presses and by drop hammers. Weldable
3S-½H	21,000	14,000	Where metal that is stronger but slightly less workable than 3S-O is usable
3S-H	29,000	16,000	Still stronger, but less workable
17S-O	26,000	18,000	Structural purposes requiring moderate strength and easy workability. Must be heat-treated after forming
17S-T	58,000	36,000	General structural use. Replaced for many parts by 24S-T
17S-T Alclad	55,000	32,000	Structural use, especially exterior skin. Being replaced by 24S-T Alclad
17S-RT Alclad	57,000	32,000	Less ductile than 17S-T
24S-O	26,000	18,000	For highly stressed structural parts requiring considerable forming. Must be heat-treated after forming
24S-T	65,000	41,000	Is standard for most aircraft parts
24S-RT	68,000	42,000	Slightly stronger but less ductile than 24S-T. Has appreciably greater yield strength
24S-T Alclad	60,000	40,000	Where great resistance to corrosion is desired in structural parts made from sheet. Forms the skin for many aircraft
24S-RT Alclad	68,000	41,000	Stronger than 24S-T Alclad but less ductile
52S-O	29,000	18,000	Parts requiring bumping. Tubing for fuel, oil, and instrument lines. Has high endurance limit. Weldable

* Figures given here have been approved by the Aluminum Company of America and in some cases are slightly different from figures published previously.

Whenever possible the airplane companies prefer to have heat-treating done by the aluminum mill. However, after aluminum-alloy sheet has been heat-treated, it cannot be worked, bent, or formed so easily as before. Consequently some parts must be formed before being heat-treated. In such instances the aircraft firm does heat-treating in its own shops.

Students usually become familiar with heat-treating through the heat-treating of rivets. Rivets designated as "D" or "DD," as explained later in this chapter, are heat-treated in the aircraft factory and then kept at a low temperature in a refrigerator, and are brought out just before they are used.

Annealing.—This is a heating and cooling operation which is done to remove hardness and strains that come as a result of forming. It softens and refines the metal. The temperature to which metal should be heated for annealing, the means of cooling, and the rate of cooling depend upon the composition of the metal. Aluminum is cooled much more rapidly than steel.

Handling in the Shop.—Scratches on pieces of sheetmetal are enough to cause their rejection by Army and Navy inspectors in the aircraft plants, since a scratch is a possible source of corrosion. To prevent the scratching of metals, workbenches, vises, and other working spaces are covered in such a way that no rough edges will harm the sheet. It is common practice to cover benches with heavy paper, to protect vise jaws with pieces of aluminum sheet or other soft metal, and to protect finished parts.

One of the first lessons in the use of tools is to make sure that screw drivers, snips, chisels, and other tools do not slip and scratch the metal. When parts are finished, they are not thrown carelessly to the floor or into a box but are piled neatly together so that surfaces are protected.

NICKEL ALLOYS

Several special alloys are used for aircraft purposes. One of these is *Inconel*, which is a nickel alloy containing chromium and iron. It is used for exhaust manifolds because it can withstand sudden changes of temperature, great heat, and the corrosive effects of condensation. Nickel is also alloyed with steel for wing ribs, bolts, and other aircraft and engine parts.

MAGNESIUM ALLOY

Dowmetal is a magnesium alloy that is one-third lighter than aluminum. It has a high strength-weight ratio and is used in aircraft work generally in the form of castings. The metal worker may be assigned to finish parts or fittings of this metal. It is principally used for fuselage fairings, secondary structural parts, and housings. In both England and Germany, magnesium is used to a greater extent in airplanes than it is in this country. It is expected that a much greater use will be made of it here.

AIRCRAFT STEELS

Although the bulk of aircraft sheetmetal work is concerned with the aluminum alloys, a mechanic should also be familiar with certain steels that are in common use.

Steels are identified by their S.A.E. number. Under the auspices of the Society of Automotive Engineers, all steels in common use throughout American industry have been given a number. Once you know what the numbers mean, you can tell the properties of a steel from the number. The two most commonly used aircraft steels are 1025 and 4130.

Under the S.A.E. numbering system, the first figure tells the class to which the steel belongs.

1—Carbon.
2—Nickel.
3—Nickel-chromium.
4—Molybdenum.
5—Chromium.
6—Chromium-vanadium.
7—Tungsten.
9—Silicon-manganese.

The second figure indicates the approximate percentage of the principal alloy. The last two or three figures denote the average carbon content in hundredths of 1 per cent.

Thus 1025 means a carbon steel (since the first figure is a 1, denoting carbon). The second figure is 0, meaning there is no principal alloy. The last two figures, 25, show that the amount of carbon runs between 0.20 to 0.30 per cent. The carbon content may fluctuate 0.05 above or below the formula.

The steel that you will use most often is 4130. The first figure shows that this is an alloy steel using molybdenum, and the second figure denotes that there is 1 per cent of molybdenum. The last two figures indicate about 30 per cent of carbon. This steel has some chromium in it; but chromium is a secondary alloy, and only the principal alloy shows in the numbering formula.

Chromium is a metal that is added to steel to produce hardness. It also makes the steel more resistant to corrosion. Molybdenum is an element that has a magic touch when added to steel. When combined in proper amounts with chromium, it produces a hard, strong steel that can be heat-treated successfully and welded easily. The 4130 steel is generally called *chrome-moly*.

STAINLESS STEEL

The sheetmetal mechanic may be called upon to handle stainless steel, and he should know how it differs from aluminum-alloy sheet. Stainless steel is valuable in the aircraft industry because it is almost indestructible from corrosion. It is used for wing-tip floats, ailerons, elevators, and trailing edges of wings. Stainless steel does not need to be shop-primed during construction or painted after completion.

This metal is also used for the fire walls of many airplanes, as its high melting point offers more protection in case of an engine fire than if an aluminum-alloy fire wall is used. Stainless steel is often used for exhaust collector rings.

It is made from steel that has a low carbon content, with the addition of about 18 per cent chromium and 8 per cent nickel. It is often designated as 18-8. It can be joined easily by shot or spot welding. It is tough and springy and is not so easy to work with as aluminum alloy, but because of its strength it can be used in thinner gage sheet than aluminum alloy.

PROTECTION OF METALS

Corrosion is an ever present problem in aircraft construction. Everything possible is done in the factory to prepare metal parts for a long life. We have already discussed protecting aluminum sheet by the Alclad method and by anodizing.

Painting is the other principal method. When painting is used, the metal may or may not be anodized previously, although anodizing provides an excellent base for paint. It is not possible to paint successfully on the shiny aluminum-alloy surface, and a primer coat is first applied. This is most often a coat of zinc chromate, which is sprayed on the metal. Zinc chromate primer is a greenish liquid with a synthetic base thinned for spraying by the addition of 2 or 3 parts of toluol. It dries in about 5 min., and it also has the advantage of being from 50 to 75 per cent lighter in weight than other primers. It is almost always covered by one or more additional coats of either lacquer, enamel, or zinc chromate that has had aluminum paste mixed with it.

Red oxide oil-base primer is sometimes used, although it is not now so common as the zinc chromate primer. It has an iron oxide or a lead base, is thinned 25 to 50 per cent with turpentine, and dries in 15 to 20 hr. It improves if it is baked.

Interiors of fuselages and wings that cannot be inspected easily are usually sprayed with zinc chromate and then painted. The frames of ailerons, rudders, and other fabric-covered surfaces are invariably painted. Outside surfaces that are easily visible during inspections may not be painted. Often they are waxed.

Shop Priming.—Before two pieces of sheet are riveted together, the parts that will be covered by the overlapping are given a coat of zinc chromate called *shop primer*. This is an extra precaution to prevent corrosion from developing at points where the sheet has been cut or drilled. Cutting or drilling exposes the interior of the sheet. Since Alclad is really a sandwich of aluminum alloy covered by a thin coating of pure aluminum, the interior of the sheet is exposed at the edges. When sheets are riveted together, it is impossible to inspect or paint the covered portions, and shop priming adds a plus factor in the war against corrosion.

Dopeproofing.—In fabric-covered fuselages, such as are used in private planes and in military trainers, and in fabric-covered control surfaces, the dope used on the fabric will cut through an undercoating of paint and act like a varnish or paint remover. To prevent this from occurring, the metal surfaces coming in contact with the dope are protected with aluminum foil or dopeproof paint. Commercial adhesive tape is also used where sharp edges occur.

Shop Protection.—To protect aluminum-alloy stock during assembly operations a coating of clear fuselage varnish slightly pigmented with Prussian blue is sprayed on one or both sides of the sheet. The color is added to provide a light tint so that the mechanic can see what points he has sprayed. The film of varnish protects the metal from small abrasions that occur in handling. If the sheet is seriously scratched, the damage is apparent immediately, whereas it might not be discovered in the unpainted metal. When assembly operations are completed, the Prussian blue on the interior surface that is not to be painted is left on the metal but is washed off if the metal is to be painted or if on the outside surfaces of the airplane. Specifications for priming and painting are given on blueprints, as was pointed out in Chap. 1.

ARMY-NAVY SPECIFICATIONS

Parts for military planes in this country must be manufactured to meet standards set by the Army and Navy. These are called *AN specifications.* Some parts are drawn to Air Corps specifications alone, and these are abbreviated AC. Other specifications have been set by the Naval Aircraft Factory, and these are abbreviated NAF. However, the largest group of standards are AN. The sheetmetal worker does not need to know all details concerning AN parts, but he must realize that when blueprints call for a specific AN part, that part alone must be used. Army and Navy inspectors working in aircraft factories are quick to reject any parts other than those specified on the drawings.

In all AN parts the figure following the letters "AN" refers not only to the part number but to the page in the Army-Navy specification book where information about the part is given. The mechanic gradually learns the numbers of parts with which he is working, but when in doubt he can always refer to the book.

A-N RIVET CODE

Although riveting is discussed fully in Chap. 11, this is a convenient place in the book to present a general description of the AN rivet code.

Aircraft sheetmetal workers should learn the AN rivet code. At first glance it may seem complicated; but actually only a few types of rivets are in general use, and for these the code can be learned quickly. Rivets are specified by letters and figures, of which the following is one example: AN425DD4-6.

The three figures following AN designate the kind of head on the rivet.

AN420	Countersunk head (iron and copper).
AN425	Countersunk head (aluminum alloy and aluminum).
AN430	Round head (aluminum alloy and aluminum).
AN435	Round head (iron and copper)
AN442	Flat head (aluminum alloy and aluminum).
AN455	Brazier head.

Drawings of these heads are shown in Chap. 11.

The letter or letters "A," "AD," "D," "DD" marked on blueprints signify the aluminum alloy that is used in the rivet. These are as follows:

The letter "A" designates an aluminum rivet of 2S or 3S aluminum. These rivets have a smooth head and are sometimes stamped 2 or 3 on the shank, denoting 2S or 3S. They are driven *as received* and do not need to be heat-treated.

The letters "AD" designate a half-hardened rivet that has been heat-treated at the aluminum factory. This rivet is of A17S-T alloy and is driven as received. It is not heat-treated in the aircraft plant. It has an indentation, or dimple, in the center of the head.

The letter "D" signifies a 17S rivet, which is commonly called an *icebox* rivet. It is made from 17S-O material which is heated in the aircraft factory to 930°F. and then quenched in cold water, then put in an icebox and kept frozen until ready for use. It must be used within 15 or 20 min. after it is removed from the icebox. The heat-treating process is further explained in Chap. 11, on How to Rivet. This rivet has a hump, or a tit, on the center of head for identification.

The letters "DD" designate a 24S rivet, which is also an icebox rivet. It is also heat-treated in the aircraft factory and stored in a refrigerator until ready for use and must be used within 5 min. after it is taken from the icebox. It is identified by two raised bars, or dashes, on opposite sides of the head (DD = double dash.)

Summary:

A	Smooth head, 2S or 3S aluminum, drive as is. (Do not heat-treat.)
AD	Dimple on head, A17S-T alloy, drive as is. (Do not heat-treat.)
D	Hump on head, of 17S alloy, icebox rivet. (Heat-treated in aircraft factory.)
DD	Two raised bars on head, of 24S alloy, icebox rivet. (Heat-treated in aircraft factory.)

The figure in the rivet code after the letters "A," "AD," "D," or "DD" signifies the diameter of the shank in thirty-seconds of an inch. Thus in the specification AN425DD4-6, the figure 4 signifies 4/32 in. in diameter, or a 1/8 in. rivet.

The figure after the dash signifies the length of the rivet in sixteenths of an inch. In the paragraph just above, the rivet is 6/16 in. (3/8 in.) in length. If the length of the rivet is 5/32 in., for example, which cannot be expressed in sixteenths of an inch, the number following the dash is a fraction, -5/32.

Example: AN425AD3-5

AN	Army-Navy specification.
425	Countersunk head.
AD	Half-hardened rivet, drive as is.
3	3/32 in. in diameter.
-5	Length of rivet is 5/16 in.

AN455DD5-7

AN	Army-Navy specification.
455	Brazier head.
DD	Icebox rivet.
5	5/32 in. in diameter.
-7	7/16 in. in length.

A-N BOLTS

Aircraft drawings call for bolts by a numbering system. Thus a bolt might be specified as follows: AN10-13. The AN signifies Army-Navy specification. The first figure following AN specifies the diameter in sixteenths of an inch. In the foregoing example, the 10 means 10/16 (or 5/8 in.). The number following the dash signifies the length of the bolt in steps of 1/8 in. These steps run 1 to 7, representing 1/8 to 7/8, but 8 and 9 are skipped, and a bolt 1 in. long is represented by 10. Figures over 10 represent more than 1 in. Thus the 13 of the preceding example means a bolt 1 3/8 in. long.

A few examples follow:

AN5-7	A bolt of 5/16 in. diameter, 7/8 in. long.
AN3-4	A bolt of 3/16 in. diameter, 4/8 in. long.
AN11-14	A bolt of 11/16 in. diameter, 1 4/8 in. long.
AN8-10	A bolt of 8/16 in. diameter, 1 in. long.
AN8-20	A bolt of 8/16 in. diameter, 2 in. long.

Just as -8 and -9 are omitted, so -18 and -19 are omitted. A length of 1 7/8 in. is -17, and the next step is -20.

All the foregoing are hexagon-headed bolts with holes for cotter pins. To designate a bolt without a cotter-pin hole the letter "A" is added. Thus: AN10-13A.

Head Markings.—The markings on bolt heads denotes the kind of material used in the bolt. An asterisk (*) or an × on the head of an Army-Navy or Air Corps bolt indicates that the material is S.A.E. 2330 (nickel steel). Two dashes on the head show that the material is 17S aluminum alloy. A plain head indicates that the material is 24S aluminum alloy.

In the bolt code if there is no letter in addition to the AN, the bolt is of steel. D signifies 17S aluminum alloy, and DD signifies 24S aluminum alloy. The letters "D" take the place of the dash, thus: AN4DD5.

In the bolt code,

AN3 to AN16, inclusive, are reserved for hexagon-headed bolts.
AN23 to AN36 are reserved for clevis bolts.
AN42 to AN49 are reserved for eye for pin.
AN73 to AN81 are reserved for drilled hexagon-headed bolts.

A-N NUTS

Aircraft nuts must be made to strict specifications. They are made of steel, dural, and brass. If no letter is used in addition to the AN, it is understood that the nut is of 4130 chrome-molybdenum steel. If the letter "D" precedes the dash number, the nut is dural, and the letter "B" signifies brass. Steel aircraft castle nuts are indicated as AN310. Dash numbers indicate the diameter of tap used in sixteenths of an inch and run from -3 to -16. Thus AN310-7 is a steel castle nut size 7/16 in.

AN315 is a plain aircraft hexagon-headed nut, steel or dural. AN316 is an aircraft check or lock nut made of steel. AN320 is an aircraft castle shear nut, steel or dural. AN340 is a machine-screw hexagon nut, brass or steel. AN350 is a wing nut made of steel, with a hole in one wing for safety wire. AC365 is a self-locking hexagon nut made of S.A.E. 1020 steel, 17S-T dural, or brass. AC366 is the same as 365 except that the steel is 1112 and the nut has two tabs that are riveted to the structure when the nut cannot be reached with a wrench or when the material is too thin to tap a thread. AC367 is the same as 366 except it has an 82 deg. depression in the end opposite the fiber insert.

A-N MACHINE SCREWS

Machine screws used for aircraft are usually cadmium-plated steel, although some are made of aluminum alloy. Machine-screw numbers range from AN500 to AC566. The screws range in size from 1 to 10 gage, machine-screw sizes, plus $\frac{1}{4}$, $\frac{5}{16}$, and $\frac{3}{8}$ fractional diameter.

On blueprints the size of machine screws is coded with the symbol AN or AC followed by the part number that indicates the type of screw. Then comes the screw size. Fractional diameters are given as 416 ($\frac{4}{16}$ in., or $\frac{1}{4}$ in.), 516 ($\frac{5}{16}$ in.), or 616 ($\frac{6}{16}$ in.). Length is signified by the dash number, given in sixteenths.

For example: AC503 10-8 is an Air Corps screw, type 503, size 10 and is $\frac{8}{16}$ in. in length. AN502 416-14 is Army-Navy type 502, $\frac{1}{4}$ in. in diameter, and $\frac{14}{16}$ (or $\frac{7}{8}$) in. in length.

AN502	Fillister head	NF thread.
AC503	Fillister head	NC thread.
AN505	Countersunk head	NC thread.
AN510	Countersunk head	NF thread.
AN515	Round head	NC thread.
AN520	Round head	NF thread.
AC525	Washer head	NF thread.
AC526	Brazier head	NF-NC thread.
	Phillips head	
AN530-535	Self-tapping	

(NF is National fine thread. NC is National coarse thread.)

Parker-Kalon screws (shop abbreviation: PK's) are often used to hold sheets of metal together temporarily during construction. Their chief advantage lies in the fact that they cut their own threads as they are turned into position. A small fiber washer is often used under the head so that the screw will not burr the sheet. This type of screw is also used for permanent fastening of instrument panels and cabin linings and with various kinds of plastic materials.

OTHER A-N PARTS

Too many standard parts are listed in the AN book to be repeated here. The mechanic will gradually learn the AN numbers as he becomes familiar with the part. A listing of the more commonly used parts follows:

INDEX OF A-N STANDARD PARTS

AN3 to AN16	Bolts, hexagon head.
AN23 to AN36	Bolts, clevis.
AN73 to AN81	Bolts, drilled head.
AN100	Thimble, wire cable.
AN110 to AN111	Bushings.
AN115	Shackle, cable.
AN130 to AN140	Cable.
AN150	Turnbuckle assembly fork.
AN155	Barrel-turnbuckle.
AN160 to AN161	Fork, turnbuckle.
AN165	Eye, turnbuckle for pin.
AN210	Pulley, control.
AN310 to AN367	Nuts.
AN380 to AN415	Pins.
AN420 to AN455	Rivets.
AN502 to AN566	Screws.
AN570	Bushing.
AN671 to AN708	Tie rods.
AN735 to AN745	Clamps.
AN750 to AN755	Clips.
AN860 to AN868	Flanges.
AN935 to AN975	Washers.

NOMENCLATURE

Experienced mechanics "speak the language" of aviation. Through years of working around airplanes they have learned scores of terms connected with many phases of aeronautics. One way for the beginning mechanic to get along faster in his job is to know aviation nomenclature, or terms. A few airplane parts are identified in Fig. 24. In one drawing it is impossible to identify many parts, but those shown are a beginning. It is suggested that sheetmetal mechanics learn as many terms as possible, especially those of airplane parts.

A list of nearly 200 terms, with their definitions, is given in the Appendix, beginning on page 269. The mechanic can profit from studying this list.

Review Questions

1. Name seven properties of metals that are important in aviation work and define each briefly.

2. What is the difference between stress and strain?

3. Name five stresses and define them in relation to airplane design.

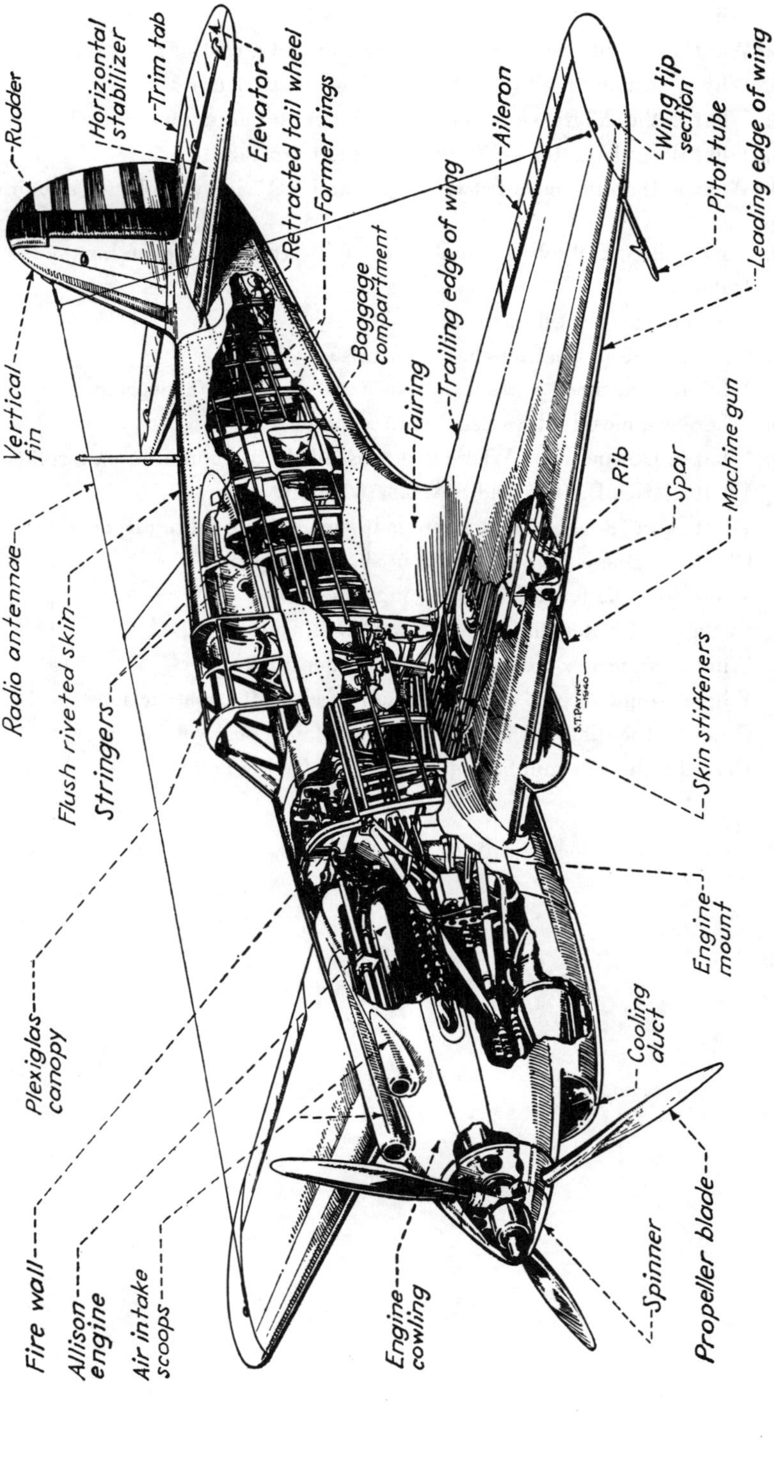

Fig. 24.—Some of the principal parts of a Curtiss P-40.

4. What is an extrusion and how is it made?

5. What is the difference between a forging and a casting?

6. Why is aluminum alloy used in airplane construction?

7. What is the difference between aluminum and aluminum alloy?

8. What does the letter "S" signify in the term 17S-T?

9. What is the difference between "T" and "O" in symbols for aluminum alloys?

10. Which class of alloys is usually formed in presses and drop hammers?

11. Define "Alclad."

12. Why are sheetmetal parts anodized?

13. How does heat-treating change metals?

14. Why are scratched parts usually rejected by aircraft inspectors?

15. Where are nickel alloys used in an airplane?

16. What is Dowmetal? Where is it most likely to be used in an airplane?

17. What do S.A.E. 1025 and S.A.E. 4130 signify?

18. What is an 18-8 steel and where is it sometimes used in airplanes?

19. Of what value is zinc chromate in shop priming?

20. What does the term "dopeproofing" mean?

21. In the rivet code what does AN455AD34 signify?

22. What is an icebox rivet and how is it identified?

23. Where would AN435 rivets be used in aircraft construction?

24. Describe the different identification markings on rivet heads.

25. Describe the AN numbering system for aircraft bolts.

CHAPTER 4

HOW TO MEASURE

The sheetmetal mechanic must know how to measure accurately if he is to hold an aviation job. If he comes into aviation from other kinds of work, he may be amazed at the close measurements that are consistently required in building airplanes. In measuring sheetmetal for an air-conditioning system in an office building there are sometimes variations from $\frac{1}{4}$ to $\frac{1}{2}$ in. in the finished piece. Such leeway in measuring cannot be permitted in aircraft building.

A "tolerance" is the amount of permissible variation in measurement. Thus, if a measurement is to be 1 in. with a tolerance of $\pm \frac{1}{64}$ in., the mechanic may have a leeway of $\frac{1}{64}$ in. on either side of exactly 1 inch. The measurement could be 1 in. plus $\frac{1}{64}$ in. or 1 in. minus $\frac{1}{64}$ in. A variation of $\frac{1}{64}$ in. is the greatest that is permitted in many airplane parts. Some parts are measured in terms of $\frac{1}{1000}$ (0.001) part of an inch.

Accurate measurement is necessary for several reasons. In mass production there is no time to cut and file individual parts until they fit into their intended place on the airplane, nor can holes be reamed if they do not line up. Parts are made in widely separated departments, and each must fit without further handwork. In fact, subassemblies are often built outside the factory by subcontracting firms. A manufacturer of ailerons or rudders may be located on the East Coast and send his products to an airplane factory on the West Coast. If his airplane parts are to fit, the measurements must be within the tolerance limits permitted on the blueprints.

Parts that fit loosely tend to wear out rapidly. In control surfaces, such as rudders, elevators, or ailerons, if the movable parts are too tight, they may bind and cause trouble. Military airplanes are often built to closer tolerances than commercial planes in order to accommodate fire-control apparatus, guns, and bombs, which require extremely accurate installation.

Other reasons for accurate measurement are the weight and the performance problems. If one wing of a plane is longer and heavier than the other, the airplane will not fly properly. If the two sides of a horizontal stabilizer or an elevator are not the same, poor control will be a result.

KINDS OF MEASUREMENT

Five kinds of measurement concern the sheetmetal mechanic.

Linear measurement is from one point to another along a line. In aircraft work, such measurements are expressed in parts of inches, in inches, and in feet. The wing span of a pursuit plane may be expressed as 56 ft. 3½ in. The distance between two bolt holes may be 17$\frac{3}{64}$ in. Measurements are sometimes made as close as $\frac{1}{100}$ (0.01) in., but for ordinary work $\frac{1}{64}$ in. is the smallest fraction used for this type of measuring.

Square measurement concerns the number of units in a surface area. A square foot has 144 sq. in. A piece of Alclad sheet 6 by 72 in. will have 432 sq. in. in its area. The area of a square or a rectangle is easily obtained by multiplying the length times the width. Square inches may be reduced to square feet by dividing the number of square inches by 144.

Cubic measurement is the space enclosed within three dimensions: height, width, and breadth. A gasoline tank that is 2 ft. high, 2 ft. wide, and 4 ft. long contains 16 cu. ft. The capacity is obtained by multiplying the three dimensions together. Cubic measurement in the United States is usually in cubic inches, cubic feet, or cubic yards.

Weight is a measurement in pounds, ounces, or other units, such as tons. For example, an airplane may have an empty weight of 2,500 lb. and gross weight of 4,000 lb.

Circular or *angular* measurement is concerned with arcs and angles. A circle is a plane figure bounded by a curved line, every point of which is an equal distance from the center. The line that bounds a circle is called its *circumference*. A straight line from one side of a circle that passes through the center and touches a point on the opposite side is called a *diameter*. Any portion of the circumference is called an *arc*. The entire circumference of a circle is divided into 360 units called *degrees*. An *angle* is the opening between two straight lines that meet at a point. A *right angle* is equal to 90 deg.; an angle less than 90 deg. is an *acute* angle, or a *closed* angle; an angle of more than 90 deg. is an *obtuse* angle, or an *open* angle.

60 seconds ($''$)	= 1 minute ($'$)
60 minutes	= 1 degree ($^\circ$)
90 degrees	= 1 right angle or quadrant
360 degrees	= 1 circle

MEASURING TOOLS

Rules.—The most common rule in shop use is made of steel and is 6 in. in length. It is used both for measuring and as a straightedge for marking or scribing. On one edge the distances are graduated in sixty-fourths of an inch and on the other in sixteenths or thirty-seconds. A popular type of 6 in. shop rule has a cross member that can be slid up and down to serve as a depth gage. Rules are made in larger lengths, usually 24, 36, and 48 in. For measurements over 4 ft., a flexible steel rule is used. Steel rules should be held on an edge and not flat for measuring. In this position the scale is easier to read and closer measurements can be taken. It is also advisable to take the measurement from any convenient point, except the extreme end of the rule which may have been cut wrong or may have been worn from careless handling.

Steel Tapes.—These are manufactured in 25, 50, and 100 ft. lengths. As with the shorter, flexible rules, the tape is wound around an enclosed reel and operates by a spring and crank arrangement. The most common length is 50 ft. Steel tapes are useful in laying out jigs, for measuring large sheets and long extrusions, and for checking measurements of major parts during final assembly.

Squares.—Several kinds of squares are used in aircraft sheet-metal work. The first is the solid square, which is a steel rule with a short metal handle fastened at right angles. It is much the same as the carpenter's try square. The adjustable square has a beam (which is the handle section) that can move back and forth along the blade. It can be fastened at any position by means of a clamp screw. The combination square is really eight tools in one. It can be used for a variety of operations including measuring, squaring, mitering, marking angles, gaging depth and height, leveling, locating centers with a center head, and scribing (see Fig. 25). A number of measuring tools are shown in Chap. 6.

Dividers.—Dividers are used for measuring distances between two points or for transferring distances from a rule to the work or from the work to the rule. They can also be used for scribing circles and arcs. An adjustable screw keeps the points set at the desired distance. When circles or parts of circles are to be drawn on sheetmetal, it is often the shop practice to cover a portion of the sheet with blue vitriol or layout ink. Then, when one point

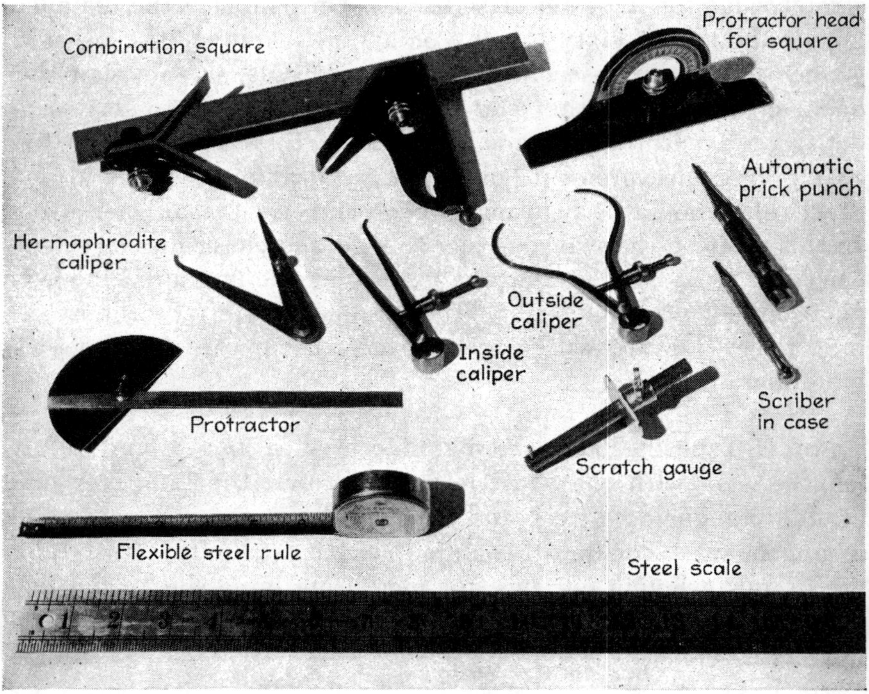

Fig. 25.—A group of measuring tools that may be used by sheetmetal mechanics.

of the dividers is put in the center mark made by a prick punch, and the other used as a scriber to mark out the circle, the line shows clearly through the ink, which later can be washed off. Dividers are used in several sizes. They are an essential tool to the sheetmetal mechanic (see Fig. 42).

Trammels.—Trammels are used for measuring or laying off distances and for scribing large arcs and circles, when the distance is too great to be reached by dividers. A trammel consists of a bar along which two adjustable points may be moved. Each can be tightened to the bar in order that the points may be locked into position. Some trammels are provided with a number of interchangeable points. Divider points, caliper points, pencil points, pen points, and ball points can be interchanged and used for different kinds of work. A ball point may be used at one end of the trammel if an arc or circle is to be swung on a sheet having a drilled hole as a center. The ball point used should be slightly larger than the hole, so that it can ride around the edges without going through or jumping out (see Fig. 44, Chap. 6).

Calipers.—Calipers are used for measuring distances in positions where dividers would not be satisfactory. They are made in several different styles, and the simplest calipers have the general appearance of dividers, except that *inside* calipers turn out at the points and *outside* calipers turn in like ice tongs. Inside calipers are used for measuring the inside diameter of holes or cutout sections. Outside calipers are used to measure outside dimensions, such as the thickness of a steel bar or a tube (see Fig. 25).

Pocket-slide calipers are beam calipers with a graduated slide with jaws at right angles to the beam. They may be used for taking either inside or outside measurements. The slide is graduated to 1/64 in. They are useful in aircraft sheetmetal work for checking the sizes of small standard parts.

Micrometer Calipers.—There are three common types of micrometer calipers: the outside, the inside, and the outside thread type. They are used for precision measurements, although micrometers are made that will take measurements up to 12 and 14 in.

How to Read a Micrometer.—The principles on which all micrometer calipers are used are the same, and this explanation will be given for small outside micrometer calipers of the type used by sheetmetal workers, which are capable of measuring to 0.001 in.

A micrometer caliper is shown in Fig. 26. The part to be measured is placed between the anvil and the spindle. Then the thimble or ratchet is turned to the right until it just meets the object being measured. Tight clamping pressure should not be used. The diameter of the object is then read from the scale on the barrel. The spindle has a pitch, or thread cut, of 40 to

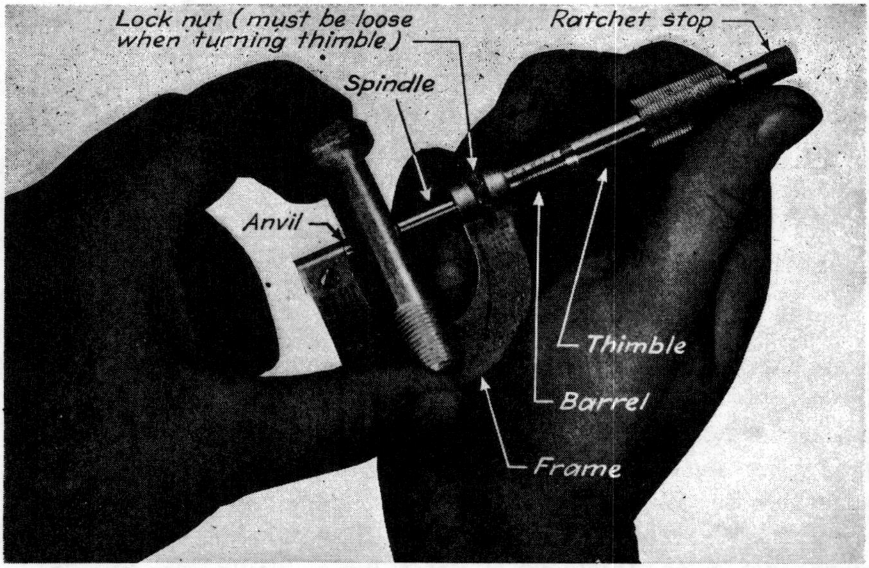

FIG. 26.—A micrometer with the principal parts identified. This is the proper way for a micrometer to be held.

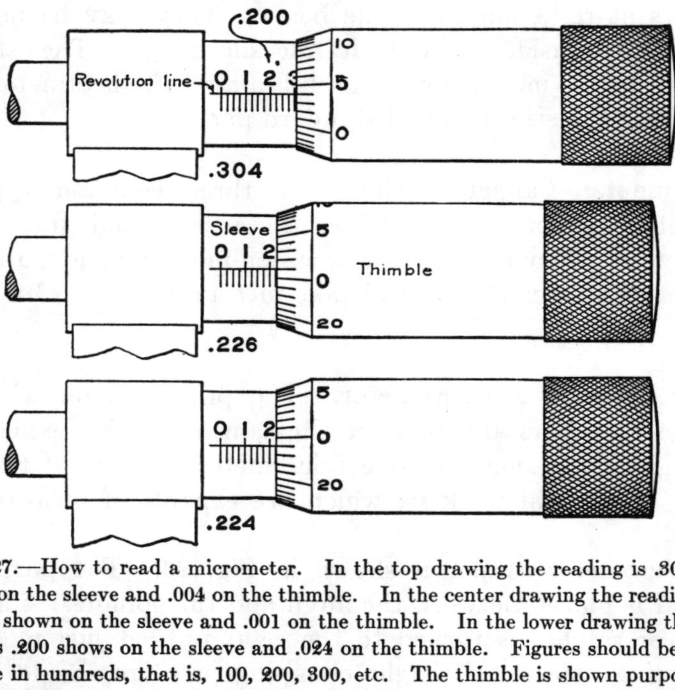

FIG. 27.—How to read a micrometer. In the top drawing the reading is .304, as .300 is shown on the sleeve and .004 on the thimble. In the center drawing the reading is .226, as .225 is shown on the sleeve and .001 on the thimble. In the lower drawing the reading is .224, as .200 shows on the sleeve and .024 on the thimble. Figures should be taken off the sleeve in hundreds, that is, 100, 200, 300, etc. The thimble is shown purposely close to the lines in these drawings, as those are the points where a mistake is most likely made. Note carefully the position of the zero line in each reading. (*These drawings are through the courtesy of the J. T. Slocomb Co., Providence, R.I.*)

the inch on the portion inside the barrel. One turn of the thimble moves the spindle $\frac{1}{40}$, or 0.025, in. The marks on the barrel show the number of turns that the thimble has made because, as the thimble is turned to the right (or tightened), more figures on the barrel are covered, whereas, when the thimble is turned to the left for larger measurements, more figures are uncovered.

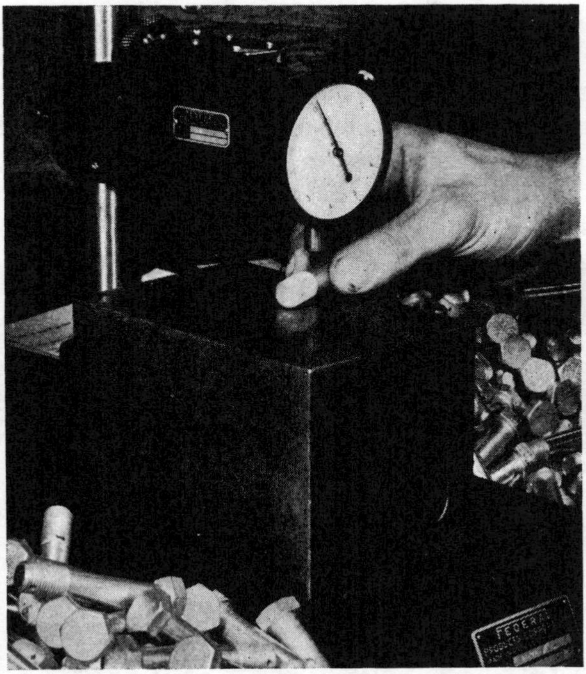

FIG. 28.—A dial measuring gage, made by Federal Products Co., in use at the Curtiss-Wright plant in Buffalo. In production work, where a large number of items must be inspected, a dial indicator is faster to use than a micrometer. After the gage is properly set, the hand on the dial will indicate variations plus or minus the dimension that has been specified.

Every fourth graduation is marked 1, 2, 3, 4, etc. As each mark is 0.025 in., the first four mean 0.025 × 4 equals 0.100 in. The third means 0.300. The thimble has a beveled edge, which is marked with 25 horizontal lines, numbered by fives. Each of these means $\frac{1}{25}$ of a turn, or $\frac{1}{25}$ of $\frac{1}{40}$ equals 1/1,000 in. To read the measurement, multiply the marks on the sleeve or barrel by 25 and add the number of graduations indicated on the edge of the thimble. The final reading thus obtained is then in thousandths of an inch (see Fig. 27).

A Vernier micrometer is one with additional horizontal parallel lines on the barrel, which permit readings to 1/10,000 in. (0.0001 in.). It is used principally by machinists. The sheetmetal worker, especially the beginner, does not use such fine measurements and does not need to learn to use such an instrument. How to read a Vernier micrometer is explained in the catalogue of firms manufacturing measuring tools.

Depth Gage.—There are two kinds of depth gages. One has a micrometer attachment so that measurements as fine as $\frac{1}{1000}$ in. can be made. The other is a steel rule with a sliding cross member and measures to $\frac{1}{64}$ in. These tools are used to measure to the bottom of holes, slots or channels, and other depressions.

FIG. 29.—A height gage being used by an inspector in the Boeing factory to check the accuracy of finished parts. Note other measuring tools on the left.

Height Gage.—A height gage is a vertical steel bar marked in inches and parts of inches and works like a Vernier caliper, or gage. The lower end is mounted to a base, and the carrier can be moved up and down. It is used for measuring the height of objects (see Fig. 29).

Thickness Gage.—It is often necessary to measure the clearance between two objects. A thickness gage is used for this purpose. It consists of a handle and a number of thin leaves of steel, which vary from 0.001 to 0.025 in. in thickness. By using a combination of several leaves, any thickness up to the total of all the leaves can be obtained. Such a gage is used to determine the clearance between a rivet head and a sheet or for aircraft sheetmetal construction that requires checking to make sure that the joints are tight together.

Sheetmetal and Wire Gage.—Both sheet and wire are made in a number of different sizes. The simplest form of gage is a circular or a rectangular metal disk, with slots of different sizes cut in the outer edge. By fitting a piece of sheet or a wire into the various slots, the thickness or the diameter can be quickly determined.

Surface Gage.—This tool is used to establish and mark out centers and for scribing lines when laying out work. It is used in connection with a surface plate, which is a flat sheet of heavy steel, used as a working base for taking accurate measurements. The gage consists of a base and a vertical spindle, which can be tightened in different positions. An adjustable rod with a needle point is attached to the vertical arm. It is used in sheetmetal work, principally for checking forgings or extrusions that have been machined.

Protractor.—A protractor is used for laying out angles or for measuring angles. The simplest type is of metal or celluloid and is a half circle marked off in degrees. An inexpensive form of protractor for shop use is made of stainless steel and has an arm fixed to a pivot. It is easier to use and is read more accurately than the protractor without an arm. For precision work, a protractor is used that has a Vernier attachment by which angles can be read to $1/12$ deg. or finer. The protractor head of the combination square is widely used for aircraft layout work and for assembly.

There are numerous kinds of special gages for measuring and checking work in aircraft plants. Those described above are the most common and are all that need concern a beginning mechanic. In fact, the Vernier gages, except for the micrometer calipers, are seldom used by the beginner, but the sheetmetal man should know what they are and, in general, how they are used.

A Few "Don'ts" for Use in Measuring

1. Don't use a wood ruler or yardstick for measuring, as the ends may be worn, and often they are inaccurately marked.
2. Don't transfer measurements from a blueprint to your work. The blueprint may be wrinkled, or the paper may have shrunk when it was being dried.
3. Don't measure in a poor light.
4. Don't hesitate to buy good tools; they are worth the money.
5. Don't lay the scale flat on the work; keep it on the edge.
6. Don't measure from the extreme end of the rule; it may be worn or damaged.
7. Don't bend a steel scale or use it for a pry.
8. Don't clamp a micrometer too tightly.
9. Don't throw precision measuring tools down carelessly.
10. Don't allow measuring tools to become dirty.

Review Questions

1. What is a tolerance?
2. When applied to a measurement, what does $\pm 1/64$ signify?
3. Which is a closer tolerance: $1/64$ or 0.015?
4. Why are aircraft parts made to close tolerances?
5. What are some of the common units of measurement and measuring tools used in aircraft work?
6. Distinguish between the use of rules and steel tapes.
7. How are squares used in measuring? What is an adjustable square?
8. For what purposes are dividers used?
9. What are trammels?
10. Describe the different kinds of calipers and their uses.
11. For what purposes might a sheetmetal mechanic use a depth gage?
12. Describe a thickness gage and its use.
13. How is a wire gage used?

14. For what kinds of measurements is a protractor used?
15. Why is it poor practice to measure dimensions on a blueprint?

Shop Work

Measuring is required in each of the five projects listed in Chap. 15. Additional measuring practice can be secured from laying out several of the sheet-metal parts that are shown on the blueprints on Chap. 1.

CHAPTER 5

TEMPLATES

In experimental work or when the first airplane of a new type is built, it is usually necessary for the mechanic to lay out individually each sheetmetal part and fitting. This is simply a process of transposing the engineering drawing to the metal. For intricate parts it is necessary to have a broad knowledge of measuring and drawing and to possess the ability to read blueprints. Regardless of the finished shape of a part that is made from sheetmetal, a flat layout showing the contour or outline, the points of bending, and the location of holes is required. Such a process is necessarily slow. Consequently, when the first ship, or prototype, is completed and accepted, more efficient production methods are used. To speed production in making a quantity of interchangeable sheetmetal parts and aircraft fittings, patterns that are called *templates* are used.

A template is simply an exact copy, usually in flat form, of a sheetmetal part or section of a part. Templates are patterns made of sheet steel, aluminum-alloy sheet, or plywood. They are used to make any number of accurate reproductions, without the necessity of making a separate layout for each one. The gage and the type of material chosen for the template depend on the durability required and on the kind of use to which it will be put.

TYPES OF TEMPLATE

There are five types of template in general use:

1. The *layout, or marking, template* is used as the name suggests, for laying out points or scribing lines on the sheet for measuring, cutting, drilling, or forming operations.

2. The *contour template* is used in the capacity of a gage for checking the contour, such as angles of bending, fillets, or curvatures of formed parts.

3. The *drill template* is used as a guide in drilling operations.

4. The *trim template* acts as a guide in cutting, filing, and finishing operations.

5. The *trim-and-drill template* combines in one template both of these functions.

A *master template* is made first to close tolerances, often to a plus or minus 0.001 in. If, for example, a door for a fuselage were to be made of 17S-T aluminum-alloy sheet, the master marking template might be made of $\frac{3}{16}$ in. sheet steel, carefully checked by the engineering department. Then, from the master template, a number of lighter gage *shop templates* would be made of $\frac{1}{8}$ in. steel. Templates should always be made of sufficiently heavy-

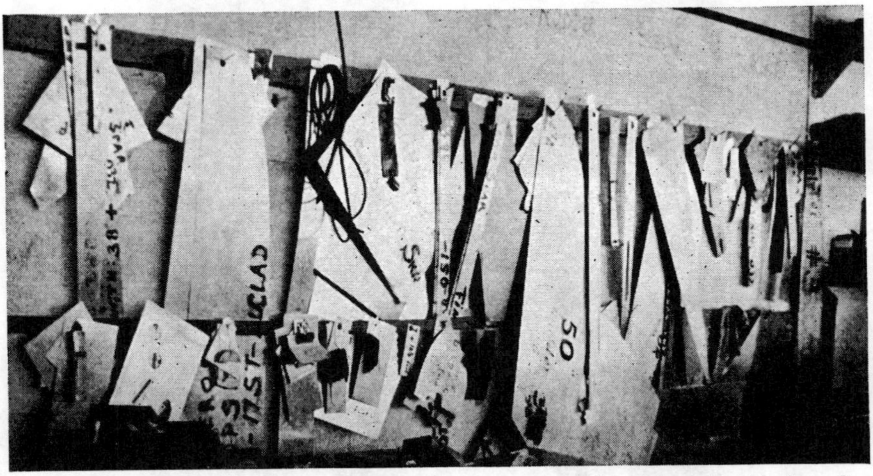

FIG. 30.—A group of layout templates hanging on a wall at Luscombe Airplane Co. Each of these flat patterns bears the name, number, and symbol of the part for which it is used.

gage sheet to avoid their being easily bent or otherwise damaged in normal handling and use. By using shop templates for the door pattern, production can be greatly speeded, since the layout of each individual sheet, required in older methods, is unnecessary. From an economy standpoint, too, templates effect a great saving. If templates of irregular shape are used, they can be placed on a sheet of metal and moved around in various positions until the greatest amount of material is utilized. Placing a number of templates or the same template in several positions in this manner on one sheet is called *nesting*. For this work the direction of the grain must also be taken into consideration to lessen the possibility of cracking, as explained in Chap. 13.

Making Templates.—In making templates, one side of the stock should be coated with layout fluid, which is an inklike liquid, or with a thin, even coat of dull or flat paint on which thin or fine lines can be visibly scribed. Chap. 6 describes this process.

The tools required for laying out templates are similar to those used for ordinary sheetmetal layout work, described in the next chapter, except that a higher degree of precision is essential in

FIG. 31.—A marking template made of sheet steel is being held on top of a small sheet of dural while the workman scribes around the template. (*Photograph made at Republic Aviation.*)

both instruments and work. Template layout tools generally required are: a prick punch, a center punch (preferably automatic), a duplicating center punch to match the size of pilot holes to be drilled in the templates, a light ball-peen hammer, a combination straight and right-angle scriber, one 6 in. and one 24 in. flexible steel scale graduated in thirty-seconds and sixty-fourths of an inch, one 6 in. scale graduated in hundredths of an inch, a protractor, one pair of 3 in. and one pair of 8 in. dividers, one 6 in. and one 12 in. try square, one pair of outside calipers, one pair of hermaphrodite calipers, a straightedge, a trammel with adjustable points, a flexible spline and weights, a magnifying glass, and a table of decimal equivalents.

A long straightedge should preferably be made of steel, although one made of laminated wood will serve the purpose if it is kept in good condition. The trammel bar should be of sufficient length to check the extreme measurements of the part being made. All pointed tools should be kept at needle-point sharpness.

Tolerances.—Drawings of aircraft sheetmetal parts usually specify tolerances plus or minus of $\frac{1}{64}$ in. for fractional dimen-

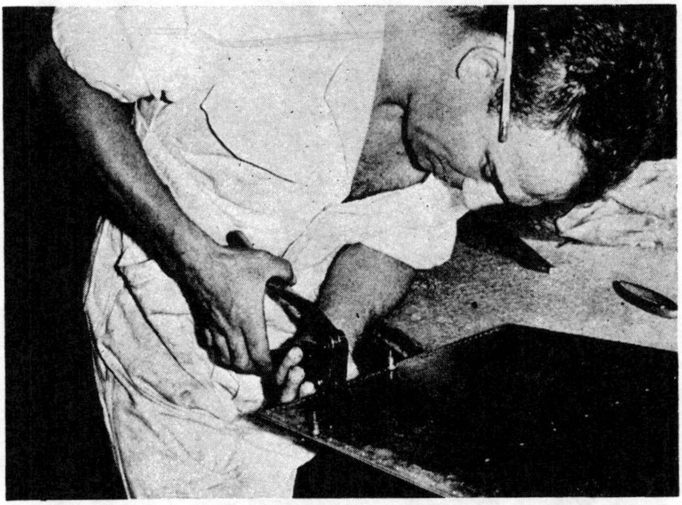

FIG. 32.—This mechanic at the Luscombe factory is punching rivet holes. The template is fastened on top of the dural sheet and held in place by Cleco fasteners. Rivet holes are already drilled in the template and serve as a guide for punching holes in the sheet beneath.

sions, ± 0.015 in. for decimal dimensions, and $\pm$ one-half of 1 deg. for angles. However, tolerances permitted in making templates must be even closer. For instance, if a template were made $\frac{1}{64}$ in. oversize from a drawing, taking advantage of a $\pm\frac{1}{64}$ in. tolerance, then if a part made from the template were finished $\frac{1}{64}$ in. over the template size, the finished part would then be $\frac{1}{32}$ in. over the size specified in the drawing. The usual practice is to lay out templates with a fractional tolerance of one-half of $\frac{1}{64}$ in. ($\frac{1}{128}$ in.), which is about as small as the naked eye can easily see. A magnifying glass is of assistance in doing this type of work, and it is indispensable when decimal dimensions are specified.

To ensure production schedules and to prevent waste of materials, only men who are thoroughly experienced in layout work should be permitted to make templates, regardless of the simplicity of the design.

The Glenn L. Martin Co.'s photographic process for reproducing exact-scale engineering drawings is also one of the simplest methods of making templates. The part drawings are reproduced to exact size on white-coated aluminum-alloy sheet. This

FIG. 33.—A drill template in use at the Glenn L. Martin plant. The sheet stock is under the template. The operator uses the holes in the template as a guide in drilling. A jig or fixture is also used here to hold both the stock and the template in place.

photodrawing layout can then be cut out and used directly as either a contour or a marking template. If a heavier gage template is required, a steel or a dural sheet may be inserted under the photodrawing layout and clamped in place. Using the photodrawing as a guide, small holes are then drilled through both sheets, along and tangent to the layout lines. When the photodrawing is lifted, the contours are clearly marked on the lower sheet by the drill. The actual part forms, or templates, are then cut out of the sheetmetal. When this method is used, redrafting for layout is unnecessary (see Figs. 34 and 35).

The Lockheed Aircraft Co. has developed a process for making shop templates by an electrolytic transfer. Drawings are scribed on specially coated metal sheets. Then through an electrolytic process, during which the two sheets are held together

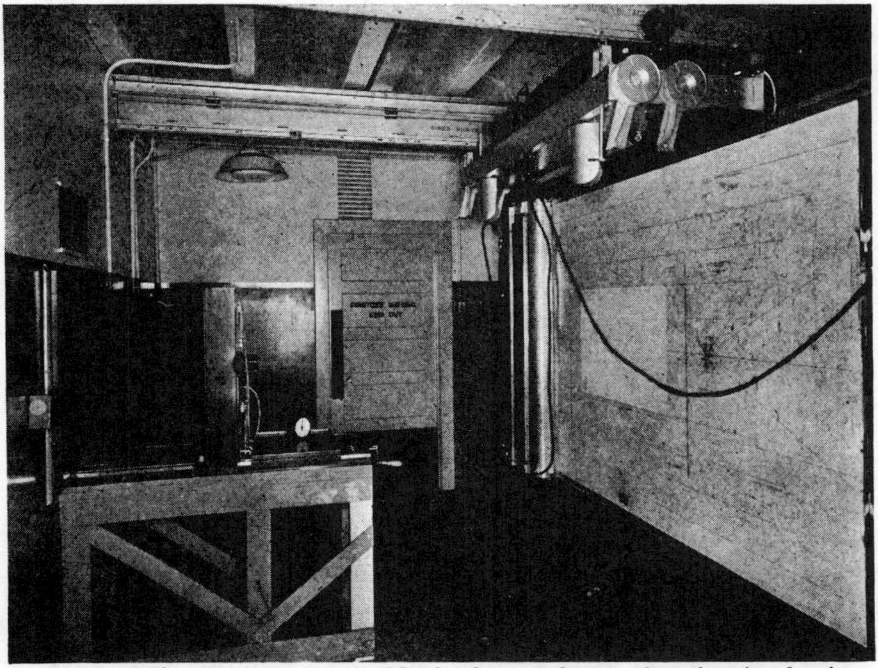

FIG. 34.—The camera used at the Martin plant to photograph engineering drawings, which are fastened to the board at the right. Copies of the drawings in exact size, or scaled down, are reproduced on white-coated metal sheets from which templates can be made, as shown in Fig. 35.

in a press, all markings are transferred to the metal sheets from which the shop templates are cut. This is a fast, accurate, and yet inexpensive way to make shop templates (see Fig. 36).

Identification of Templates.—Templates for parts of an airplane are numbered to correspond to the part and job number. They are kept in a stock room and classified as to the various component parts of the ship such as the fuselage, the left wing, the right wing, the fin, the rudder, etc. Each rib of a wing may require a different set of templates, which can be drawn from the template rack or stock room as needed.

To speed production and to decrease errors when using drill templates, several factories paint circles around each drill guide hole. A different color or paint is used for each drill size on the template.

In addition to the usual identifying part and code numbers marked on templates, symbols or abbreviations the same as those used for blueprints are generally used. These may be found in Chap. 1 beginning on page 13.

FIG. 35.—White-coated metal sheets, lying on the benches, are placed on top of thin sheet steel and holes are drilled that outline the drawing. Then the under sheet is removed and a template made from it. The dark templates on the nearest table were made in this way. (*Glenn L. Martin photograph.*)

HOW A TEMPLATE IS USED

If a number of doors, for example, are to be made for a fuselage, the aluminum-alloy sheet that will form the skin of the door is blanked out, that is, cut on the power squaring shear to the approximate size. A trim-and-drill template is then placed on top of perhaps 15 or 20 such sheets. A roughed-out plywood or wood pattern is placed underneath. Machine-screw holes are then drilled at several guide points in the template through all layers of the stock with a portable drill. These holes are usually made at points that will later be enlarged for bolt or lightening holes. Flat-headed machine screws are used to hold all the pieces together, the heads being drawn flush in the wood pattern. The wood pattern also serves to protect the bottom outside sheet of the stock. This is important in the case of Alclad.

The sheet stock with the steel and the wood templates bolted or clamped in place is next taken to the drilling department, where

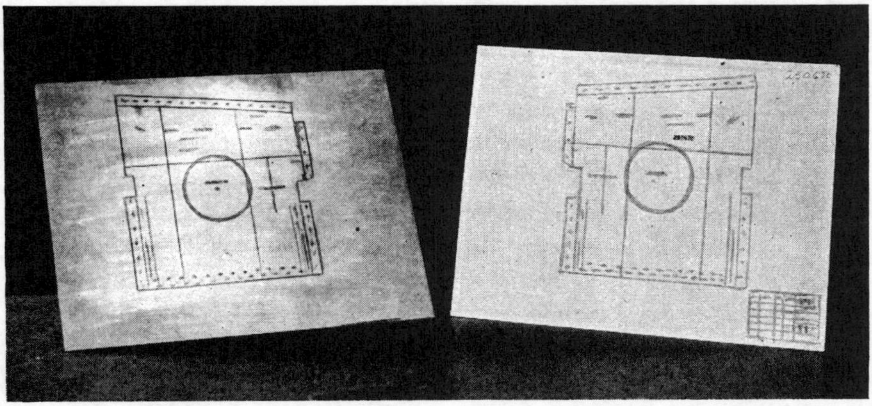

FIG. 36.—At Lockheed, templates are made by an electrolytic transfer. Drawings are scribed on metal sheets, such as the one at the right. Then the master sheet is moistened and put in a press with another sheet held firmly against it. The press is closed and through electrolytic process the drawing is transferred to the second sheet, as shown at the left. This sheet can then be cut out and drilled and used as a template. Any number of duplicates can be made from the master copy and templates up to 4 by 12 feet can be accommodated in the press.

it is placed on the table of a drill press with the steel template at the top. Holes for riveting stiffeners and holes for bolts are in their exact locations in the template, making it easy to use the template holes for a guide to drill the sheet stock. Rivet- and bolt-hole locations are often drilled oversize in a drill template to permit a hardened bushing or a sleevelike drill guide to be inserted in the hole of the template to prevent wear from the drill. The actual drill size, No. 30 for ⅛ in. rivets, for example, is then brought down through the bushing. If this method were not used, the drill template would soon wear out, since the holes would become elongated from continued use and vibration or eccentricities of drilling.

The stock must next be cut to the exact shape of the template. Cutting is quickly accomplished on the router. If a radial overhead swing-type router is used (see Fig. 61, Chap. 7), the stock is placed on the routing table and clamped in position with the wood-pattern side against the router table. The steel trim template on top serves as a guide for the routing collar to ride against as the router is moved around the template and the sheet stock is cut back even with the edge of the template. If a stationary vertical-spindle router is used, the trim template is placed down against the routing table and the work is moved around the cutter using the template as a guide.

When all drilling and cutting operations indicated on the trim-and-drill template have been completed, the template and the wood patterns are removed from the stock. In some cases additional templates can be used successively on the same stock where cutting and drilling operations are used. If forming operations such as bending or pressing are also required, one or more additional contour templates may be used not only as patterns but also as gages in measuring bends and curves.

Templates are often erroneously referred to as *jigs* or *fixtures* by factory mechanics. In a limited sense, they sometimes act in those capacities. Fixtures are adjustable holding devices used for drilling or cutting operations. Templates should not be confused with assembly jigs, which are discussed in Chap. 12.

Templates are often used in the manufacture of steel and aluminum-alloy fittings even though the fittings are made with hand tools. They may be held in place on top of the stock by hand or clamped directly to the stock. Cutting lines can then be scribed closely around the contour of the template, and holes drilled where they are indicated. The template can then be removed, and the work finished by hand. Or a cutting or filing template of harder material may be clamped to the stock to act as a guide in hand finishing.

Templates are indispensable to the present mass-production pace because of the speed and ease with which they can be used. The fact that a knowledge of blueprint reading is not usually required when templates are used in making airplane parts makes it possible for mechanics of little previous training to be useful soon after they get their first job.

Review Questions

1. What is a template?
2. Name five kinds of templates and briefly describe the purpose of each.

3. From what materials are templates made?

4. Are tolerances closer in making a templates or in making a part from the same template?

5. How are templates made at the Martin and Lockheed plants?

6. How are drill templates protected so they will not wear out rapidly?

7. How are templates secured to a pile of sheets being cut or routed?

8. How are templates marked for identification?

9. What is the difference between a master template and a shop template?

10. Is it probable that an aircraft factory would have more than one shop template for the same part?

11. Explain the difference between a template and a fixture.

12. Explain what is meant by the following abbreviations that may be found on templates: Csk., Fwd., Flg., Jog., Ltg. H., Sta., TS. Up., RR., RL., O.B.

Shop Work

Project 5 of Chap. 15 calls for the making of templates for the two ends of the fairing. These templates may be made now, following the methods set forth in this chapter, if the instructor so desires. Templates may also be made for several of the sheetmetal parts shown in the blueprints of Chap. 1.

CHAPTER 6

AIRCRAFT SHEETMETAL LAYOUT

In aircraft construction the term *layout* means the interpreting and the transcribing of blueprinted engineering drawings or written instructions from operations sheets to the metal that will be made into a part of the airplane. Actually, layout consists of making drawings on metal. To do layout work the mechanic must possess mechanical skill, a general knowledge of blueprint reading, and a working knowledge of the basic principles of mechanical drawing and know the working properties of materials and practices of aircraft sheetmetal work. Layout work is done by beginning mechanics only if a template cannot be used, as a template makes a job simpler.

Mechanics who have not previously worked on aircraft sheetmetal parts will soon find that the ability to do layout work is essential if they are to progress beyond the job of being a machine operator or a riveter to become a leadman. Certain airplane sheetmetal parts are not adaptable to the use of templates in their fabrication, for example, fittings that require intricate bends at various angles or that have elaborate curvatures. Layout practices must also be part of the knowledge of the assembly mechanic who fits the skin to a fuselage, a wing, or a control surface. A knowledge of layout is also essential if the mechanic is required to check the finished product for accuracy, even though templates can be used in making the part originally. The large experimental departments, too, rarely use templates but depend on layout, since usually only a few of the same type of parts are required.

LAYOUT PRACTICES

Layout of a part on a flat sheet of metal consists principally of marking the sheet so that the flat shape, or pattern, of the part is indicated for all drilling, cutting, bending, and forming operations. It is a working drawing in the truest sense, because you work to its lines and marks. Accuracy in all details is essential. The layout on sheetmetal may be made from printed instructions on a job or operations sheet, as previously mentioned, but it is more often taken directly from a blueprint.

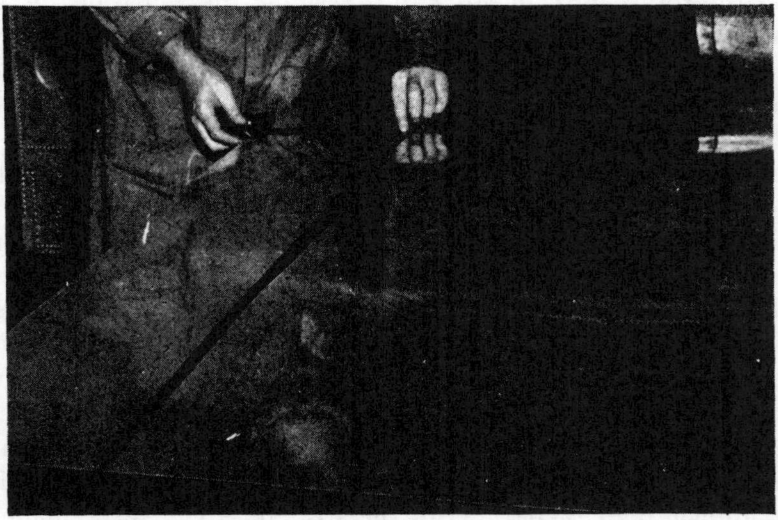

FIG. 37.—A flexible steel tape, with a right-angle hook on the end, is used for measuring and laying out blank on sheet stock.

Details of layout are often left out to be developed in the shop. The mechanic may, for example, find that he must add several dimensions, then figure the bending allowance for the material

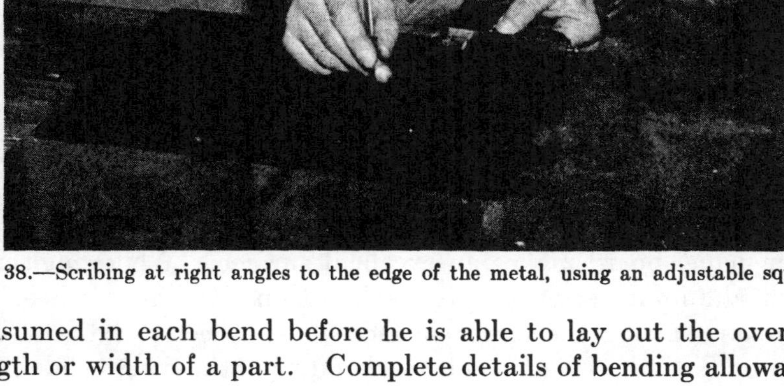

FIG. 38.—Scribing at right angles to the edge of the metal, using an adjustable square.

consumed in each bend before he is able to lay out the over-all length or width of a part. Complete details of bending allowance are given later in this chapter. He may also find it necessary to subtract the height of the two side flanges of a channel section from the total width in order to determine the width of the web, which may not be given on the print.

One of the fundamental principles of layout is knowing where and how to start measuring and marking the sheet. It will be noticed by those who have had mechanical-drawing experience that there is a similarity between most drawing instruments and sheetmetal layout tools, although the basic instruments of the drafting department, such as T squares, triangles, and French curves are not used in aircraft metalwork. Points that are known to be in a line or an edge that is known to be straight usually serve as the first step in starting the layout. If it is necessary to lay out a comparatively small part or fitting on a large sheet of aluminum alloy, one edge, if not straight, can be cut on the squaring shear and tested with a steel straightedge. All measurements can then be based on the *straight edge* of the sheet. Lines at a known angle or parallel to the straight edge can be made by marking off points from a combination square held firmly against the straight edge of the sheet.

If it is impossible to obtain a straight edge on a sheet to start a layout, or if the distance from the edge is too great, a *reference line* may be used. The reference line may be made by connecting any two points with a straight line. Perpendiculars may be erected to the reference line, by using a compass or dividers, thus forming a cross (see Problems 1 to 4 at the end of this chapter). Once the cross is accurately laid out, it may be used as a basis for almost any type of fitting layout. A disadvantage in using a reference line lies in the fact that there is no straight edge against which a 90 deg. square, a combination square, or a protractor head can be firmly placed for marking.

Protection during Layout.—Every precaution must be taken to avoid marring aluminum-alloy sheet, and even steel sheet should be carefully handled. Sheet stock must be placed on a smooth, flat-topped layout bench. If the parts are small, a metal surface plate is most desirable for this purpose. Tempered composition panel board makes an excellent surface. Where high-mill-finish aluminum or Alclad is used, a thin padding of sheet felt prevents scarring the under surface of the sheet. Extreme care must be used to prevent accidental bending of the sheet in handling.

Large sheets should be moved by two men. Layout tools and portable drills must be kept off sheet stock. Sheetmetal workers should even avoid wearing rings and wrist watches, since they may be a hazard around machinery and are apt to scratch polished metal surfaces.

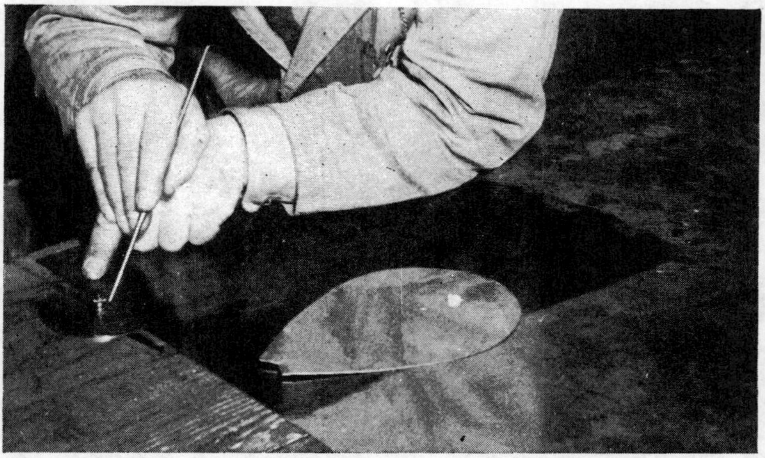

FIG. 39.—To lay out angular measurements, a layout protractor marked in degrees is used with a steel scriber.

Layout Marking Fluids.—Because of the high polish of most aircraft aluminum-alloy and steel sheet, difficulty is experienced in marking the sheet without first coating the metal with layout fluid, which is an inklike liquid. The visibility of center points and lines scribed through points that are prick-punched is greatly increased by marking on a surface that has been prepared with layout fluid. Before beginning the layout on aluminum-alloy sheet the surface to be marked is usually coated with a blue dye having a high alcohol content, which promotes rapid drying. The dye is applied sparingly with a spray gun, a rag, or a small sponge. The coating should be uniform and light. A mixture of Prussian blue pigment and nitrate dope thinner can easily be made in the shop to serve as layout fluid.

Sheet steel can be given a thin coat of white lacquer, flat white paint, or chalk or coated with copper sulfate with a dauber made by wrapping a rag around the end of a short stick. Copper sulfate causes the sheet to turn a greenish brown but does not harm the metal. It is generally recognized as the best medium. It may be removed from the finished part by washing in clear water. Other layout fluids can be removed in the same way or, when the base of the fluid is pyroxylin, by using nitrate dope thinner.

FIG. 40.—An automatic prick punch is used to locate the center prior to scribing a circle, as shown in Fig. 42.

The means of marking sheetmetal used in aircraft construction is of great importance and must be given careful consideration. Pencils, crayon, chalk, scribers, prick punches, and center punches are all used, but certain general rules must be followed. Dimension points and centers are located with a pencil point or a prick punch. Arcs or circles are drawn with a compass or dividers. Prick punching is the most accurate means of locating points, but the punching should be done lightly on thin sheet to prevent denting or swelling of the sheet. This is done with a small pointed punch sharpened to a finer point than a center punch. Center punching should be avoided if possible at points where holes will not later be drilled, thus removing the mark. "Automatic" center punches are usually used by layout men. This type of center punch does not require tapping with a hammer but works on a telescoping internal-spring principle. It is operated by hand, simply by pressing down on the top of the punch.

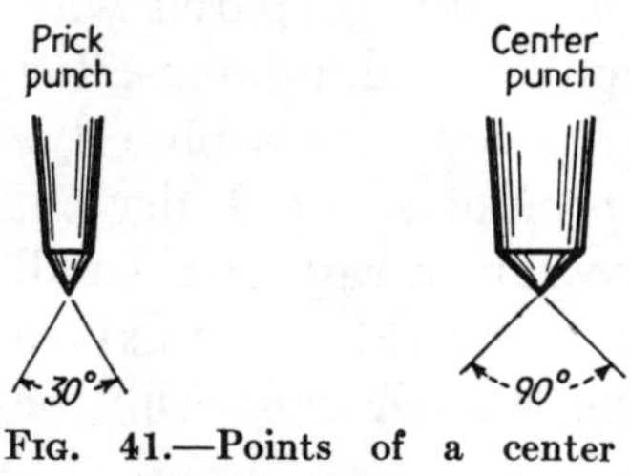

FIG. 41.—Points of a center punch and a prick punch.

Center-punch marks are used as centers for drilling holes. Prick-punch marks are used as points to be connected by lines and as centers for a compass or a pair of dividers in swinging an arc or a circle. The indentation caused by the prick punch helps to hold one leg of the dividers in place. The broader depression made by the center punch helps to prevent a drill of small diameter from riding away from the point being drilled. A protractor may also be used at a center-punched or prick-punched point to lay out an angle or for the spacing of rivet or bolt holes.

Scribing.—Lines must be drawn to represent the exact width, length, and shape of the part to be made. These lines usually

FIG. 42.—Using dividers to scribe an arc on flat sheet.

form the outside dimensions to which the part is cut to size. They can be made with any type of sharp-pointed steel scriber held diagonally against and toward the edge of a template or a steel scale or other straightedge (see Figs. 38 and 39). Center lines, bending lines, and other points that will not be removed from the finished part should not be scribed but may be made with red crayon or a 2H pencil if the material is Alclad or other aluminum alloy. Even the most shallow line that is cut in the surface of the metal may cause cracking and eventual failure. Any scribed lines that remain on the part after cutting and forming should be removed with extreme care by means of emery or crocus cloth.

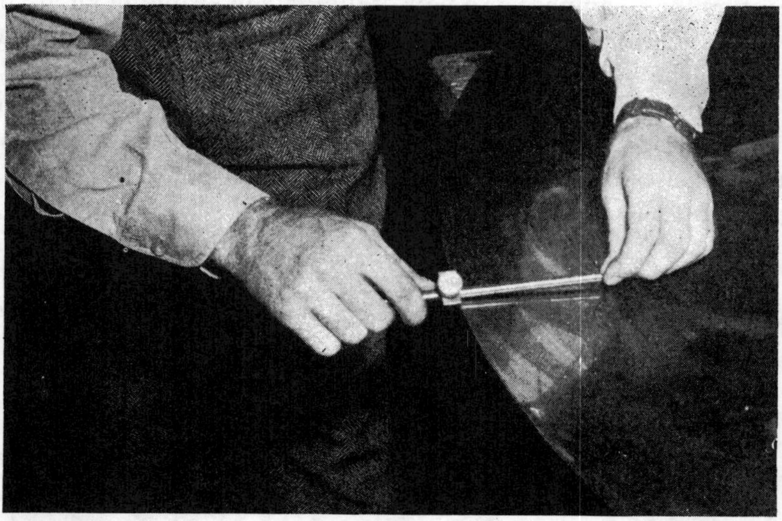

FIG. 43.—Using a scratch gage to scribe a line parallel to the edge of the stock.

FIG. 44.—Trammels may be used to transfer measurements from a scale or another part to the work. Trammels are also used to swing arcs when the radius is too great to be handled by dividers.

If the lines cannot be removed easily, the part should be condemned. Pencil lines may be made at any point, since they do not damage the surface of the sheet. Lines made with a steel scriber are generally more accurate than pencil lines and are not easily obliterated accidentally during the layout.

Curved lines that are not marked by using a template can be made by laying out a series of closely located centers and connecting them with a line. However, dividers or a compass are usually used to scribe circles and curves. Curves greater in radius than the scope of the dividers may be made by swinging a trammel bar fitted with scribing points or pencil points. Centers greater than 1/4 in. are located by drawing arcs or circles at the 90 deg. intersection of straight lines.

BENDING ALLOWANCE

The most frequently encountered forming operation in aircraft construction is bending. Since close tolerances are required on aircraft parts, bending becomes a responsibility of the mechanic doing the layout. Bending angles in sheet or strip stock is a comparatively simple mechanical operation. The layout requires measuring the stock to be formed in order that its exact length may be determined before any bending is attempted. Such measurements cannot be calculated without a knowledge of bending principles and techniques.

All aircraft sheetmetal materials cannot be bent to the same radius. The minimum radius of the bend is controlled by the type of material used and thickness of the metal being bent. A soft sheet of aluminum (3S-O) can be bent to a small or sharp radius equivalent to the thickness of the metal. For 0.032 sheet the smallest bending radius is 1/32 in.

For harder heat-treated sheet, such as 24S-T aluminum alloy, the bending radius must be at least twice the thickness of the metal. For example, 0.062 24S-T sheet has a minimum bending radius of 1/8 in.; 0.062 plus 0.062 equals 0.124, and since the decimal equivalent of 1/8 in. is 0.125, a 1/8 in. radius may be used. If this sheet were bent to a 1/32 in. radius, failure in the form of cracking would result. Tension stress and bending stress play an important part in the bending operation. If you open your hand out flat with your fingers together, then slowly close your fist, you will see that the skin on the back of your hand is stretched and drawn tight. The skin on the palm of your hand, however, is wrinkled and compressed. The skin on the back of your hand is stretched and in tension because it must bend around a larger outside radius than the skin in the palm of your hand, which follows the smaller inside radius. Somewhere in a line between your palm and the back of your hand the tension changes to the compression. Along this line, which is termed the *neutral axis*, there is neither tension nor compression. The same principles that affected the movement of the skin on your hand are involved in bending metals.

Bending is accomplished by a number of methods; but before metal aircraft parts are bent to shape, the amount of material

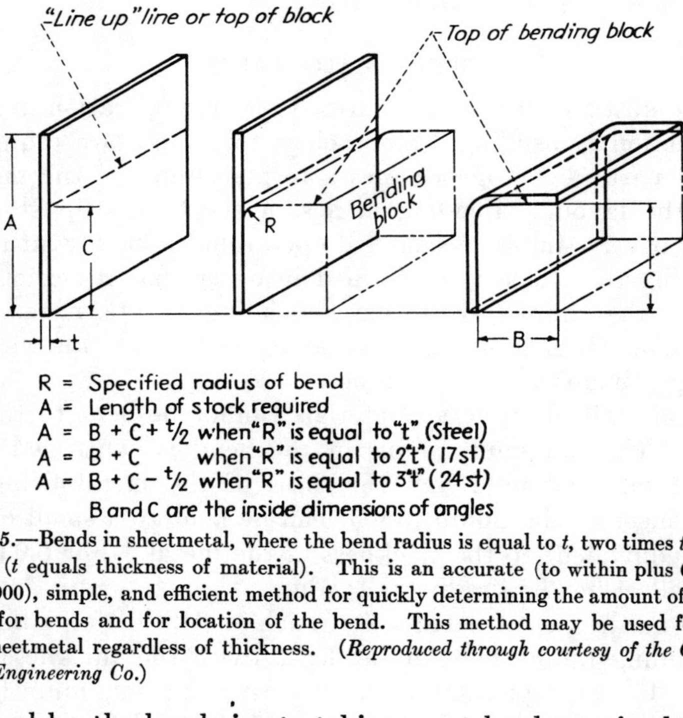

FIG. 45.—Bends in sheetmetal, where the bend radius is equal to t, two times t, or three times t. (t equals thickness of material). This is an accurate (to within plus 0.005 and minus 0.000), simple, and efficient method for quickly determining the amount of material required for bends and for location of the bend. This method may be used for laying out all sheetmetal regardless of thickness. (*Reproduced through courtesy of the Grumman Aircraft Engineering Co.*)

consumed by the bends in stretching must be determined for the thickness and type of material. Study the diagram in Fig. 45. The mechanic must be familiar with a workable bending formula or have access to a table of bend allowance unless exact specifications regarding over-all length of the flat sheet are given in the layout. The required over-all length of the stock to be formed is not always given in an aircraft engineering drawing. However, bend-allowance tables are issued by the engineering department of the factories to mechanics engaged in layout work. Since the majority of bends are made to a 90 deg. angle, a special table, as shown in Fig. 46, is used for finding the developed length of 90 deg. bends for various bending radii and gages of stock. The chart on page 96 may be used for bends of any angle.

Complex formulae for bend allowance are rarely used by mechanics because of the simpler and faster methods presented in this chapter.

	Radius																				
BWG.	1/32	3/64	1/16	5/64	3/32	7/64	1/8	9/64	5/32	11/64	3/16	13/64	7/32	15/64	1/4	9/32	5/16	11/32	3/8	7/16	1/2
.330																	.499	.512	.525	.549	.579
.284																.466	.479	.492	.506	.529	.557
.259															.422	.435	.449	.462	.476	.499	.529
.238														.390	.396	.410	.423	.437	.450	.473	.504
.220													.361	.368	.374	.388	.401	.415	.428	.451	.482
.203												.333	.340	.347	.354	.367	.381	.394	.408	.431	.461
.180											.299	.306	.313	.319	.326	.339	.353	.366	.379	.403	.433
.165										.274	.281	.288	.294	.301	.308	.312	.335	.348	.361	.385	.415
.148									.247	.254	.260	.267	.273	.280	.287	.300	.314	.327	.340	.364	.394
.134								.223	.230	.237	.243	.250	.257	.263	.270	.283	.297	.310	.324	.347	.377
.120							.199	.206	.213	.220	.226	.233	.240	.246	.253	.266	.280	.293	.307	.330	.360
.109						.179	.186	.193	.199	.206	.213	.220	.226	.233	.240	.253	.263	.276	.243	.317	.347
.095					.156	.162	.169	.176	.182	.189	.200	.203	.204	.216	.223	.236	.250	.263	.276	.300	.330
.083				.135	.141	.148	.154	.161	.168	.175	.181	.188	.195	.201	.208	.222	.235	.248	.262	.285	.315
.072			.144	.121	.128	.134	.141	.148	.155	.161	.172	.175	.181	.188	.195	.208	.222	.235	.248	.272	.302
.065		.100	.106	.113	.119	.126	.133	.139	.146	.153	.164	.166	.173	.180	.186	.200	.213	.226	.240	.263	.293
.058	.084	.092	.098	.104	.111	.117	.124	.131	.138	.144	.155	.158	.164	.171	.178	.191	.205	.218	.231	.255	.285
.049	.073	.081	.087	.093	.100	.107	.113	.120	.127	.133	.144	.147	.153	.160	.167	.180	.194	.207	.220	.244	.274
.042	.065	.072	.078	.084	.091	.098	.105	.111	.118	.125	.136	.138	.145	.152	.158	.172	.185	.198	.212	.235	.266
.035	.056	.064	.070	.076	.083	.090	.096	.103	.110	.116	.127	.130	.136	.143	.150	.163	.177	.190	.203	.227	.257
.032	.053	.060	.066	.072	.079	.086	.093	.099	.106	.113	.119	.126	.133	.139	.146	.160	.173	.186	.200	.223	.253
.028	.048	.055	.061	.068	.074	.081	.085	.094	.101	.108	.114	.121	.128	.135	.141	.155	.168	.182	.195	.218	.249
.025	.044	.052	.057	.064	.071	.077	.084	.091	.097	.104	.111	.118	.124	.131	.138	.151	.164	.178	.191	.214	.245
.022	.040	.048	.054	.060	.067	.074	.080	.087	.094	.100	.107	.114	.121	.127	.134	.147	.161	.174	.188	.211	.241
.020	.038	.045	.051	.058	.065	.071	.078	.085	.091	.098	.104	.111	.118	.125	.132	.145	.158	.172	.185	.208	.239
.018	.035	.043	.049	.055	.062	.069	.076	.082	.089	.096	.102	.109	.116	.122	.129	.143	.156	.169	.183	.206	.236

TABLE FOR FINDING THE DEVELOPED LENGTH OF 90° BENDS
Subtract the correct figure in the table from the sum of the length of legs.

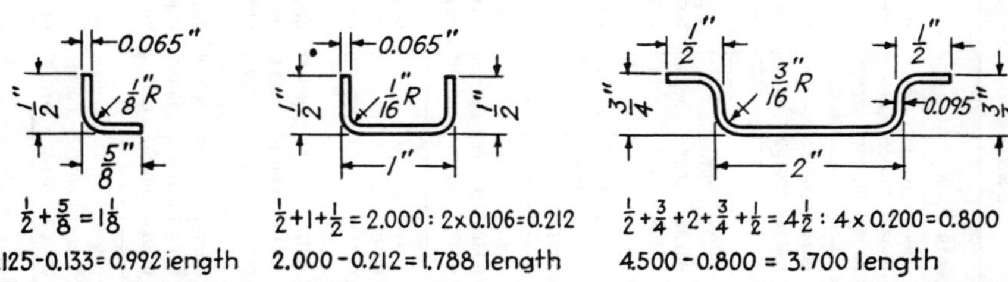

FIG. 46.—Developed length of 90 deg. bends. (*Courtesy of Grumman Aircraft Engineering Co.*)

Be sure that you have located all points of bending on the drawing of the part to be made before starting a layout.

The accuracy of the finished part depends on the layout. Extreme care must be taken to see that all profile and bending lines are carefully drawn and all centers for holes accurately located before any drilling, cutting, or forming operations are started. Inaccurate or slovenly layout always ends in a worthless

THE GLENN L. MARTIN CO.

BEND-ALLOWANCE CHART—(For any degree angle of bend)

R \ T	.010	.012	.015	.018	.020	.022	.025	.028	(1/32) .031	.032	.035	.040	.045	.049	.050	.051	.057	.062	.064	.065
1/64	.00035	.00037	.00039	.00041	.00043	.00044	.00047	.00049	.00051	.00052	.00055	.00058	.00062	.00065	.00066	.00067	.00072	.00076	.00077	.00078
1/32	.00062	.00064	.00066	.00068	.00070	.00072	.00074	.00076	.00079	.00079	.00082	.00086	.00090	.00093	.00093	.00094	.00099	.00103	.00104	.00105
3/64	.00089	.00091	.00093	.00096	.00097	.00099	.00101	.00103	.00106	.00107	.00109	.00113	.00117	.00120	.00121	.00121	.00126	.00130	.00132	.00132
1/16	.00117	.00118	.00121	.00123	.00125	.00126	.00128	.00131	.00133	.00134	.00136	.00140	.00144	.00147	.00148	.00149	.00153	.00157	.00159	.00160
5/64	.00144	.00145	.00148	.00150	.00152	.00153	.00156	.00158	.00160	.00161	.00163	.00167	.00171	.00174	.00175	.00176	.00181	.00184	.00186	.00187
3/32	.00171	.00173	.00175	.00177	.00179	.00181	.00183	.00185	.00188	.00188	.00191	.00195	.00199	.00202	.00202	.00203	.00208	.00212	.00213	.00214
7/64	.00198	.00200	.00202	.00204	.00206	.00208	.00210	.00212	.00215	.00216	.00218	.00222	.00226	.00229	.00230	.00230	.00235	.00239	.00241	.00241
1/8	.00226	.00227	.00230	.00232	.00233	.00235	.00237	.00239	.00242	.00243	.00245	.00249	.00253	.00256	.00257	.00258	.00262	.00266	.00268	.00269
9/64	.00253	.00254	.00257	.00259	.00260	.00262	.00265	.00267	.00269	.00270	.00272	.00276	.00280	.00283	.00284	.00285	.00290	.00293	.00295	.00296
5/32	.00280	.00282	.00284	.00286	.00287	.00290	.00292	.00294	.00296	.00297	.00300	.00304	.00307	.00311	.00311	.00312	.00317	.00321	.00322	.00323
11/64	.00307	.00309	.00311	.00313	.00314	.00317	.00319	.00321	.00324	.00324	.00327	.00331	.00335	.00338	.00339	.00339	.00344	.00348	.00349	.00350
3/16	.00335	.00336	.00339	.00341	.00342	.00344	.00346	.00348	.00351	.00352	.00354	.00358	.00362	.00365	.00366	.00367	.00371	.00375	.00377	.00378
13/64	.00362	.00363	.00366	.00368	.00370	.00371	.00374	.00376	.00378	.00379	.00381	.00385	.00389	.00392	.00393	.00394	.00398	.00402	.00404	.00405
7/32	.00389	.00391	.00393	.00395	.00396	.00398	.00401	.00403	.00405	.00406	.00409	.00412	.00416	.00419	.00420	.00421	.00426	.00430	.00431	.00432
15/64	.00416	.00418	.00420	.00422	.00423	.00426	.00428	.00430	.00433	.00433	.00436	.00440	.00444	.00447	.00448	.00448	.00453	.00457	.00458	.00459
1/4	.00443	.00445	.00447	.00450	.00451	.00453	.00455	.00457	.00460	.00461	.00463	.00467	.00471	.00474	.00475	.00475	.00480	.00484	.00486	.00486
9/32	.00498	.00500	.00502	.00504	.00505	.00507	.00510	.00512	.00514	.00515	.00517	.00521	.00525	.00528	.00529	.00530	.00535	.00539	.00540	.00541
5/16	.00552	.00554	.00556	.00558	.00559	.00562	.00564	.00566	.00569	.00570	.00572	.00576	.00580	.00583	.00584	.00584	.00589	.00593	.00595	.00595
11/32	.00607	.00608	.00611	.00613	.00614	.00616	.00619	.00621	.00623	.00624	.00626	.00630	.00634	.00637	.00638	.00639	.00644	.00647	.00649	.00650
3/8	.00661	.00663	.00665	.00667	.00668	.00671	.00673	.00675	.00678	.00679	.00681	.00685	.00689	.00692	.00693	.00693	.00698	.00702	.00704	.00704
13/32	.00716	.00717	.00720	.00722	.00723	.00725	.00728	.00730	.00732	.00733	.00735	.00739	.00743	.00746	.00747	.00748	.00752	.00756	.00758	.00759
7/16	.00770	.00772	.00774	.00776	.00777	.00780	.00782	.00784	.00787	.00788	.00790	.00794	.00798	.00801	.00802	.00802	.00807	.00811	.00812	.00813
15/32	.00825	.00826	.00829	.00831	.00832	.00834	.00837	.00839	.00841	.00842	.00844	.00848	.00852	.00855	.00856	.00857	.00861	.00865	.00867	.00868
1/2	.00879	.00881	.00883	.00885	.00886	.00889	.00891	.00893	.00896	.00896	.00899	.00903	.00907	.00910	.00911	.00911	.00916	.00920	.00921	.00922
17/32	.00934	.00935	.00938	.00940	.00941	.00943	.00945	.00947	.00950	.00951	.00953	.00957	.00961	.00964	.00965	.00966	.00970	.00974	.00976	.00977
9/16	.00988	.00990	.00992	.00994	.00995	.00998	.01000	.01002	.01005	.01005	.01008	.01012	.01016	.01019	.01019	.01020	.01025	.01029	.01030	.01031
19/32	.01043	.01044	.01047	.01049	.01050	.01052	.01054	.01057	.01059	.01060	.01062	.01066	.01070	.01073	.01074	.01075	.01079	.01083	.01085	.01086

FIG. 47.—Bend-allowance chart, for any degree angle of bend. Examples for the use of this chart are shown in the next figure. (*Courtesy of the Glenn L. Martin Co.*)

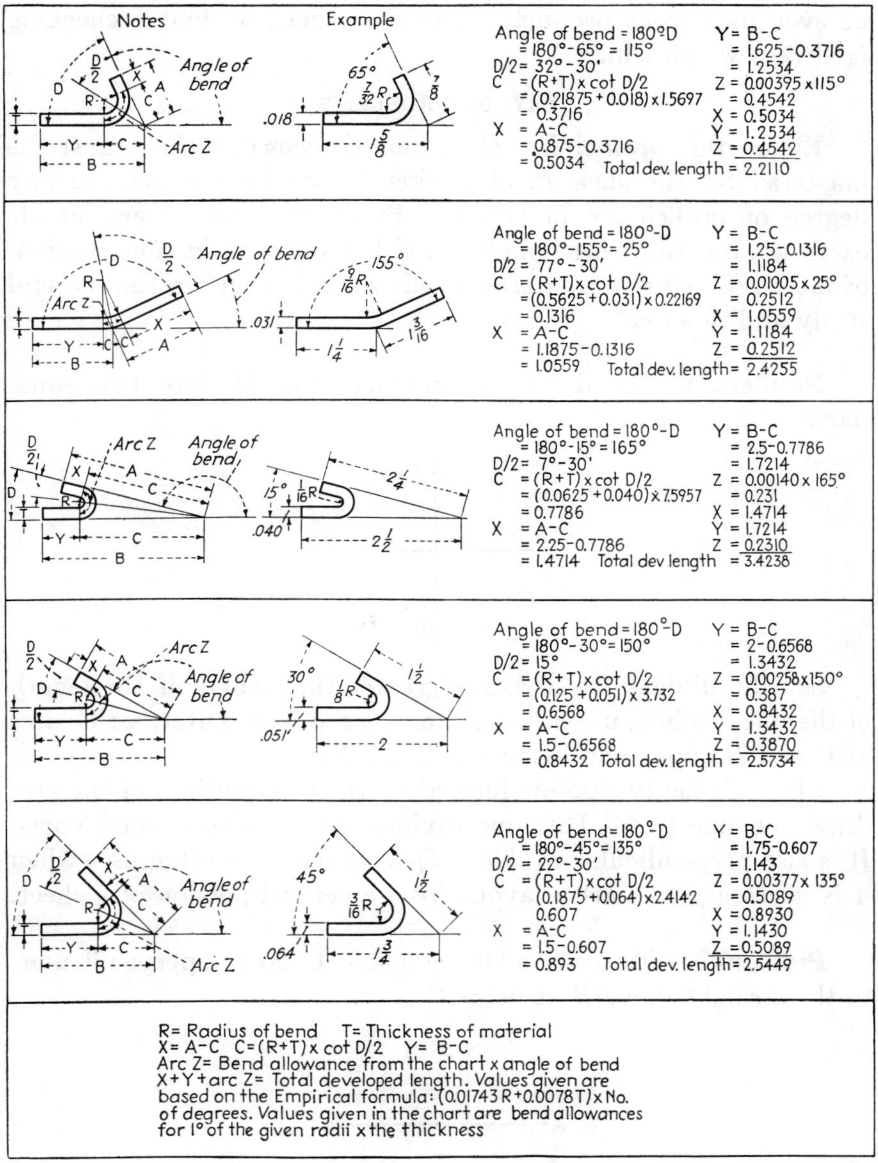

FIG. 48.—How the bend-allowance chart is used. (*Drawings courtesy of the Glenn L. Martin Co.*)

or even dangerous product. The time spent in double checking is always worth while.

LAYOUT PROBLEMS

Elementary principles of geometric construction must be mastered by the sheetmetal worker before he can achieve any degree of proficiency in layout. Problems 1 to 17 are simple exercises, but they form the basis, either singly or in combination, of most problems encountered in this work. They warrant careful study and practice.

Problem 1.—To divide a reference line *AB* into two equal parts.

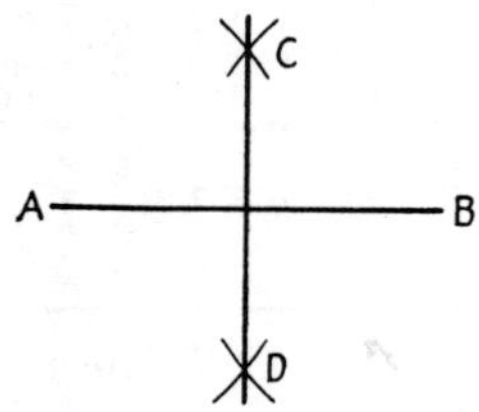

Set the dividers to a radius greater than one-half the length of the line. Then, using first *A* and then *B* as a center, scribe arcs at *C* and *D* above and below the line *AB*.

Through the two points formed by the intersections of the arcs draw the line *CD*. This line divides *AB* into two equal parts. It is also perpendicular to *AB*. This procedure is often used when it is necessary to start a layout from a central portion of a sheet.

Problem 2.—To scribe a 90 deg. angle, or erect a perpendicular, to the straight line *AB* at point *C*.

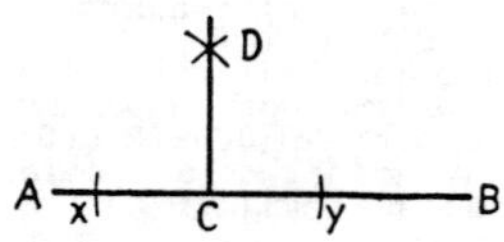

Set the dividers to any convenient radius; and with point *C* as a center, scribe two arcs, *X* and *Y*, on the line *AB*. Using points *X* and *Y* as centers and with a radius somewhat greater than before, scribe two arcs above the line *AB*. These arcs intersect at point *D*. A line drawn from *D* to *C* is perpendicular to *AB*. The angles *ACD* and *BCD* are 90 deg.

Problem 3.—To scribe a perpendicular line, or erect a 90 deg. angle, from the point *A* at the end of a line *AB*.

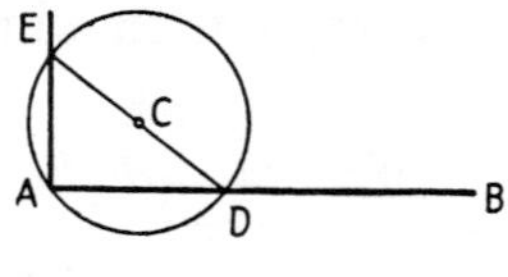

With any point *C* outside the line *AB* as a center and with *CA* as a radius, draw a circle intersecting *AB* at point *D*. Then draw a line from point *D* through point *C*, and continue it until it meets the circle at point *E*. The line drawn from *A* to *E* is perpendicular to the line *AB*. The angle *DAE* is a 90 deg. angle.

Problem 4.—To draw a perpendicular to a line *AB* from a point *C* at a distance from it.

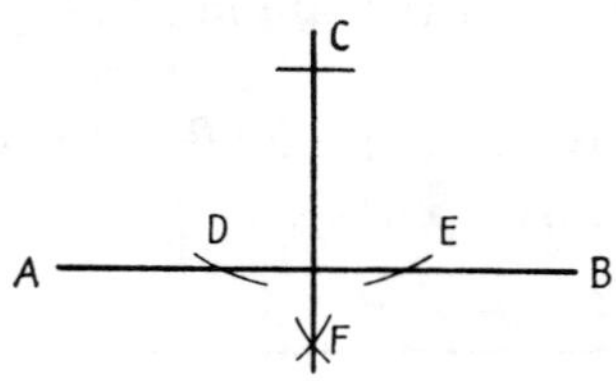

With point *C* as a center, scribe arcs that intersect the line *AB* at points *D* and *E*. Then with *D* and *E* as centers and with a radius longer than one-half the distance between *D* and *E*, scribe arcs that intersect at point *F*. A line drawn from *F* to *C* is perpendicular to the line *AB*.

Problem 5.—To lay out a line parallel to the line *AB* at a given distance from it.

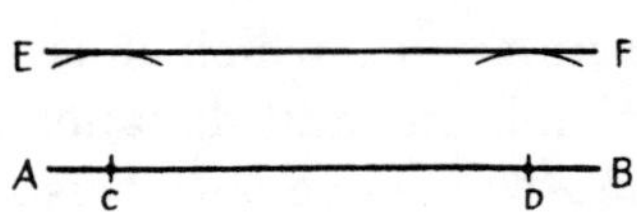

Set the dividers at the given distance. Using as centers two points *C* and *D*, swing arcs above the line *AB*. Next, lay a straightedge so that it is just touching, or tangent, to both arcs.

The line *EF* drawn or scribed along the straightedge is parallel to the line *AB*.

Problem 6.—To form an angle with a line *AB* that is equal to a given angle *FGH*.

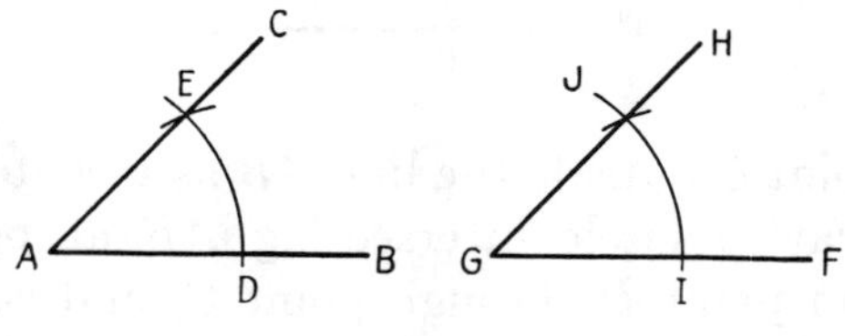

Using point *G* as a center and with any radius less than *GF* or *GH*, scribe an arc *IJ*. Then with *A* as a center and with the same radius, scribe an arc *DE*, approximately equal to the arc *IJ*. With *I* as a center, set dividers to the intersection of the arc *IJ* and the line *GH*. Using this radius and *D* as a center, scribe a short arc across the arc *DE*. Through points *A* and *E* scribe the line *AC*. The angle *BAC* then equals the angle *FGH*.

Problem 7.—To divide a line *AB* into any number of equal parts (in this example, five parts).

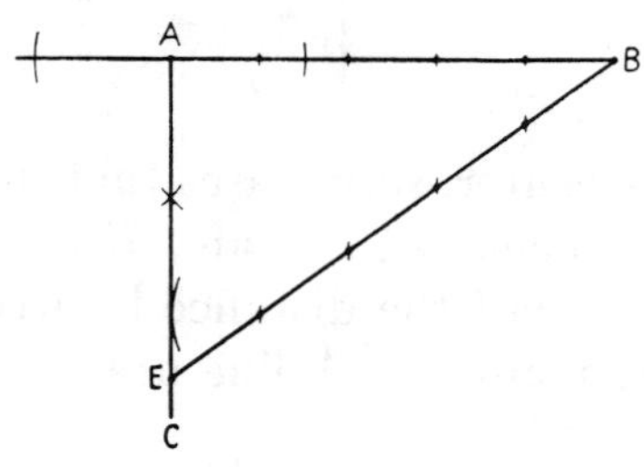

From point *A* construct a perpendicular *AC*. Then chose some unit of measurement which when stepped off five times will meet the line *AC* at a point *E*. This unit may be 1 in., 1¼ in., 1½ in., or any other unit with which it is easy to work. From a point on line *EB* which is one unit distance from point *E* draw an arc tangent to the line *AC*. Then with this same compass setting, begin at point *A* and step off five points on the line *AB*. If measurements have been made accurately, each step on *AB* will be one-fifth of the length of the line. This method may be used for spacing rivets.

Problem 8.—To draw a line at 45 deg. to a given line *AB*.

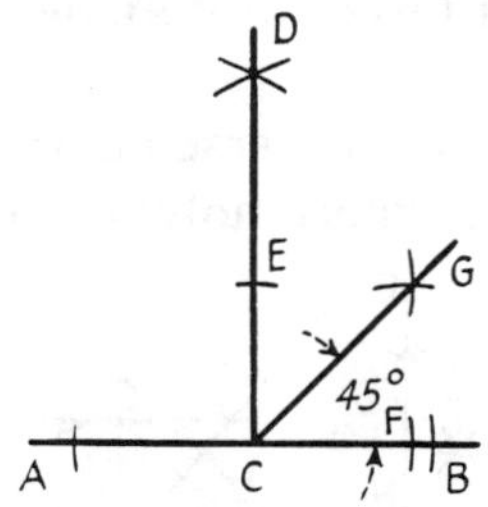

On the line *AB* locate a point *C* near the middle of the line.

Using methods described previously, erect a perpendicular *CD*. Then with *C* as a center and using a convenient radius, draw arcs that intercept the lines *DC* and *CB*. Label these points *E* and *F*.

With *E* and *F* as centers, draw arcs of the same radius that intersect at a new point *G*. The line *CG* forms a 45 deg. angle *BCG*. This same method will bisect any angle.

Problem 9.—To draw a line at 60 deg. to a given line *AB*.

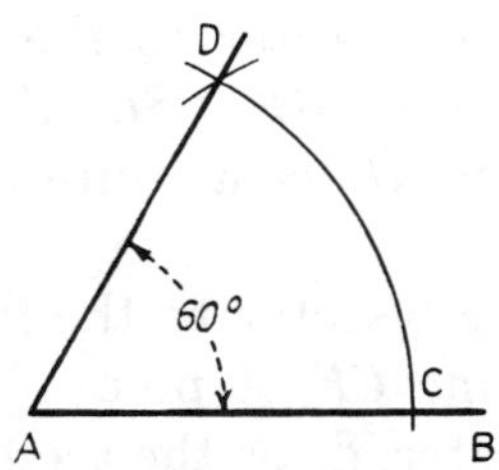

With *A* as a center, draw an arc that intersects the line at point *C* and that continues some distance above the line. Then using the same radius and with point *C* as a center, intersect the arc at point *D* with another arc. When the line *AD* is drawn, it will form a 60 deg. angle *CAD*.

Problem 10.—To draw a line at 30 deg. to a given line *AB*.

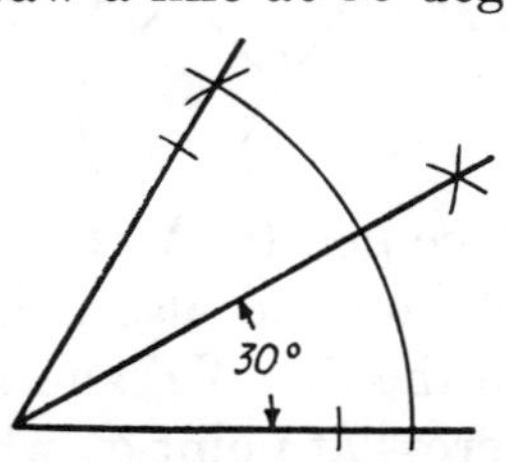

Draw a 60 deg. angle, following the method given in Problem 9.

Then bisect this 60 deg. angle by using the method described in Problem 8, which will bisect any angle.

Problem 11.—To draw a reverse curve. This method may be used to form radius relief where notches occur in sheetmetal.

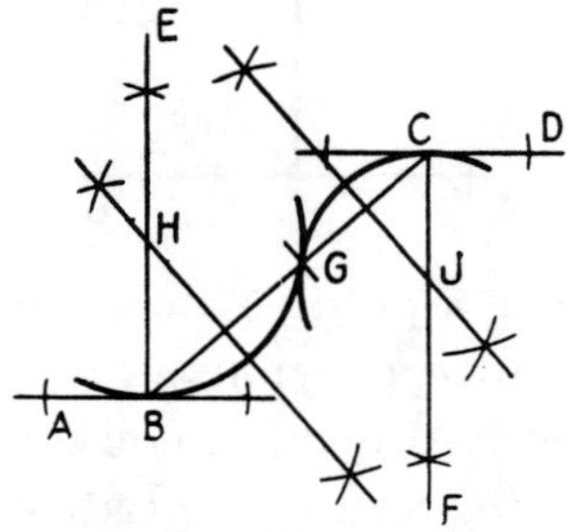

Draw two parallel lines *AB* and *CD*. From point *B* erect a perpendicular *BE*. From point *C* erect a perpendicular *CF*. Then join *B* and *C* with a straight line.

Locate a point *G* on the line *BC* through which the curve is desired to pass.

Erect a perpendicular bisector to the line *BG* and mark the point *H* where it intersects *BE*. Set the dividers to a radius equal to *HB*; and, using *H* as a center, draw the arc through *B* and *G*.

Erect a perpendicular bisector to the line *CG*, and continue it until it intersects the line *CF* at point *J*. With the radius *CJ* and with point *J* as a center, draw the arc through points *C* and *G*. The curve *BGC* is a smooth, reverse curve.

Problem 12.—To find the center of any true arc.

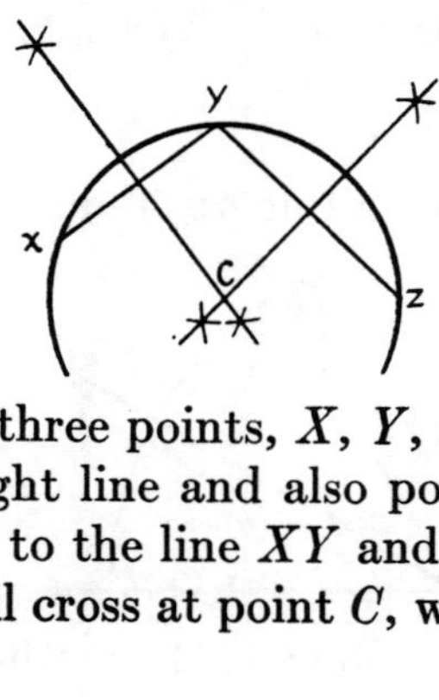

On any arc locate three points, *X*, *Y*, and *Z*. Connect points *X* and *Y* with a straight line and also points *Y* and *Z*. Draw a perpendicular bisector to the line *XY* and also to the line *YZ*.

These new lines will cross at point *C*, which is the center of the arc.

Problem 13.—To construct an arc tangent to two straight lines.

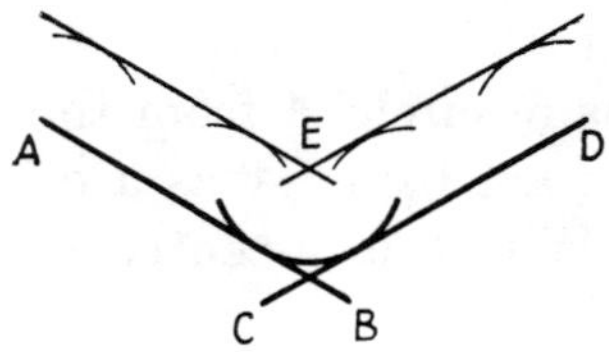

Draw lines *AB* and *CD* at any angle to each other. Using methods described earlier, draw a line parallel to *AB* and a line parallel to *CD* at a distance from them equal to the radius of the tangent arc. The intersection of the two new lines is point *E*.

With *E* as a center, draw the tangent arc.

Problem 14.—To construct a concave arc tangent to two circles.

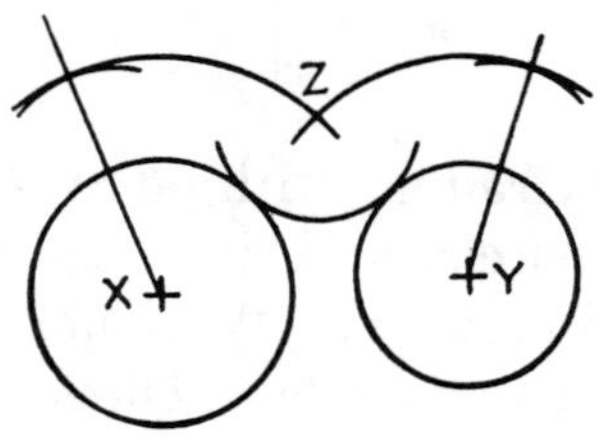

Draw two circles of different sizes, and label the centers *X* and *Y*. Draw a circle parallel to circle *X* and at a distance from it equal to the radius of the tangent arc. Then draw a circle parallel to circle *Y* at a distance from it equal to the radius of the tangent arc. The intersection of the two new circles is point *Z*. With *Z* as a center, draw the desired tangent arc.

Problem 15.—To construct a convex arc tangent to two circles.

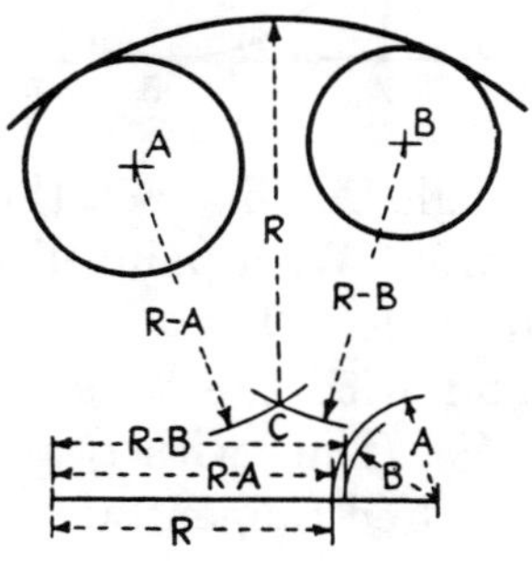

Draw two circles *A* and *B* of different sizes. Subtract the radius of circle *B* from the radius of the tangent arc, and draw an arc using *B* as a center.

Subtract the radius of circle *A* from the radius of the tangent arc, and then draw an arc using *A* as a center. These two arcs intersect at point *C*. With *C* as a center, draw the tangent arc.

Problem 16.—To draw a tangent to a circle from a point outside the circle.

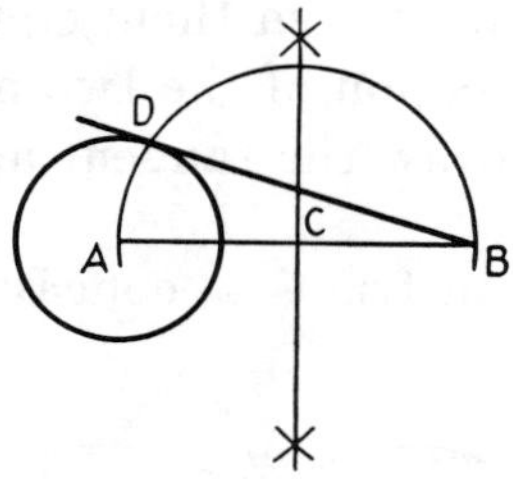

Draw a circle of any radius, with point *A* as a center. Locate a point *B* outside the circle, and draw the line *AB*. Bisect line *AB* to locate the mid-point *C*. With point *C* as a center and with radius *CA*, draw a semicircle. The semicircle intersects the original circle at point *D*, which is the point of tangency. Then draw *BD*.

Problem 17.—To draw an arc tangent to a right angle.

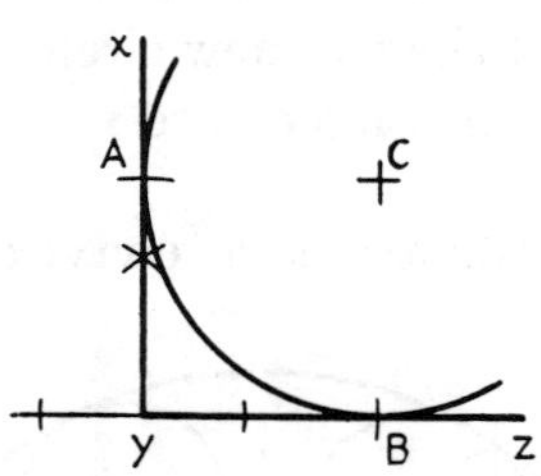

Construct a right angle *XYZ*. Set the dividers to a radius of the desired tangent arc. With point *Y* as a center, draw arcs on each leg of the right angle. These are points *A* and *B*. With *A* and *B* as centers and with the same radius, draw arcs that intersect each other at *C*. Then with *C* as a center and with the same radius, draw the desired tangent arc.

Review Questions

1. In aircraft work, what does the term *layout* signify?

2. If templates are available, is it necessary to do layout work?

3. Why is a knowledge of layout technique of value to a mechanic?

4. What is a reference line?

5. What are some of the commonly used layout tools?

6. What is marking fluid and why is it used?

7. When may lines be drawn with a steel scriber?

8. How are curved lines drawn?

9. Why is a formula used in figuring a bending allowance?

10. Describe the purpose of each of the different kinds of bending-allowance chart given in the text and explain how they are used.

11. Describe the term *nesting*.

12. How are holes indicated on the stock that is to be drilled?

Shop Work

Layouts of various kinds are called for in Projects 2, 3, 4, and 5 of Chap. 15. Additional layout practice may be secured from the sheetmetal parts shown in the drawings of Chap. 1. Students should work out all 17 problems given in the preceeding pages.

CHAPTER 7

HOW TO CUT SHEET

When sheets of aluminum alloy are received from the factory, they are almost never of a size that permits them to be used without additional cutting. Consequently, the cutting of sheet-metal is one of the most common operations carried on in an aircraft plant.

There are several methods of cutting sheet. The most common is by the *squaring shear*, which consists of a bed or table with one knife edge on which the metal rests and a knife bar at the rear of the bed. The square-edge knife descends vertically and cuts with a guillotine action as it passes the knife edge of the table. This type of shear cuts only in a straight line. It is used principally for blanking, but extremely accurate parallel or angular cuts may be made. The shear may be operated by stepping on a foot treadle, or it may be power operated. Figure 49 is a typical example of a squaring shear used for aircraft sheet-metal work.

Sheet is usually inserted from the operator's side of the shear. If it has been marked for cutting, the line on which it is to be cut is placed directly under the knife blade. The sides may also be lined up by the use of *squaring arms* or metal guide bars that slide in grooves on the bed of the shear, which can be secured by hand-adjusted screws or quick-setting gages. Sheet does not necessarily need to be marked for cutting, as a gage bar, or stop, can be adjusted properly on the side nearest the operator so that, when the piece of sheet rests firmly against it, the shear blade will fall at the proper measurement. The bed of the shear is often marked with a graduated scale, as an aid to measuring.

Long pieces of sheet may be inserted from the rear of the shear, pushed through until the end rests against the front fence, and then cut.

Some squaring shears are equipped with back gage bars for close gaging behind the knife. They can easily be adjusted by a hand wheel or a crank and checked by a dial reading to $\frac{1}{64}$ in.

For shearing sheet that has been marked by a scribed line, the larger power shears are often equipped with a *light-beam shearing gage.* It operates by the simple device of casting a sharp shadow along the scribed line. The fixture is focused so that bright and dark areas are clear and distinct even in well-lighted factories and it eliminates adjustment and sighting from end to end of the sheet.

FIG. 49.—A large Cincinnati power squaring shear in use at the Curtiss factory in Buffalo. Sheet stock may be cut up to the full length of the shear. Small pieces of sheet, piled on the near side of the operators, are being blanked. Only the far end of the shear was being utilized when this picture was taken. Note the plunger hold-down stops in front of the comblike guard. The shearing blade is operated by stepping on the foot treadle.

Although this machine is sometimes called the *squaring shear,* it also cuts any angle that is desired. Both the front and the rear gage bars and the side squaring arms are adjustable for taper shearing.

The sheet is held in place during the cutting operation by a bar of padded *hold-downs,* or fingers, located just in front of the blade. On some shears, these fingers are operated by a lever, and on other power-driven shears the hold-downs are hydraulically operated and automatically descend just before the cutting blade strikes the metal. They deliver a heavy, uniform pressure along the full length of the sheet, thus preventing slippage of the work, regardless of any variation in thickness.

To prevent aluminum-alloy sheets from being scratched, a fiber top may be fitted to the table, or heavy wrapping paper held in place with masking tape may be used. The hold-down fingers should be covered with soft leather cups. On hydraulic

FIG. 50.—Although large in size, Cincinnati shears have delicate adjustment controls. A power back gage is operated with finger-tip control for setting the size of the cut. Dials at the top read in sixty-fourths of an inch.

hold-downs, the oil pressure may be reduced in the plungers to avoid denting soft or thin-gage sheet.

Most power-driven shears are carefully guarded with a comb-like steel fence in front of the knife bar, so that the operator will not catch his fingers under the knife. Foot-operated squaring shears are often fitted with a strip of paralyn across the front of the knife bar. The transparent paralyn permits the operator to see markings on the sheet, yet prevents him from getting his hands close to the knife.

Power shears are generally used in longer sizes than the foot-operated machines, which are not used larger than 10 ft. in length. Operators working on the latter type should be careful to keep their feet from beneath the treadle as it is pushed down, as the bar often goes nearly to the floor.

For aircraft work, squaring shears are used up to 18 ft. in length, and the smallest size in general use is 36 in. A shear always has a definite capacity, as to the thickness of the metal to be cut. To exceed this may ruin the blade or break the machine. If, for example, the capacity of the shear is limited to 1/8 in. (0.125 in.) mild steel, and 3/16 in. (0.1875 in.) mild steel is cut, the shear may be ruined. It would be incorrect, too, if 0.125 chrome-molybdenum steel were sheared, since the greater hardness of this metal would spoil a shear blade that was not intended for it.

HAND BENCH SHEAR

The hand bench shear is similar in operation to a paper cutter. It has one fixed metal blade and a movable knife, hinged at the back, which is pulled down by a handle to cut the metal. This is the most common type for cutting small pieces of sheetmetal. Metal is marked and then held so that the blade will fall exactly on the proper line. The frame of the bench shear is offset to provide clearance for the severed edges of long sheets during slitting operations. This, however, does not prevent one side of the sheet from being bent down and distorted. Consequently, the bench shear is most often used for cutting small pieces of steel for fittings.

For cutting stock that is narrower in width than the length of the blades, the lever of the shear can be pulled all the way down. When cutting larger pieces, a continuous series of short bites should be made, since complete closing of the blades tends to tear the sheet at the end of each cut.

Each bench shear has a definite cutting capacity designated in gage and material. This capacity should never be exceeded.

Rod, wire, or cable should never be cut between the knife blades of a bench shear. Many shears are provided with holes in the blades that can be aligned for the insertion of round stock to be sheared.

The *throatless shear* works on the same principle as the straight-blade bench shear except that the blades are curved. This design allows the metal to be turned in any position for the cutting of curved shapes. It is best used with a series of short cuts. For straight-line shearing, it is not so efficient as the straight-blade bench shear but it cuts with less distortion and ordinarily does not leave a burred edge requiring additional burring or filing (see Fig. 51).

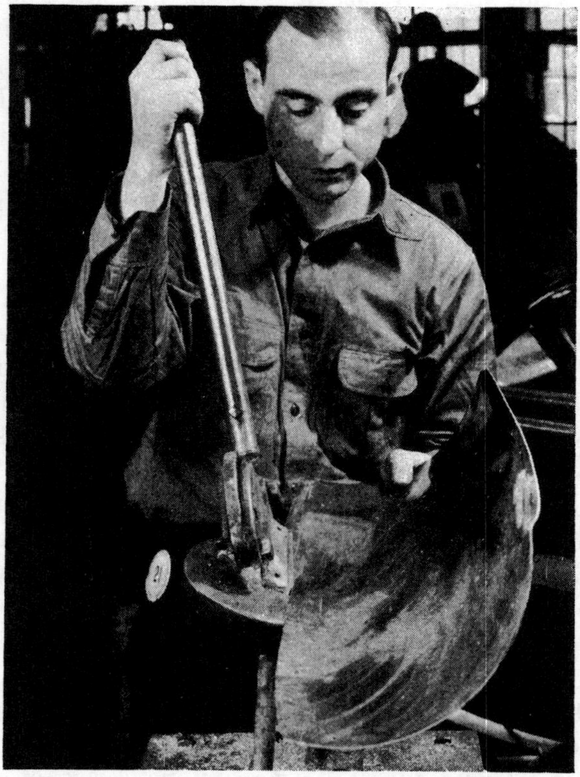

FIG. 51.—A hand-operated throatless bench shear at Curtiss-Wright, Buffalo.

METAL SNIPS

Regardless of the size of the aircraft factory, there is always a considerable amount of sheetmetal that must be cut with hand shears, or *snips*. There are several kinds of snips, each of which serves a different purpose. In common use, there are *straight*, *curved*, *hawk's bill*, *scroll pivoter*, *trojan*, and *aircraft snips*. The last named is also known as *Bellanca* or *Dutch* snips. Straight snips are used for cutting straight lines when the distance is not great enough to use a squaring shear and for cutting the outside of a curve. The other types are used for cutting on the inside of curves of small radii or for cutting difficult positions, some of which are illustrated. Snips are never used on heavy sheet.

The flat part of the blade is always held at right angles to the surface of the metal. The blades of ordinary right-hand snips are arranged so that the material on the left curls up and the material

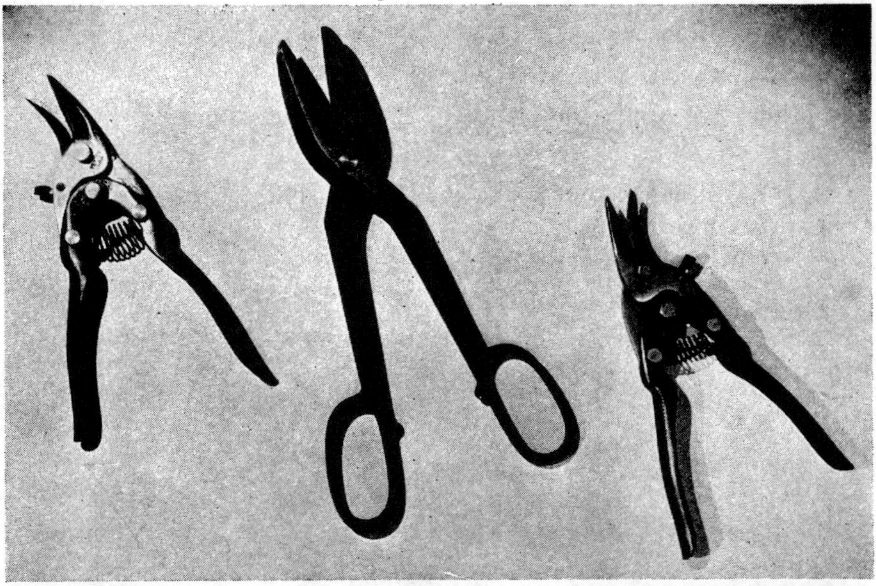

FIG. 52.—In the center is a pair of straight snips. On the left is a pair of left-hand snips, which will make a circular cut to the *right*. On the right is a pair of right-hand snips, which will make a circular cut to the *left*. Aircraft snips are the most commonly used tool for hand cutting of aluminum-alloy sheet.

on the right bends downward. When trimming sheet, the snips should be used so that the scrap material curls up, thus preventing the sheet from becoming distorted and at the same time enabling the mechanic to see the marked cutting lines. Skill in cutting straight lines comes easily with practice, but following curved lines is more difficult. In cutting the inside of a circle, a hole is made near the edge of the circle with a hollow punch or a drill, and one point of the snip is inserted from the underside. Then a larger opening is cut, and the snips are worked toward the marked line.

In the *scroll pivoter* snips, the blades lie flat, the exact opposite of the ordinary cutting blades. It is easily pivoted and very useful in snipping around corners and circles and for making angle cuts.

Aircraft snips, also known as Bellanca or Dutch snips, are used more than any other type by the sheetmetal worker. Their short curved jaws, compound lever action, and rubber-covered grips make them very useful for cutting irregular shapes from aluminum-alloy sheet. They are made in both right- and left-hand types. The right-hand snip is designed to cut to the left, and the left-hand snip is designed to cut to the right. They are equipped with a spring in the handles to open them after each bite and a hook to keep them closed when not in use.

FIG. 53.—An electric Unishear being used for cutting galvanized-iron sheet for templates at the Glenn L. Martin Co.

In general work it is best to use straight snips where possible for roughing out, then finish close to the cutting line with aircraft or scroll pivoter snips. The last two types are not recommended for straight cutting.

All types of snips should be kept in a closed position with the jaws protected when not in use. Material over 0.040 in. in thickness should be cut by some other means, such as a squaring shear, a beverly shear, or a band saw.

PORTABLE ELECTRIC SHEARS

Portable electric shears are in reality a pair of metal snips that are operated electrically by a self-contained electric motor. A button or a trigger controls the cutting. This type of shear is flexible and can be used for cutting curves and complicated patterns. It is portable but may also be mounted in a bench stand. In this position, the metal can be fed into the cutting jaws (see Fig. 53).

HACK SAWS

Hack saws are used for hand cutting steel and heavy-gage aluminum-alloy stock. They are also used for cutting extrusions,

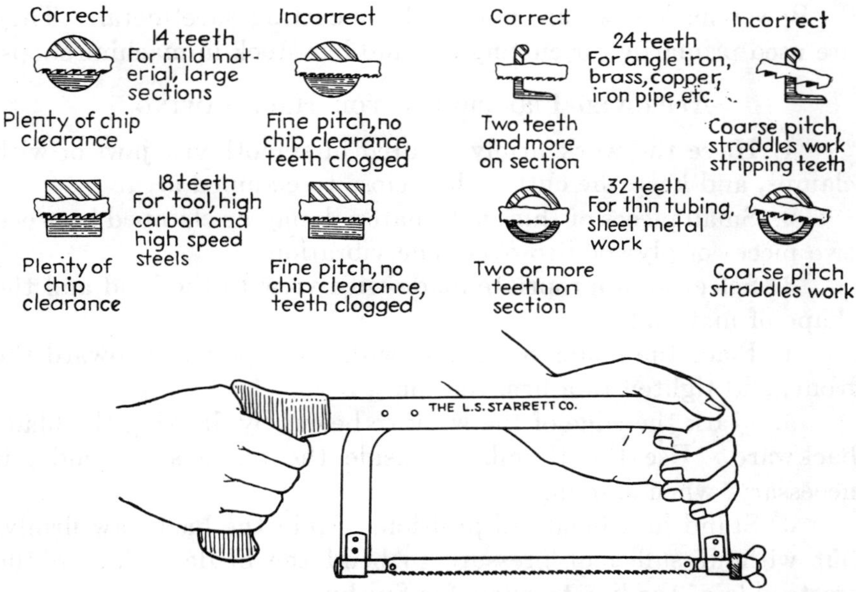

FIG. 54.—The efficient operation of the hack saw depends on the selection of the blade and the speed and angle at which the blade is moved across the work. The blade is tightened by use of wing nut at the right in the lower drawing. The blade can be given a one-quarter turn and locked in position, which makes cutting easier in certain operations. (*Illustration based on Starrett drawings.*)

bolts, and rivets. Hack saws are used only in straight-line cutting. Their frames have pistol grips and are adjustable to take blades of several lengths. The blade chosen must be suited to the metal that is to be cut. Blades vary in the number of teeth per inch from 12 to 32. Soft metal, such as aluminum, requires blades with fewer teeth per inch, so that the metal will not easily clog the teeth. A hard steel requires more teeth per inch than aluminum. As an aid in starting the cut, some hack-saw blades have fine teeth close to one end and larger teeth on the remainder of the blade.

The shape of the stock is also a factor in the selection of the blade, as illustrated in Fig. 54.

Blades should be fastened firmly in the frame, and the operator should take long, easy strokes, using the full length of the blade. If he bears down too hard, an unnecessary amount of friction will develop. Blades are adjustable in position, so that they can be turned at right angles to the usual cutting position. Where a wider cut is required, such as for a screw-driver slot in a bolt head, two blades may be used in the frame at one time.

Power hack saws are not used for cutting sheetmetal. They are used primarily for cutting rod and bar stock in machine shops.

Approved Procedures for Hack-sawing

1. Have the work firmly secured in smooth vise jaws or with clamps, and keep the cutting line close to clamped area.

2. Small pieces of thin-gage material may be clamped between two pieces of plywood to overcome vibration.

3. Select an appropriate blade with view to the kind and the shape of material.

4. Place the blade in a frame with teeth pointing toward the front, and tighten to a firm tension.

5. Mark the edge of the work to be cut by drawing the blade backward. Use the thumb alongside the blade as a guide, if necessary, when starting.

6. Stand in a balanced position. Hold the hack saw firmly, but without sufficient pressure to bend the blade. Cut on the waste side of the line to allow for finishing.

7. The blade cuts only on the forward stroke. Relieve the pressure and raise the blade slightly from the work on the return stroke. Use your body, not just your arms.

8. Use the entire length of the blade for each full stroke.

9. For efficient cutting, use 40 to 60 strokes per minute. Faster cutting will cause friction that will remove the temper from the blade.

10. Do not use dull blades. When the blade becomes dull, it should be discarded and replaced with a new one.

METAL BAND SAWS

A metal band saw has an endless blade, for continuous cutting. It is similar to the type of band saw used for cutting wood, except that the metal saw has a blade tempered for cutting metals.

The band saw consists essentially of two disks or drums mounted one above the other, over which the saw band travels as would a belt. The lower drum is driven by an electric motor.

FIG. 55.—A Doall continuous band saw being used to cut a number of stacked sheets. Compressed air is ejected from the flexible tube to blow away the chips. The chain feed, fastened around the work and operated by a foot pedal, helps to pull the sheets into the saw blade. When especially fine cutting is being done, the operator can swing a magnifying glass into position. The operator is also aided by an electric light.

For average aircraft work the diameters of the drums range upward from 18 in. Both drums are enclosed in a metal housing. One side of the saw band passes through a table located between the drums, which is usually set at right angles to the saw band for cutting vertically but may be tipped for angular cutting. The work to be cut is placed on the table and moved by hand into the blade, which cuts as it travels downward. A roller guide that can be adjusted to a point just above the work is provided for the blade. The guide reinforces the saw band and also acts as a guard.

The band saw is used for irregular cutting of a wide variety of metals in both light and heavy gage. It can be used for cutting single sheets of 0.020 in. or more in thickness or for cutting as many as 100 sheets placed one on top of the other and fastened together.

For cutting out lightening holes or for other internal cutting, the endless band must be broken and threaded through a small starting hole drilled in the work. The blade band must then be joined either by welding or by brazing. Welding is preferable, since it is stronger.

Small electric welding devices are used in which the ends of the blade may be clamped and butted together during welding. After being butt-welded, the area of the weld is annealed and the *flash*, or surplus material, ground off to the original size of the band. The joining operation takes only about 1 min, to complete on modern butt-welding units.

The Doall machine is a widely used and versatile metal-cutting band saw for contour cutting in the aircraft industry. In addition to its use for continuous sawing, it is also used for continuous filing and polishing operations described in the next chapter.

The Doall machine has all the qualities of the conventional band saw plus many additional refinements that equip it for precision work in a great variety of aircraft sheetmetal and machining operations.

Doall machines are used in several sizes, the size depending on the throat depth. Their capacity is greater and a much higher degree of accuracy can be obtained than with regular metal-cutting band saws. A power-feeding arrangement may be used to draw the work into the saw, and contour cutting may be mechanically controlled with some setups, such as circle cutting.

A working light and a magnifying glass are used to provide greater accuracy at the cutting point. A compressed-air blower is attached to keep the cutting line clear of chips.

The machine is equipped with a variable job selector that may be used to determine the speed and the type of saw for each job.

Saw Blades.—The Doall saw blades are available in coils of 50 and 100 ft. lengths and range in widths from 1/16 to 1/2 in. A required length of saw band may be easily cut from the coil and butt-welded as previously explained. The saw-welding unit is mounted as an integral part of the machine.

FIG. 56.—How a Doall band saw is used to cut out holes. A small hole is drilled within the circle to be cut, then the band saw is threaded through the hole, and the two saw ends are welded together in this same machine. A skilled operator can cut elaborate designs of any pattern to close tolerances.

Selection of Saws.—The first step in precision sawing is the selection of the proper saw for the job. Several variable factors, such as temper, width, set, and number of teeth, make it desirable to understand the scope and applications of each of these variables.

In general, band saws are made in three tempers, as follows:

A. Very hard, for cutting:
High-chrome high-carbon steels.
Other alloy steels of high carbon content.
High-speed steels.
Stainless steels.
Hard steels.

B. Hard, for cutting:
Tool steels.
Alloy steels of low carbon content.
Cold-rolled steels.
Machine steels.
Cast iron.
Hard brass.
Bronze.

C. Medium hard, for cutting:
Soft brass and copper.
Aluminum.
Thin welded sections.

The width of the blade to be used is determined first by the feed. The widest blade possible should always be used because the strength is proportional to the width of the blade. The second consideration is the curvature to be cut. The diagram in Fig. 57 shows the selection of the proper width of blade for the minimum radii marked for cutting.

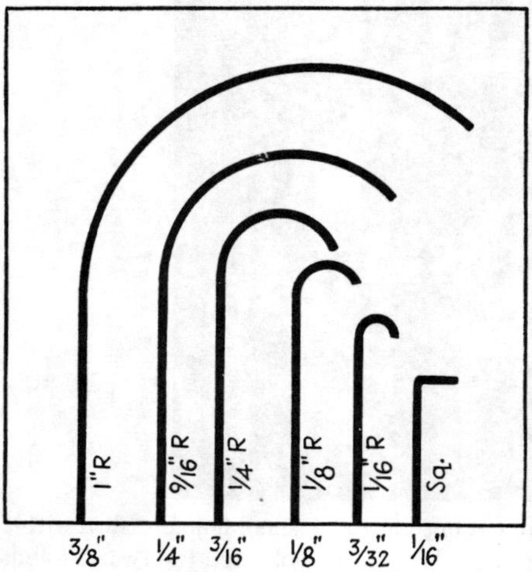

FIG. 57.—Radii capacity of band saws. Widths of saw blades are given at the bottom of the chart. For example, a blade ⅜ in. wide will easily cut a 1 in. radius. A skilled operator can cut even smaller radii than shown.

Saw Teeth.—There are three distinct types of tooth construction used for general aircraft work:

1. *Raker Tooth.*—One straight tooth alternates with two teeth set in opposite directions. The straight tooth clears the kerf of chips. The *kerf* is the space in the work occupied by the saw blade. This tooth construction is used exclusively for cutting all iron or steel except thin sheets, tubing, angles, and extrusions.

2. *Wave Tooth.*—This is the "group" set, one set of waves to the right and the next set to the left, etc. It gives the smallest possible tooth spacing and is used for cutting sheets, tubing, stainless steel, etc.

THE DOALL JOB SELECTOR LISTS THESE 45 MATERIALS WITH THEIR SAW-CONTROL FACTORS

Material to be cut	Pitch, teeth per in.	Kind of tooth	Temper	Sawing speed, ft. per min.
Aluminum alloys, aircraft	6–24	Straight	B	400–1,500
Aluminum castings	6–12	Straight	C	300–1,000
Aluminum, pure (over 1 in.)	6–10	Straight	B	500–1,500
Aluminum sheets	12–32	Straight or wave	C	300–1,500
Aluminum tubing	18–32	Straight or wave	C	400–1,500
Asbestos sheets	8–14	Raker	A	100– 200
Babbitt lead	8–10	Straight	C	400– 600
Bakelite (plastics)	8–18	Straight	A	400–1,500
Brass castings	8–14	Straight	B	400– 600
Brass, sheet	14–32	Straight or wave	C	400–1,500
Brass, soft screw stock	10–18	Straight	C	300– 500
Brass tubing	14–32	Straight or wave	C	400–1,500
Bronze, manganese	10–14	Raker	A	150– 400
Bronze castings	10–14	Straight or raker	A	200– 600
Builders board	8–12	Straight	A	200–1,500
Copper	8–18	Straight	A	75– 300
Cast iron	8–14	Raker	A	100– 200
Cast nickel iron	8–14	Raker	A	50– 150
Drill rod	14	Raker	A	65– 150
Fiber	8–10	Straight	A	250– 450
High-chrome high-carbon steel	6–14	Raker	A	50
High-chrome steel	6–18	Raker	A	50– 100
High-speed steel	8–10	Raker	A	60– 150
Iron sheets	14–32	Straight	A	100– 600
Lamination iron	14–24	Raker	B	75– 500
Machine steel	12–14	Raker	B	100– 220
Malleable iron	12–14	Raker	A	150– 250
Metal wood	14	Raker	B	400– 750
Mica	10–12	Straight	A	300– 600
Mild steel (not rolled)	10–14	Raker	B	125– 200
Monel metal	10–12	Raker	A	50– 150
Monel sheets	14–24	Raker	A	50– 750
Nickel silver	18–24	Raker	A	100– 200
Nickel steel	12–14	Raker	A	75– 140
Nitralloy	12–14	Raker	A	50– 110
Porcelain	10–14	Straight	A	50– 300
Pipe	14–18	Raker	B	100– 200
Rubber, hard	8–12	Raker	A	100– 200
Silver	12–18	Raker	B	150– 400
Slate	10–18	Straight	A	75– 200
Stainless steel	14–24	Raker or wave	A	50
Steel, structural	10–14	Raker	B	200– 300
Steel, thin sheet	14–32	Raker	B	400–1,500
Tool steel, air	12–14	Raker	A	75– 150
Tool steel, oil	12–18	Raker	A	75– 150
Zinc	12–24	Straight	C	450–1,500

3. *Straight Tooth.*—This is the smallest set; one tooth set to the right, the next to the left. It is for brass, copper, plastics, and nonmetals and is used for forming blocks.

Band saws are cut in 6, 8, 10, 12, 14, 18, 24, and 32 *pitch*, or teeth, per inch.

Operating Speeds.—An essential factor in the success of precision contour sawing is the use of the correct operating speed. The saw must travel at the rate of 50 ft. per minute when cutting high-chrome high-carbon steel; for cutting aluminum and dural sheet, the saw must travel at the rate of 1,500 ft. per minute. Within this wide range of cutting speeds, each different kind of metal and each thickness of job require a different cutting speed (see the chart on page 119). If an incorrect speed is used, the saw will tend to burn or will not cut efficiently. The Doall machine is equipped with a variable-speed control and a dial tachometer indicator to show the exact travel of the saw.

Approved Procedures for Band-saw Operations

1. The selection of the band-saw blade depends upon the kind and the shape of the material to be cut. For efficient cutting, only a blade having the proper number of teeth per inch can be used (see reference table for blade selection, page 119). In general, the softer the material the fewer the teeth per inch, but the thinner the material the more teeth per inch. At least two teeth should be in contact with the work. Use the coarsest set saw possible to permit maximum chip clearance and reduce friction. The thicker the material the coarser the teeth should be.

2. It is important that the blade of the band saw be just tight enough to hold a straight cut. The tension, however, should be just enough to keep the blade from slipping on the drums. Excessive tension is unnecessary and is apt to cause the blade to break.

3. The guides should be checked to see that the blade will run perfectly straight and not bind. Guide bearing wheels should turn freely without binding. The teeth should never be allowed to rub on the guide blocks.

4. Set the machine to the appropriate cutting speed, if it is adjustable. For general work, the harder the material to be cut the slower the speed should be.

5. Check the surface of the table for a 90 deg. position with the saw, or adjust to the proper angle. Be sure that the table is secured after adjustment.

6. Lower the saw guide and guard until it just clears the work; then secure it.

7. Wear goggles if a glass shield is not provided and keep them over your eyes all the time that the machine is cutting.

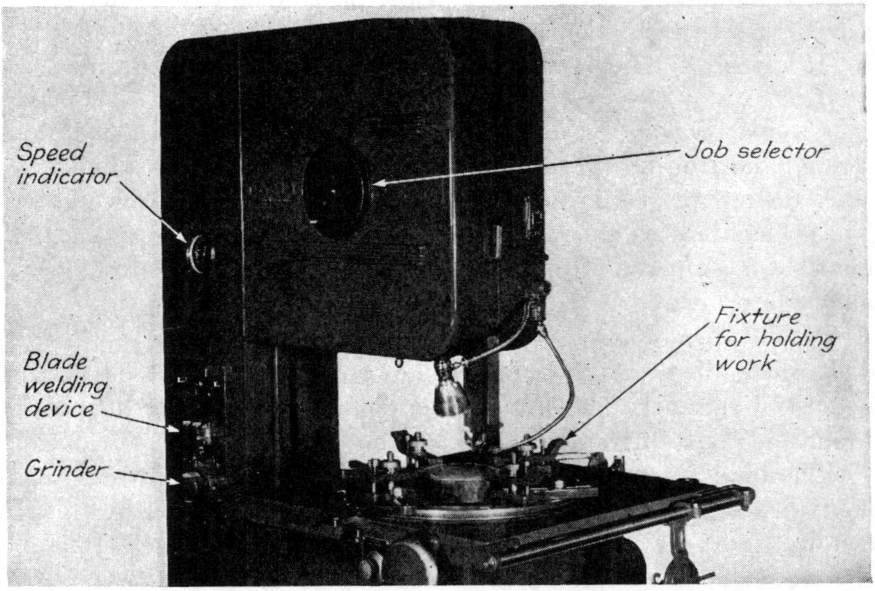

FIG. 58.—Details of a Doall machine. Saw blades are butt-welded in the device at the left. The "Job Selector" dial on the upper part of the machine provides the operator with information as to the pitch, kind of tooth, temper of the saw blade, and speed for 45 different materials. After he has chosen the proper saw, he controls the speed, which is shown on the speed-indicator dial. The work table can be tilted four different ways. The chain around the work is part of the self-equalizing power feed, which automatically turns the work being cut.

8. Start the machine and make sure that the band is running true on the drums before any cutting is started.

9. If several pieces of plywood or dural sheet are to be "ganged," or cut at one time, they should be fastened securely together to prevent weaving in the cut.

10. The material to be cut should be held down firmly and fed slowly into the blade.

11. Without forcing the work, cut as closely as possible along the outside waste edges of the line, but without removing the line. Cut slowly on small radii.

12. When turning the work to follow curves, be sure that the blade does not twist, or breakage is apt to result.

13. If the curve to be cut is too sharp to clear the blade width, the work may be backed out along the original cutting track. Waste material outside the cutting line can be notched out to permit shorter cuts along the line.

14. Keep your eyes on the work all the time, and keep your fingers well clear of the blade. If the part being cut is small, use a feeding setup or blocks of wood to guide the work.

15. Relax the tension on the blade when the saw is not in use.

Circular Saws.—Circular saws are used to a limited extent for straight cutting in aircraft sheetmetal work. The saw blade is a steel disk with teeth running completely around the periphery. These machines are similar to the woodworking type except that the blades are tempered for cutting metal, which is usually aluminum-alloy plate.

Some types of saws have high-speed steel teeth inserted in the disks instead of a solid blade. They may be used for cutting I beams or channels. A cutting compound or a cutting lubricant should be constantly used when cutting steel.

The blade is mounted vertically so that only the cutting segment protrudes above a slotted table. The table may be raised or lowered to accommodate various thicknesses of metal. It may also be set at any angle up to 45 deg. for bevel cutting.

Another type of circular saw is the overhead *swing saw*, which the operator swings down to the work in an arc. It is frequently used for cutting steel or dural tubing.

Abrasive cutting disks are often used instead of steel blades on swing saws. They have no teeth but derive their ability to cut from the abrasive grit that is impregnated in the plastic disk. They are quite durable and will cut stainless-steel tubing of heavy wall thickness.

NIBBLING MACHINES

For roughing out fittings and other parts made from heavier gage steel and dural sheet, nibbling machines are sometimes used. The stationary machines operate on the principle of a high-speed motor-driven punch press. The cutting is done by a die that cuts a series of overlapping holes by taking small bites from the metal as the operator feeds the metal past the nibbler. He can turn the metal to any angle and can secure cuts on radii as small as $\frac{3}{16}$ in. The cutting is actually performed by an upper punch die which moves up and down to meet a lower hollow die that is stationary. The machine is operated by a foot treadle at the base of the frame.

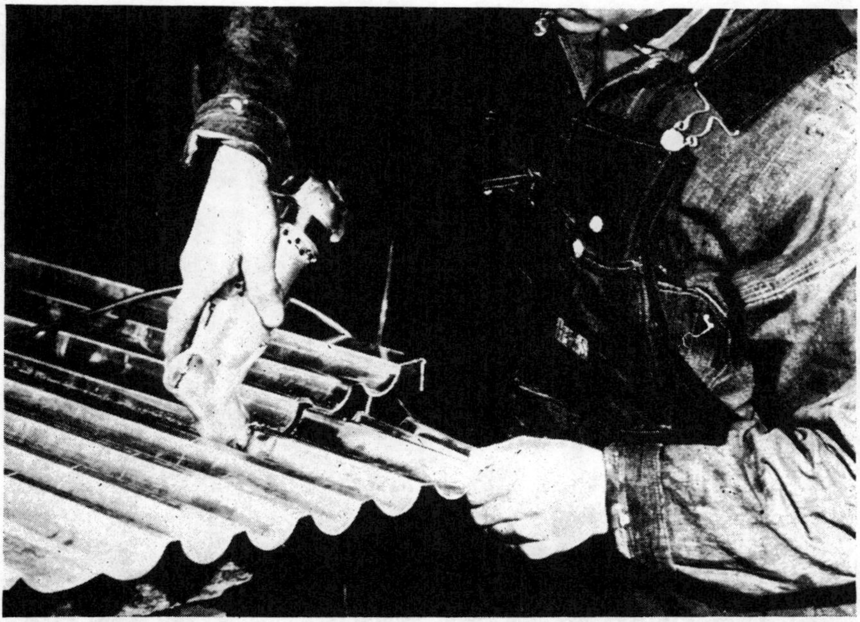

FIG. 59.—A Thor portable electric nibbler, which can be used for cutting both regular and irregular shapes, for following a scribed line or the contour of a template clamped to plain or corrugated sheet stock, or for cutting tubes. Inside cuts can be made without breaking in from the edge of the stock. Curves and circles with a radius as small as 1 in. can be cut. Nibblers are usually used for heavier gage materials.

The portable nibbler (Fig. 59) is more useful for the greater part of aircraft work. The manner of nibbling is essentially the same as the stationary type, but the nibbler is driven by a self-contained electric motor controlled with a recessed toggle switch. It is used for cutting tubing and sheet stock, both flat and corrugated.

The portable unit weighs less than 3 lb., and it can be fed into the work with one hand. It will cut regular and irregular shapes and accurately follow a scribed line or the contour of a template clamped to a sheet. It is also useful for inside cutting, since inside circular cuts can be made with a radius as small as 1 in. without breaking in from the edge of the stock. An adjustable yoke-type front head is used to accommodate various thicknesses up to No. 15 gage in aluminum alloy and up to No. 18 gage in steel.

Although nibblers are efficient for heavy-gage cutting, they leave a slightly serrated edge which usually must be filed or finished on a sanding disk or a belt sander. Unlike the majority of other means of cutting, the waste material is reduced to chips.

FIG. 60.—Close-up view of a power punch press in use at the Douglas Aircraft Co. Batteries of punch presses are in use in all large aircraft plants. Cutting dies can be installed to make cuts of different shapes and sizes. The steel plate in the foreground is the template which is used to set the adjustable guides which form the fixture against which the sheet is held as it is being cut.

DIE CUTTING

A great deal of die cutting today is done by hydraulic presses. In addition to forming, these presses actually cut the blanks to a usable size. This method is explained in Chap. 9. Thousands of small parts can be cut in one day by this means.

Die stamping is another method used for the blanking operation. Stamping machines work in much the same way as a nibbling machine, with the exception that the cutting is performed in one impact of the die. They are used for both steel fittings and aluminum-alloy sheet parts. Many parts that require hand-tool operation for completion utilize die stamping for cutting end and relief radii.

ROTARY CUTTING TOOLS

Except for the squaring shear and some uses of the band saw, most of the cutting methods described are used for cutting one or two pieces of sheet at a time and for relatively short cuts. When an airplane factory goes into production on a model, large quantities of parts must be cut to the same dimensions from aluminum-

FIG. 61.—A radial router in the Vultee factory. This cutting machine can rout a dozen or more sheets of aluminum alloy. The operator follows a template, or pattern, clamped on top of the sheets. When one set of work is finished, the entire table is revolved clockwise, which permits the routing to be continuous. The man in the foreground removes the cut sheet, the router operator cuts a new pile, and the two men on the far side load up their table with another batch of work.

alloy sheet stock, which is usually 48 by 144 in. in size. The fastest method for irregular cutting is to use a *profiling machine*, or router.

With this method as many as 25 sheets can be "ganged" one on top of the other and cut at one time, frequently producing as many as 600 separate pieces.

As explained in Chap. 7, the basic principle of profiling consists of stacking a number of standard-size sheets of aluminum alloy on a table and cutting them all to the outline of a single template. The actual cutting is accomplished by a high-speed router bit driven at approximately 15,000 r.p.m. These cutters are single-lipped spiral-fluted end mills, usually about 5/16 in. in diameter, permitting radii to be routed as small as 5/32 in.

The radial router consists of a heavy, rigid central pedestal on which are pivoted one or two jointed arms which support the router heads. The joint in the swinging arms permits the routing heads to be moved to any point within a circle of about 16 ft., except to within possibly 1 ft. of the central pedestal. The router head can be raised and lowered manually for feeding the cutter into and clearing it from the work.

The chuck shank of the router is fitted with a guide-bearing collar to bear against the template, or *router block*. Router blocks are wood templates made of composition board or fir plywood about 1/2 in. thick. The regular marking templates serve as patterns in making the blocks, which are cut out on band saws or wood shop routers. In making the router blocks, allowance is always made for the difference in diameter between the router bit and the guide collar.

The stacked sheets are drilled before routing with the aid of a drill template that is the same size as the standard stock sheet. The trim templates for the parts may then be laid out on a sheet of 1/4 in. plywood, leaving a space between them of about 1/2 in. for the router bit. As many templates as can be nested on the sheet are used. The templates are then riveted to the plywood.

The templates carry all the hole layout required for the finished part and, in addition, at least two 3/16 in. locating holes for securing router blocks during later operations.

After all indicated holes have been drilled through the template, individual router blocks are located in their proper positions and fastened by 3/16 in. lag screws, which pass through the locating holes into the wood surface of the router table. Electric or pneumatic wrenches are usually used to speed the work of inserting the lag screws.

After the routing blocks have been secured, the table is moved to the routing position and locked in place.

The operator cuts the blank by moving the router around the periphery and the internal lightening holes, or cutouts, in each block. When the routing is completed, the table is moved to an unloading station where the lag screws and the blocks are removed. The completed blanks are then burred and are ready for use.

While the operator is cutting one set of sheets, another set is being made ready for him. Many factories build routing devices to meet their individual specifications, sometimes combining drill-

FIG. 62.—Rotary power shears being used to cut sheet in the Douglas factory. The operator is following a cutting template placed on top of the work. Many complex profiling operations can be done with this machine. The gear-driven cutting disk bears at an angle against the work.

ing and routing operations in a single pedestal unit. A radial router with tables for setting up layout, drilling, and routing operations may be seen in Fig. 61.

Protective transparent face masks should always be worn when working on or near profiling machines.

As this chapter has pointed out, there are many kinds of cutting tools used today. In many instances several types of hand or machine tools may be used to produce the same results. The final choice of a tool depends upon the degree of accuracy required and the volume of the work to be done.

Review Questions

1. Why is it important for the aircraft mechanic to know various methods of cutting sheetmetal?

2. What is a squaring shear and how is it operated?

3. Will a squaring shear cut angles in flat sheet stock?

4. Is it proper to cut any kind of metal on a squaring shear?

5. For what purposes is a hand bench shear used?

6. What is a throatless shear?

7. What types of metal snips are used for aircraft work, and how do they differ?

8. For what purposes are hack saws used?

9. How are blades changed in a hack saw and in what direction are teeth pitched?

10. Describe the operation of a metal band saw.

11. How is a Doall machine used for internal cutting?

12. What are some of the factors to be considered in selecting saw blades?

13. Describe three kinds of teeth in band-saw blades.

14. What saw-control factors should be used in the cutting of aluminum tubing?

15. What is a nibbling machine and how does it cut sheetmetal?

16. Describe die cutting.

17. What is a router and how is it used?

18. How are templates used in routing operations?

Shop Work

Cutting with a variety of tools is required in the five projects of Chap. 15. Additional cutting is necessary if instructors assign the fabrication of parts shown in the blueprints of Chap. 1. It is assumed that students will be given practice jobs on every type of cutting tool available in school shops.

CHAPTER 8

FILES AND HOW TO USE THEM

Filing is one of the basic sheetmetal operations that all mechanics must master. When sheets of aluminum alloy are cut on a shear, stamped out in a press, or blanked out by any other means, the edges are apt to be uneven or rough, even on fairly "clean" cuts. There are likely to be a number of small, sharp fragments of the metal left along the edges. These uneven fragments are called *burrs*. They must be removed before the sheet is considered ready for use.

Each burr is a potential source of trouble because a crack may develop at that point. When an airplane is in the air, nearly all sheetmetal parts are subject to vibration. If the vibration is severe enough, cracks in the sheet may lead to failure. Cracks are apt to start first at points along the edges where burrs have not been removed or where small indentations occur. If burrs fall at a point where a sheet is bent, cracks are very likely to develop. Burrs may be identified by running your hand lightly along the edges of a blanked sheet. You can readily feel their sharp edges.

Edge Burring.—Burrs are most easily removed from the edges of aircraft sheetmetal by the use of a *burring tool,* or *edge scraper.* There are two types of this small hand tool in regular use. The devices used for sharpening kitchen knives can be utilized for this purpose. One is a very simple tool that may be made by cutting a sharp, beveled-edge notch in one end of a 6 in. length of strap steel, which is then hardened. The V-notch end is drawn lightly along the edge of the sheet, scraping away the burrs. Such a tool is easily made.

The other type employs two small, hardened cutting wheels mounted tangent to each other at the end of a handle. As the circular cutting blades slide over the edges of the sheet, the rough burrs are cut off (see illustration on page 261).

Some skill is required to do a uniform burring job. If the pressure applied to the tool is too heavy, more material than the burred edge is removed and the sheet becomes chamfered.

When it is not convenient to use a burring tool, as in lightening holes and at other points on formed sheetmetal parts where limitations of space prevent its use, the burrs must be removed by filing. Files are also used for reducing the size of sheets and other stock to the exact dimensions of the layout.

For production work, a machine is now in use that washes off all foreign matter and compresses any existing burrs between polished steel rolls. The use of this machine for production work makes the slower method of handwork unnecessary.

CHARACTERISTICS OF FILES

Files have three major characteristics that identify them: *length*, *shape*, and *cut*.

Length.—To measure the length of a file, it is necessary to know the names of its principal parts:

1. The *tang* is the pointed part that is inserted in the wooden file handle.
2. The *point* is the end of the file opposite the tang.
3. The *heel* is that part of the file at the base of the tang which comes next to the handle.
4. The *face* of the file is the cutting area. There may be one to four faces. The length of the file then is the distance between the point and the heel. The tang is not included in the length. Most files range in length from 4 to 16 in. (see Fig. 63).

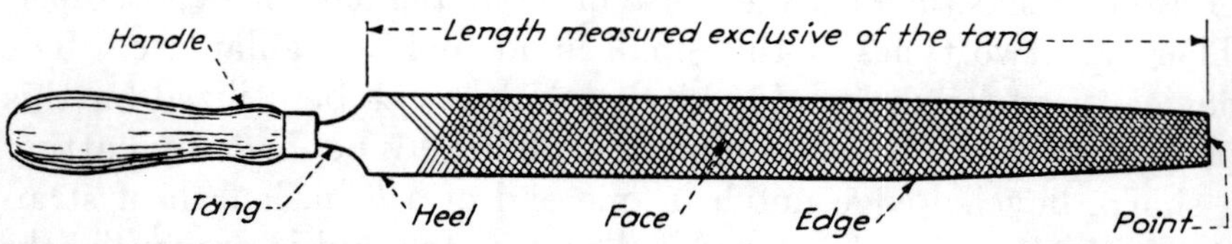

FIG. 63.—The parts of a file. This is a flat file, which is the most commonly used shape.

Shape.—The shape of the file refers to the appearance, or style (see Fig. 64).

1. *Flat files* have a rectangular cross section and are slightly tapered toward the point in both width and thickness. They are double cut on both faces, but usually only single cut on the edges.
2. *Mill files* are also rectangular in cross section and are parallel in thickness from heel to point but are usually tapered in width. They are single cut and thinner than flat files. They are

used extensively for finishing and for draw-filing steel and aluminum-alloy fittings. Mill files may also be obtained with one or two round edges.

3. *Warding files* are similar in cross-sectional shape to both the flat file and the mill file, although thinner than either. They are sharply tapered in width toward the point and are double cut.

4. *Pillar files* are equal in width but tapered in thickness. At the heel, they are thicker than any files previously mentioned. They are double cut on the faces and often have one safe, or uncut, edge. The safe edge permits a file to be used close to parts that do not require filing.

5. *Square files* are square in their cross section and are double cut on all four sides. They are generally used for enlarging rectangular holes. They may be tapered or blunt. A "blunt" file has the same width and thickness from heel to point.

6. *Round files*, sometimes called *rattail* files, are round in cross section and may be obtained either blunt or tapered toward the point. They are either single or double cut and are generally used for enlarging circular openings.

7. *Half-round files* have one flat side that functions as a regular flat file and a curved or half-round back. Half-round files are not a complete semicircle, as the name implies, the arc being about one-third of a circle. They are tapered in width and thickness toward the tip and are double cut.

8. *Hand files* are parallel in width and are tapered in thickness. They are double cut and have one safe edge. They are used more often by machinists than sheetmetal workers but principally for finishing flat surfaces.

9. *Knife files* are shaped like the blade of a pocket knife. They are double cut on both flat sides and single cut on both edges and tapered in width and thickness. They become knife-like along one edge, which has an included angle of about 10 deg. They are used for fitting work having acute angles.

10. *Taper files* are triangular in shape, tapering toward the point. They are double cut with rounded edges and are used mostly for saw filing.

11. *Three-square files* or *triangular files* have the same shape as taper files but have sharp cutting edges. They are used for cleaning out corners and angles. They may be either single or double cut.

Cut or teeth of a file are generally known under four classifications: *single-cut*, *double-cut*, *rasp-cut*, and *circular-cut* or *milled curved-tooth*. These cuts in various grades can be obtained in the majority of the lengths and shapes of files previously described.

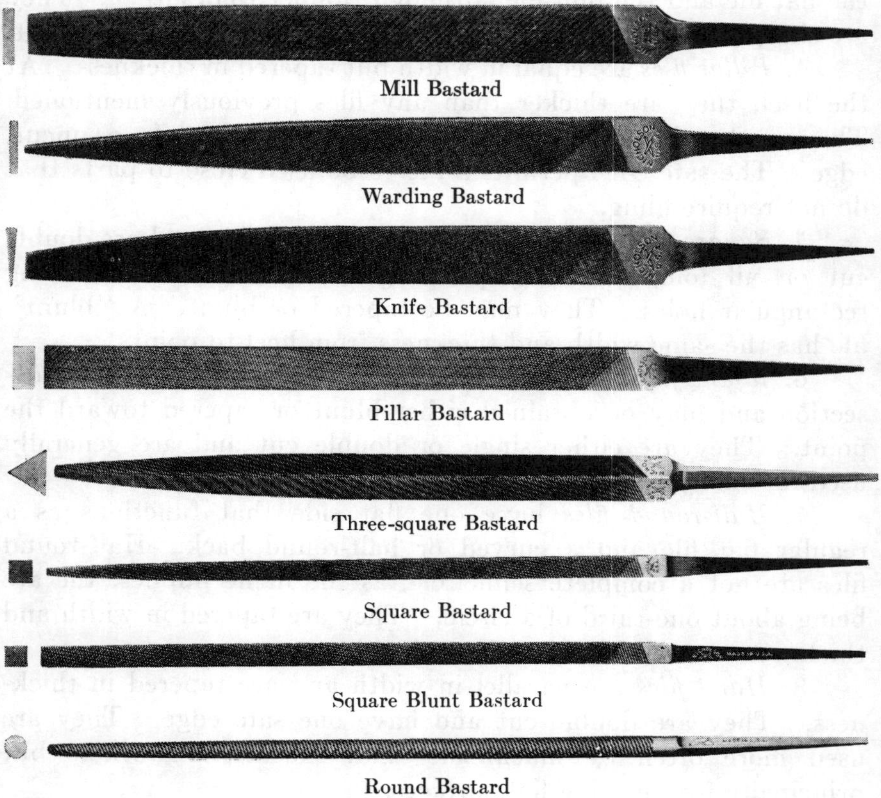

Fig. 64.—Different kinds of files. A cross-sectional view of each

1. A *single-cut* file has single rows of parallel teeth extending the length of the file at an angle across its face.

2. A *double-cut* file has two parallel rows of teeth crossing each other. The teeth of a double-cut file cut faster but not so smoothly as the single-cut (see Fig. 65).

Single- and double-cut files are further classified, or graded, for general sheetmetal use according to the distance between the rows of teeth as *bastard*, *second-cut*, and *smooth*. The files having the greatest space between the teeth are known as *bastard*, and those having the least space as *smooth*.

3. A *rasp-cut* file, or *rasp* as it is commonly known, has parallel rows of individual "punch teeth" running the length of the file and at right angles across the face. Each row of teeth is staggered across the face, so that the entire area of the face offers a coarse

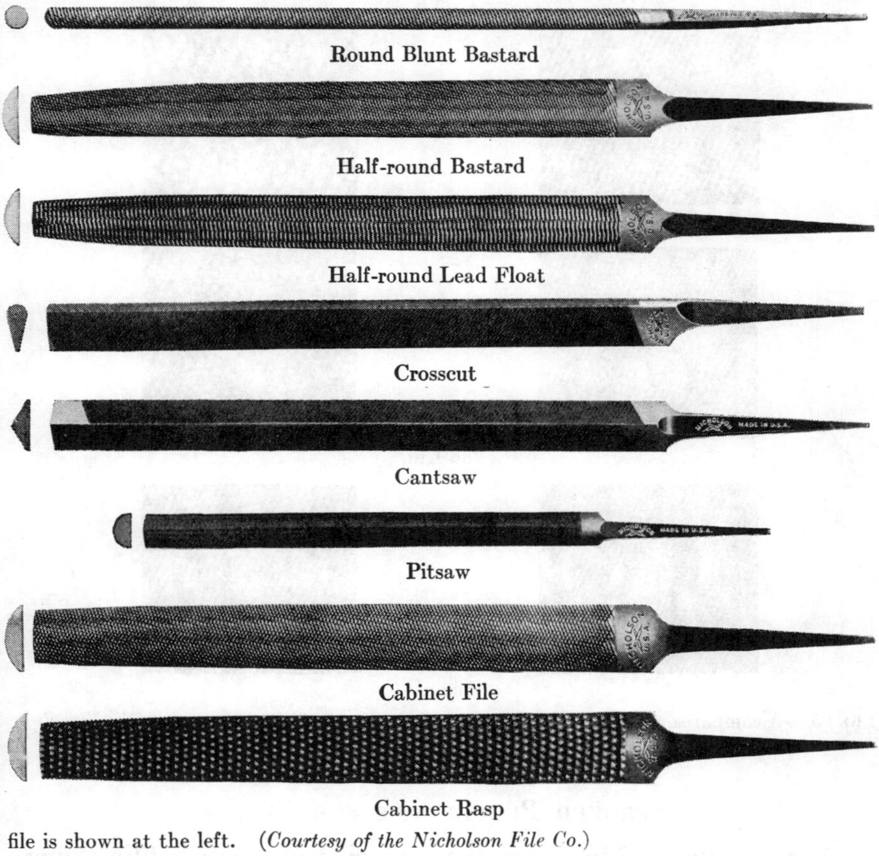

file is shown at the left. (*Courtesy of the Nicholson File Co.*)

cutting surface. Rasps are used by the aircraft mechanic for roughing out wood and plastic parts, such as micarta forming blocks. They are not suitable for metal work.

4. *Circular-cut* or *milled curved-tooth files*, generally known to the mechanic as *vixen files*, are particularly adapted for use on aluminum and aluminum-alloy castings and for the edges of sheet stock. Parallel rows of continuous curved teeth cover the face of the file. The vixen file has wide use in aircraft work, since the rake and the clearance of the teeth ensure easy and rapid cutting of the softer metals. Vixen files are usually used in flat,

pillar, and half-round styles. The flat vixen file is made in both rigid and flexible types, the latter being used only with a file holder. The pillar vixen is cut on both sides with edges left safe.

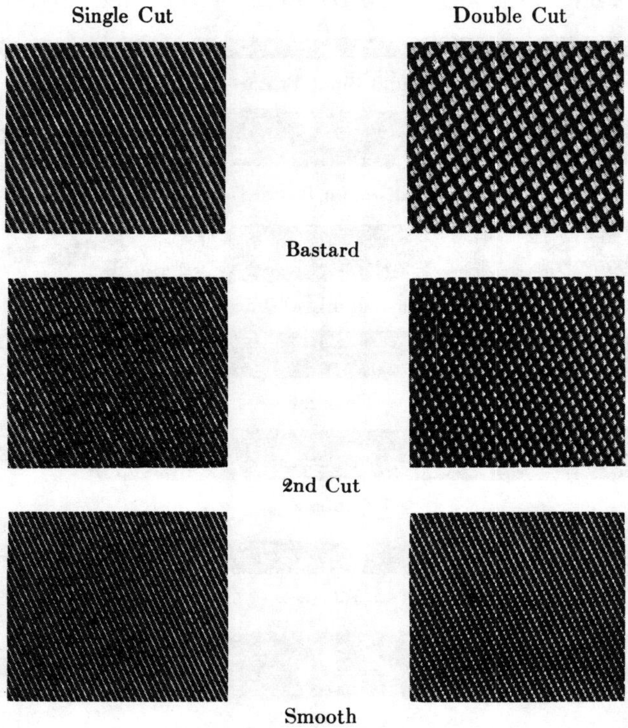

Fig. 65.—A comparison of the faces of single- and double-cut files. (*Courtesy of the Nicholson File Co.*)

Approved Procedures for Filing

1. Choosing a File.—For the majority of aircraft filing operations, the selection of the proper file ranks in importance with its actual use. The mechanic must consider the size, the style, and the cut of a file that will most effectively do the job. The size of the file normally depends upon the size of the work being filed, the available working space, and the type of material. The style, or type, of the file chosen depends mainly upon the contour, or shape, of the work. The cut, or type of teeth, in the file used should be judged by the amount of material to be removed, the contour of the work, and the material being cut. In general, coarse grades of double-cut files cut quickly but leave the surface marked. Fine, single-cut files cut slowly but leave a smoother surface.

As dural is a relatively soft metal, slightly rough files are used so that the soft metal will not readily clog the teeth. Files used for aircraft metal work should not be used for wood, as wood particles clog the teeth and make the file unfit for metal work.

2. Successive Cutting.—For average aircraft sheetmetal work, files in diminishing grades of coarseness are used. For example, a *bastard file* would be used first on a steel fitting to remove the rough edge left by a nibbling machine or power hack saw, because of its fast cutting action. As the scribed finishing line is approached, *a second-cut file* would be substituted to smooth the edge and remove scratches left by the bastard file. The final finishing of the edge would be performed by draw-filing with a *smooth file*. It must be remembered that the grades of coarseness of a file are comparable only when files of the same length are considered, since an increase in length also means an increase in coarseness.

3. Cutting Action.—The teeth of a file are so formed that they can cut only on the forward stroke. Skill must be exercised to prevent the delicate teeth from scraping on the return stroke and thus dulling the cutting edges. The file should be raised slightly from the work, when drawing it back. This is similar to the stroke used in hack-sawing where the pressure must also be relieved on the return motion.

The actual cutting teeth of a file are myriads of tiny chisellike cutting tools of ragged construction. As the higher of these uneven points wear off, an even greater number come into use. Therefore, a file that has been used for a while is actually more efficient from a chip-production standpoint than when it is new.

4. File Handles and Holders.—Files should never be used without file handles. Wooden handles with metal ferrules can be easily fitted over the sharp tang of the file and should be driven well down toward the heel. Serious injury to the hands or the arms may be self-inflicted if this precaution is neglected. In addition, the file cannot be properly held without the aid of the handle. Covering the point end of a file with friction tape or rubber where it is held by the thumb and finger will help protect your hands. This is especially recommended for use with vixen files. You may, however, apply the tape to your finger instead.

File holders fitted with handles are clamped to flexible vixen files. Flexible files of this type have no tang, but two holes close to the ends permit fastening to the file holder in a slightly bowed position. The use of the holder lessens the danger of being cut by the edges of sheet stock, on which the vixen file is frequently used.

FIG. 66.—Method of holding a file. The proper way to use a file is with long, diagonal strokes.

5. Securing Work.—Work that is filed should be secured in a rigid position. Small pieces of sheetmetal, or fittings, can best be held in a vice. Work surfaces that are narrow should be clamped close to the top of the vise jaws to prevent vibration, chattering, and the resulting noise. If the surface to be filed is straight or flat, it should be clamped so that it is parallel to the top of the vise jaws. Every effort should be made to protect the work from being scratched or otherwise marred. Even smooth vise jaws should be covered with aluminum faces, or pieces of plywood placed on both sides of the clamped work. Clamps padded in a similar manner may be used to hold larger parts or subassemblies.

6. Holding Files.—For the usual cross-filing work, the file should be held as shown in Fig. 66, with the handle resting well up against the palm of the right hand and the thumb placed on top. The left hand is held at the point of the file with the fingers curled under and the thumb pressing on top.

When the file is thin, there is a tendency to bow the file downward, causing the edges of the work to become rounded. This can be overcome by using the left thumb as a fulcrum on top of the file, while the fingers of the left hand bow the point of the file up.

On work where it is impossible to grasp the tip of the file, the handle may be held with both hands to apply additional pressure. For draw-filing the hands are placed palm down so that the file is grasped at both ends.

7. Cross-filing.—Expert hand filing requires much practice in order to cut smoothly or to file without making a curved or an uneven surface. The file should be held at an angle of about 45 deg. to the edge being filed. This is done so that a large amount of cutting surface comes in contact with the work even when it is the edge of a thin sheet. Slight pressure should be exerted on the stroke away from the body, and the file should be lifted slightly for the return stroke.

The body should move smoothly with each stroke. Deliberate, jerky motions should be avoided, and again, as in hack-sawing, too much speed is inefficient. Try to overcome a rocking motion when filing narrow surfaces. Take care, too, that your left wrist is not scratched or cut as it passes over the edge of the work.

As each stroke of the file cuts away particles of metal, small grooves are left in the surface. Continued filing in the same direction deepens the grooves, and the surface becomes increasingly roughened. By frequently changing the direction of the stroke a few degrees, this condition is largely eliminated. Changing direction is especially necessary in the filing of broad, flat surfaces and helps show where the file is cutting. The half-round and round files should be twisted slightly on the forward stroke when filing out lightening holes or concave surfaces.

8. Draw-filing.—To secure a smoother surface on an edge or on a wider flat surface that has previously been filed, *draw-filing* is used. The file is drawn sidewise across the work in a manner

Fig. 67.—A vixen file mounted in a holder is used to trim aluminum-alloy sheet rapidly.

similar to the method of using a drawknife, and, like that tool, it can be either pushed or pulled. The file should be held as explained in item 6. The best results are obtained when it is grasped quite close to either side of the work and lifted slightly for the return stroke as in other types of filing. A single-cut file, usually a mill file, is used. As it moves across the surface, the teeth produce a shearing or shaving effect. For the most efficient draw-filing, the angle at which the file is held with respect to its line of movement will vary with different files, depending on the angle at which the teeth are cut. The file is therefore not necessarily held at right angles to the work. Draw-filing of aircraft sheetmetal work is generally confined to truing the edges of steel or aluminum-alloy sheet stock for fittings and to smoothing the surfaces of extruded aluminum-alloy fittings. It should never be practiced on the face surfaces of aircraft steel fittings as a means of removing scores or indentations, since it would remove too much of the metal.

9. Polish Finishing.—Oil may often be used to advantage when filing hard steels, but it should not be used on aluminum, cast iron, or brass. With steel it acts as an aid to cutting and promotes a smoother surface. When an even smoother surface is required than can be obtained in this way, a fine grade of emery cloth saturated with oil may be wrapped around the file. The oil can later be removed with naphtha, gasoline, or kerosene.

10. Care of Files.—The file is one of the most used tools, yet it is also one of the most abused. This is probably due to mechanics thinking that since files are sufficiently tough to cut hard metals, they are also tough enough to take care of themselves. From one standpoint they are actually fragile, since they must be tempered to a highly brittle state in order to perform their work. Files should never be thrown down carelessly on the bench or into a toolbox but should always be put down carefully to prevent chipping of their teeth.

Never use a file for a driftpin or hammer on any part of it; the teeth may be ruined, or the file may break. A file should never be used as a lever for prying, since it is not designed for bending and will almost surely break. It should be kept clean and free from rust. Don't pound a file across the edge of a metal-topped bench to remove chips. If you treat a file with as much care as you would a micrometer, the file will last a great deal longer and produce better results.

11. Cleaning Files.—Work surfaces are often badly scratched because small particles of metal become clogged in the gullets between the teeth of a file. This is known as *pinning* because of the parasite pin teeth that are formed. It is a frequent occurrence when filing aluminum alloys. This condition can be avoided to a great extent if the pressure applied is properly controlled. If you bear down too hard, the teeth will clog easily. Vixen files may sometimes advantageously be drawn backward lightly over the metal to help clear the teeth. The application of chalk to the cutting face of the file will also help reduce pinning. Small

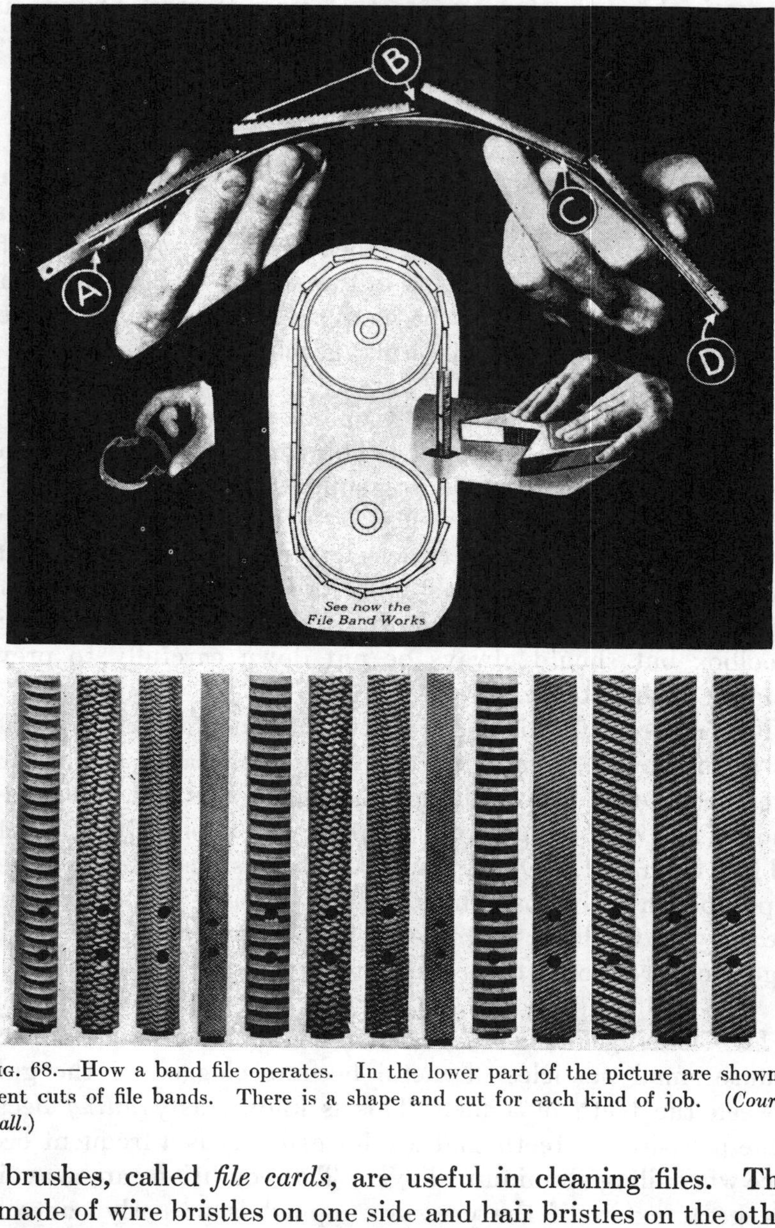

FIG. 68.—How a band file operates. In the lower part of the picture are shown 13 different cuts of file bands. There is a shape and cut for each kind of job. (*Courtesy of Doall.*)

flat brushes, called *file cards,* are useful in cleaning files. They are made of wire bristles on one side and hair bristles on the other. Particles of dirt and metal are loosened with the wire side of the brush; the other side is then used to brush them away. A small metal "scorer" is carried in the handle of the brush to remove the more stubborn pins.

12. Band Filing.—For production filing of steel and aluminum-alloy fittings and stacked, blank sheetmetal parts, a band-filing machine is used. The Doall machine previously described is also a popular band-filing machine (see Fig. 68).

In the band-filing machine, short segments of file are riveted on an endless carrier, which might be compared to a band-saw blade without teeth. When the file band is at the point of work above the table, it forms a rigid file column. This machine tool elevates the operation of filing far beyond the scope of hand filing, because the cutting pressure can be applied steadily and is continuous. The operation also tends to hold the work in position on the table.

The machine has a working depth considerably greater than is ordinarily required for aircraft sheetmetal parts. It is useful for filing operations on extruded, forged, and cast fittings and parts.

For filing the inside edges of openings, such as lightening holes, the band may be disengaged, passed through the opening, and then refastened. Bands can be obtained with various forms and cuts of files.

13. Band Polishing.—The Doall machine can also be used for polishing. An attachment that forms a rigid backup support and has a graphite-impregnated facing is used in conjunction with endless abrasive polishing bands that are 1 in. in width. The polishing bands are similar to conventional emery cloth used for hand finishing. The edges of sheet stock as well as castings and forgings can be given a much smoother finish than can ordinarily be obtained by filing.

Review Questions

1. Describe two types of burring tools.

2. Describe the four principal parts of a file.

3. The text describes 11 different shapes of files. Name as many as you can and briefly describe each.

4. Describe four kinds of cuts, or teeth, and name the kind of work for which each is intended.

5. In doing considerable filing on a steel fitting, which file would be used first, a smooth, bastard, or second cut?

6. Do files cut on the forward or backward stroke, or on both?
7. When is it permissible to leave the wooden handle off a file?
8. How is work held as it is being filed?
9. Describe the proper way to hold a file.
10. What is cross-filing?
11. When is draw-filing used?
12. Is oil used when filing aluminum alloys?
13. When does oil aid filing?
14. How are files cleaned?
15. What is band-filing?

Shop Work

The filing of either steel or aluminum alloy is called for in each of the five projects of Chap. 15. If the instructor feels that additional practice is needed, special projects can be developed with little difficulty.

CHAPTER 9

FORMING, STAMPING, AND HYDRAULIC PRESSES

Aircraft sheetmetal rarely arrives on the airplane in its original flat form. In almost every instance it is necessary to bend, or form, the sheet stock in order to utilize it for housing, streamlining, or stiffening. A sheet or strip that is bent to any angle or a sheet having a compound curvature, such as a section of engine cowling, is said to be *formed*. This is true regardless of the type of tool used for the shaping of the particular part.

Whenever possible, aircraft sheetmetal parts are fabricated by machine. In many instances, however, machine forming methods are not practicable. It is necessary that the aircraft sheetmetal worker possess at least a fundamental knowledge and a fair degree of skill in sheetmetal forming. He should also be familiar with the advantages and limitations of both hand and machine tools.

Bending Blocks.—The bending of comparatively short sections can be done without the use of elaborate equipment. After the sheet stock has been laid out and cut to size, it can be bent simply by clamping the stock rigidly along the bending line between two blocks of wood or between two smooth-faced steel dies. The material protruding beyond the blocks or the dies can then be bumped to the desired angle with light blows of a rubber, plastic, or rawhide mallet. The bumping should be started at one end close to the clamps and worked back and forth along the edge to make the bend gradual. This is continued until the protruding metal is forced down against the lower forming block. To remove irregularities, a straight-edged block of hardwood may be held edgewise against the bend. The block may then be driven against the stock by striking it with heavy blows of a wooden mallet or a hammer (see Fig. 69).

When considerable metal extends beyond the dies or bending blocks, hand pressure should be maintained by pressing down as close to the supporting surface as possible during the bumping process.

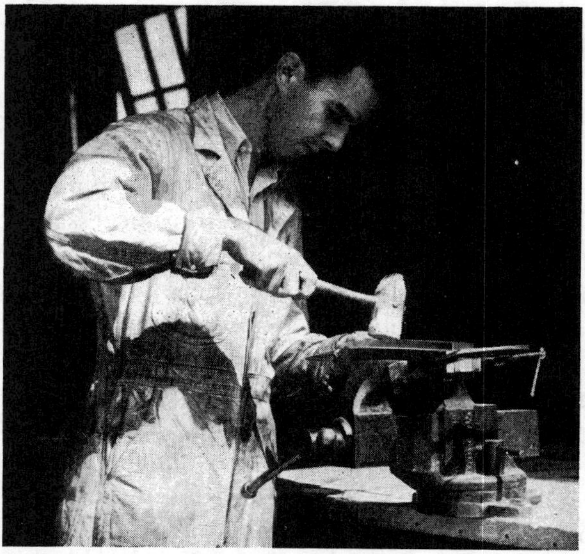

FIG. 69.—Simple forming may be done by using combinations of die blocks, which are usually made of maple, Masonite, or micarta. Bending is done by hammering.

Bending Brakes.—Sheetmetal-bending brakes are devices used for making long bends in a straight line. They are used for flanging the edges of sheet and for forming angle and channel stock from flat strips. The sheet to be bent is inserted between the two heavy steel leaves of the brake. The upper leaf, or clamping bar, is set in a fixed position during the bending operation while the lower leaf is rotated upward around the axis of the bend to the required angle. The clamping-bar leaf may be raised or lowered slightly to accommodate the thickness of the stock being bent and to hold it firmly in position against the table. Bending brakes may be operated by hand or electrically. The hand-operated type is fitted with adjustable counterbalances to assist the operator. Brakes do not usually have a capacity of more than 10 ft., since it is difficult to maintain a straight bend in greater lengths by this method. The radius of the bend can be adjusted to a limited extent by moving the clamping bar backward or forward. This is usually done by means of set screws located on either side of the machine. Half-round strip dies may be clamped along the edge of the bending leaf to form channel sections or other shapes (see Fig. 70).

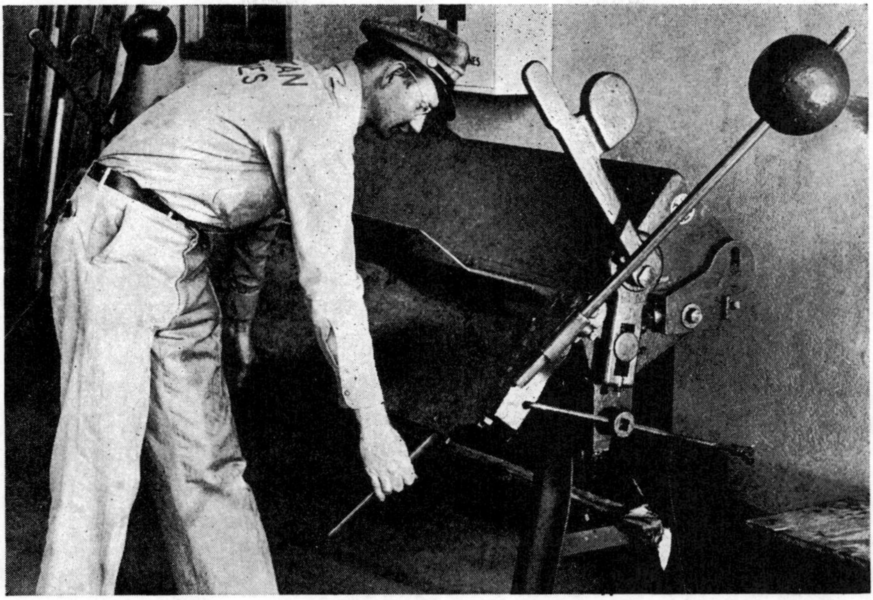

Fig. 70.—A bending brake being used by an American Airlines mechanic. He is forming an angle in sheet stock by lifting the lower leaf of the brake. The two iron balls are counterbalances that assist the operator in lifting the leaf.

Procedure for Operating a Bending Brake

1. Lay out and cut the metal to size. It should be straightened first if necessary.

2. The bending line should not be scribed but marked with a pencil or a crayon, depending on the type of material.

3. Insert the metal under the clamping bar so that the bending line is even with the edge of the table under the clamping bar.

4. Lower the clamping bar by moving the hand levers on each side, until it grips the metal securely. Check the position and the security of the work to make sure that it has not moved during the clamping operation.

5. Pull the bending leaf up with the hand lever until the metal has been bent to the desired angle. Be sure that all persons are clear of the counterweights during this operation. It is usually necessary to draw the bending leaf a few degrees beyond the required angle because of the tendency of the bent edge to spring back.

6. Push the bending-leaf lever back to its original position, and raise the clamping bar. The metal can then be removed, and the angle of bend checked.

7. If cracking failure is encountered in making the bend, it is common practice to increase the radius of the bend on the next sheet by making an angle strip of the same thickness but of softer material and using it under the clamping bar to protect the metal and increase the radius. The clamping bar can also be moved back to increase the bending radius.

Bar Folder.—The bar folder is another device used for bending or folding sheetmetal. This machine will do practically the same work as the bending brake but is generally used in sizes that can handle sheet material from 20 to 42 in. in length. Unlike the bending brake the bar folder is capable of bending sheet to a folded edge of 180 deg. It may be used for flanging or to turn the edge of a sheet to receive a wire for stiffening or to form a closed or an open lock for the seams of a fuel or an oil tank. It can be adjusted to form a narrow or a wide fold.

The main parts of a bar folder are the frame, the jaw, the folding bar, the adjustable gage, and a wedge-adjusting lever. The adjustable gage makes it possible to make folded bends varying in width from 1/8 to 1 in. An open fold may be made with the wedge adjustment to take wire from 1/16 to 1/4 in. Sheetmetal up to 3/32 in. in thickness may be worked in the bar folder, but with sheet of that thickness the sharpest bend possible is about 3/16 in.

The Press Brake.—Straight-line bending operations for production work may be carried on with a press brake. For various bending operations, specially designed, removable steel dies are fitted to the press. One die is mounted on the stationary bed of the press, and another matching punch die is fitted to an overhead slide. As the metal sheet to be bent is fed between the two dies, the overhead sliding die moves down, forcing the metal sheet against or into the die in the bed.

With suitable dies, obtuse, right-angle, or acute-angle bends can be made near the edge of a sheet or at a considerable distance from it. U channels can be formed on a press brake, and corrugated sheet is made by simply repeating the pressing operation (see Fig. 71).

Press brakes are driven either electrically or hydraulically. The electric-powered type is the more common, since great pressure is not required on light-gage aircraft sheetmetal. The pressure can be controlled to form the stock true to the dies without distortion.

Fig. 71.—A 14 ft. press brake and some of the formings that may be produced. Various combinations of the upper and lower dies may be used. For some involved shapes several sets of dies are used successively.

The press is usually operated by a foot treadle which controls the slide, leaving the operator's hands free to handle the sheet. The slide can be started or stopped at any position of its stroke by relaxing pressure on the treadle. This permits the operator to bring the punch die down close to the sheet or line to locate the bend exactly.

Sheetmetal Rolls.—In forming aluminum-alloy or light-gage stainless-steel sheet for such parts as a section of fuselage skin or the leading edge of a wing, slip rolls are used. The slip roll may consist of either three or five round steel bars or rolls geared together and mounted horizontally and operated by a crank in the manner of a clothes wringer. Larger rolling machines may be motor driven (see Fig. 72). In the three-roll type, curving is accomplished by feeding the sheet stock between the two front

FIG. 72.—Sheetmetal rolls being used for curving sections of flat sheet to form the concave bottom of a seaplane float in the Edo Aircraft factory. (*Howard Emerson Photograph.*)

gripping rolls and against the rear rolls. The sheet is forced upward in a circular bend. The gripping rolls can be adjusted to the thickness of the sheet stock. The radius of the bend can be increased by lowering the rear roller or decreased by raising the rear roller. The smallest cylinder that can be formed is limited to the diameter of the upper gripping rolls. Large-diameter cylinders can be made in any size. The sheet may be run through the machine more than once, if necessary, to obtain the desired curve.

If a cylindrical curve is to be made, the rear roll must be adjusted so that it is parallel to the front rolls. This should be done before the crank is turned. Grooves at one end of the rolls are provided to receive sheet stock that has a rolled wire edge. Deeper grooves are sometimes made so that one flange may be inserted when curving angle stock. The upper gripping roll is usually demountable at one end so that a cylinder that has been formed can be removed without distorting its shape. For example, conical shapes such as the skin at the tail of a fuselage can be formed by adjusting one end of the rear roll so that it is lower than the front rolls. The rear roll, not being parallel, permits the stock to curve up in a greater diameter at one end. Sheet that is

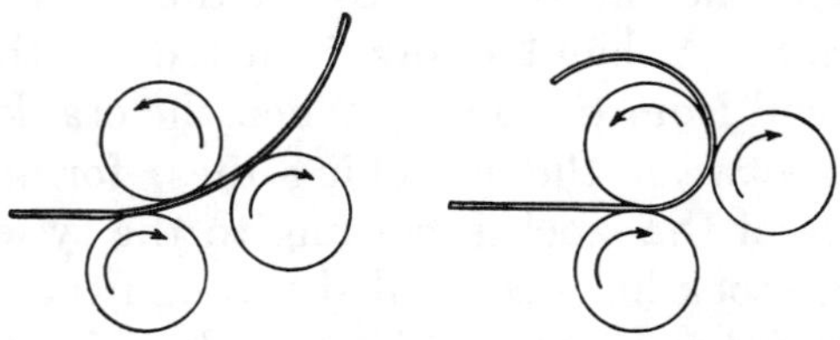

FIG. 73.—A diagram showing direction in which rolls turn as sheet is fed into them.

slightly bent can often be straightened by running the piece through the gripping rolls several times with the rear roll adjusted so that it is out of action. Sheet that is kinked or badly bent should not be straightened in this way, since it is not safe for aircraft use because of the possibility of failure. However, damaged portions may be cut away from such sheets, and the remainder salvaged for the fabrication of smaller parts. Slip rolls of the five-roll type can be adjusted to form, in one operation, shapes that are not truly cylindrical.

This is desirable in forming the leading edges of wings where there is considerable variation in curvature between the upper and lower cambers. Many variations of straight curvature can be obtained with slip rolls. Adjustments can be made to change the curving diameter while the stock is being fed through the rolls, or the stock can be removed from the rolls and rerun part way after the adjustments have been changed.

Combination Rotary Machines—Small bench-type, hand-operated, turning, or beading, machines are used extensively in aircraft sheetmetal work for flanging, crimping, flaring, folding, and wiring. These machines are used on cylindrical or flat sheetmetal to shape the edge or to form a bead along the edge.

The principal parts of the turning machine consist of two horizontal parallel shafts geared together and mounted in a housing. Various combinations of matching hardened-steel dies can be fitted to the shafts at one end. The dies are either key seated or threaded to the ends of the shafts. The upper die roll can be raised to receive the stock by means of a vertical crank screw. A sliding stop or depth gage is mounted on the lower shaft of the deep-throated machines so that the forming can be done at a uniform distance from the edge of the stock, or an adjustable stop may be mounted just behind the dies on other types. The dies are tightened on the stock by the screw-crank adjustment. A hand crank is fitted to the lower shaft at the opposite end from the dies. When the crank is turned, the stock is rolled between the matching dies, forming a bead or flanging the edge of the stock according to the type of die that is used. After the stock has been rolled through the dies, the upper die may be lowered further. This procedure may be continued until a full bead has been formed.

Flanging or beading adds considerable rigidity or stiffness to sheet parts that are not strengthened by the addition of formed or extruded stringers or stiffeners. It may be seen that flanging takes the place of angle stock used for stiffening purposes whereas beading derives its rigidity from its channel-like shape.

The turning machine can also be used to turn the edge of flat or cylindrical sheet stock to receive a wire. Two operations are necessary: first, turning up the edge of the stock, then, second, running it through a second set of dies again to fold the edge over the wire. If the stock to be wired is cylindrical in shape, the wire should first be bent in a ring of the same diameter. The stock should be tipped up and fed through the machine several times if necessary so that the edge is forced up under the wire. Although wired edges are not used extensively now, an aviation mechanic should be familiar with the process, since they are still sometimes used for such purposes as stiffening the edge of cockpit cowling.

Crimping may be done by using gearlike crimping dies. It is not a frequently used aircraft sheetmetal procedure, but it sometimes is used for shrinking the edges of sheet, which is described later in this chapter.

Draw Bench.—For forming lengths of channel, angle, or similar shapes used for stringers or stiffeners that are too long to be made in press brakes or bending brakes, a draw bench is used. Strips of flat sheet stock cut to the finished width are pulled through a series of dies that shape the strip into the desired cross-sectional form. The forming dies are made of steel, fiber, or wood, arranged progressively so that the strip is bent gradually, taking on a greater or a different bend as it passes through each set of dies. In this way undue stress is avoided that would tend to crack or tear the metal, thus causing failure.

Each set of dies is arranged so that they may be separated to insert the flat strip for starting the drawing operation. Jaws attached to the drawing head are clamped securely to the end of the strip, which is pulled along the bench of the machine by a chain-and-sprocket arrangement geared to an electric motor. The strip emerges from the last set of dies in the finished form. Extrusions, such as beaded, L and Z sections, have largely taken the place of forms made on a draw bench.

Spinning.—This is another method used for flanging or dishing circular or cylindrical forms made of aluminum-alloy sheet. The process consists of forming the metal over a wood form while both the metal and the wood die are revolving. The sheet stock is usually cut to a circular pattern. A wood forming block is then bolted to the head stock of a spinning lathe. The aluminum disk is clamped against the forming block by means of a clamp block attached to the tail stock of the lathe. Blunt forming tools of steel, aluminum, or fiber held on the tool rest are forced against the revolving disk, gradually working it over the wood form.

The disk becomes dished in shape and may, by continued pressure, be formed into surprisingly deep curved shapes. Propeller spinners, engine cowling nose pieces, and fuselage tail cones are often formed in this way. Aluminum tubes can have a flange spun on the end to provide an area for riveting. The size of the forming is limited to the diameter of the stock that the lathe will swing.

More parts are formed by hydraulic pressing and drop-hammer forming than by spinning. There are certain advantages in spinning, such as the greater uniformity of shape and the more even stressing of the metal. Spinning requires special skill.

Aluminum alloys used for spinning must be ductile. Soft forms, such as S-O, are most satisfactory. Annealed stainless steel, copper, and annealed Inconel can be spun.

The Sheetmetal-forming and Flanging Machine.—The Erco Sheetmetal Former shown in Fig. 74 performs difficult flanging and forming operations previously limited to hand production. With this small machine it is possible to reproduce flanged work done on hydraulic presses described in this chapter. It is also

FIG. 74.—An Erco Sheetmetal Former being used to crimp over the flange of a bulkhead section at the Glenn L. Martin plant. A die is attached to a plunger which operates with a horizontal motion, thus crimping the edge. A short brake is forced against a hold-down tool at a speed of 250 to 500 strokes per minute. Flanges of several types can be made by changing anvils and hold-down tools. Machines of this type are replacing much hand forming.

valuable for flanging curved or irregular-shaped parts that are not in a true plane.

It operates on the same principle as a bending brake. The forming tool, however, is less than an inch wide, bending over only a small section of the sheet at each stroke. In effect, its action might be compared to bending over the edge of a sheet progressively with a pair of pliers. A hold-down tool fitted to the head of the machine serves three purposes: it provides a guide for the work; it grips the work against an anvil during the working stroke of the brake tool; and it forms a die against which the work is finished. The standard hold-down tools have fingerlike extensions as a guide against which the edge of the work is lightly pressed to obtain the desired flange height. The brake head oscillates in tracks in the frame of the machine through an angle adjustable to 100 deg. The brake operates at a speed of 250 to 500 strokes per minute. The brake-head operating mechanism, to which the brake tool is attached, is adjusted to the angle or degree of bend desired, by means of a hand wheel in front of the machine. Holding down and release of the work are performed automatically, and the feeding is done by hand.

The blank contour of the part is accurately cut to shape before the forming operation is started. Smooth and well-formed edges are produced by bending up a small part of the sheet at each stroke. The part being formed may be run through the machine several times before completion.

Radii as small as the aluminum-alloy or steel sheet will stand can be formed without wrinkling or bending, even in complicated shapes.

STRETCHING AND SHRINKING

It has been explained previously that the process of bending metal involves both stretching and shrinking. A rubber band that is stretched to a greater length becomes thinner in cross-sectional area than when it is inert. If the rubber band is squeezed or compressed, it becomes thicker in cross section than before. This is likewise true in the forming of metals, but obviously to a lesser degree.

Most parts that are formed are shaped to two dimensions—one causing shrinking or thickening of the metal and the other causing stretching or thinning. To illustrate this principle take a piece of paper approximately 2 in. wide and 8 in. long. Fold the paper in half the long way, so that the bend forms a 90 deg. angle. In this form it may be compared to a section of formed angle stock. Hold it so that the open angle faces you. By bending both ends slightly toward you, you will observe that the upper or vertical flange bends smoothly whereas the lower or horizontal flange tends to buckle.

The upper flange is actually being stretched, but the lower flange is being bunched together. If you now press the wrinkles into flat pleats in the lower flange, the angle section will remain formed in a curve. In effect, this is what happens to aluminum alloy of the same shape.

To curve the aluminum alloy, however, the flange that corresponds to the pleated flange in the paper is *crimped* with crimping pliers, so that small bulges are made at intervals along the edge of the flange. This action shortens the flange that is crimped, causing the angle to curve. The flange that has not been crimped curves easily without buckling.

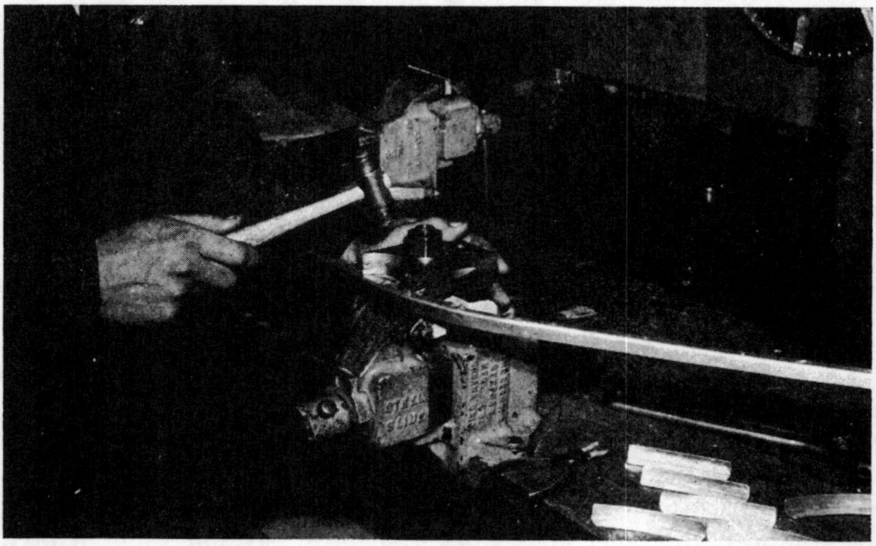

FIG. 75.—A shrinking block in use. After the inside edge of this formed L-angle stock has been crimped, it is clamped between the two metal blocks shown here. The upper block has a U-shape cutout, which allows space for the crimps to be hammered flat in the flange. Many variations of this tool are used.

The crimped bulges must next be removed. If the bulges are hammered flat, the angle would straighten out and resume its original form. In order to retain the desired curve in the angle and eliminate the bulges, a *shrinking* block is used. A shrinking block is composed of two flat steel blocks, one of which can be bolted on top of the other. The upper block is cut away to form a U-shaped opening. This permits one bulge of the flange to be inserted at a time under the upper block. The crimped bulge can then be worked out flat by hammering. Because the two legs of the top block hold the metal firmly in place, the metal cannot slide out under the top block. Since the metal cannot flow out, it becomes thickened locally, and the curve is retained (see Fig. 75).

Best results are obtained if the mechanic uses a plastic mallet and strikes light, glancing blows to flatten the metal. The process is repeated for each successive crimp until the entire flange is flat. The bend, or curve, of the angle should be checked frequently by comparing it with a properly formed angle as a contour template.

FIG. 76.—Several types of hammers used in shrinking, stretching, and flattening during metal-forming operations. Left to right: wooden mallet, weighted rawhide mallet, planishing hammer, light rawhide mallet, plastic stretching hammer, plastic planishing hammer.

For finishing stock that has been curved in shrinking blocks or for curving extruded stock, a V-block method is generally used, as shown in Fig. 78. With this method crimping is not required. The metal stock may be held on a V-shaped block made of hardwood or of lead, while the edge of the flange to be shrunk is struck light, glancing blows with a plastic or a rawhide mallet.

To bend or curve angle stock so that one flange of the angle is on the outside, continue the experiment with the paper angle. Fold another piece the same as before, and hold it again so that one flange is up and the lower flange is toward you. Now attempt to bend both ends away from your body. The paper will wrinkle because the flat lower flange cannot be stretched. If, however, the paper is torn through the lower flange, a semblance of a curved

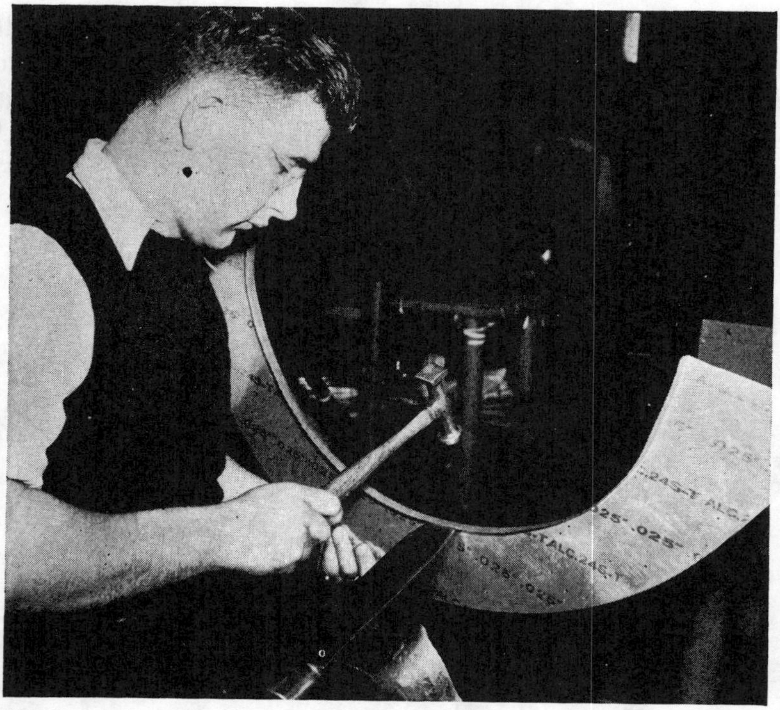

Fig. 77.—Removing wrinkles from the flanged edge of a former ring at Republic Aviation. A planishing hammer and a bumping stake are used.

Fig. 78.—A mechanic at Republic using a rawhide mallet over a V-shaped bumping block to curve an extruded angle. The curve is made by gradually hammering around the edge of the flange.

shape can be obtained. This illustrates the fact that the corresponding metal flange in an angle must be spread, or stretched, when it is to be bent, or curved, in this manner.

Bending an outward curve in metal stock is more easily accomplished than bending the inside curve previously described.

FIG. 79.—Using a weighted rawhide mallet over a V block to bend a bulb-angle extrusion to an irregular shape. A steel-angle template of the exact contour lies on the bench. The mechanic can test his work by fitting it into the template. (*Photograph made at Republic Aviation.*)

One flange of the angle stock may be held over a metal dolly or a square-headed stake and hammered. The hammered flange will stretch, and the metal will cover a greater area. As the flange stretches, or expands, it will cause the other flange to curve.

A faster method of curving the stock in the same way may be done with a pneumatic planishing hammer (see Fig. 80). One flange is moved along between the reciprocating jaws of the hammer. The pressure can be regulated to control the force of the blows to prevent damage to the stock.

Flanges may also be formed in sheet stock by compressing the stock between two matching steel dies. The dies may be held in a vise or in quick-acting screw clamps or drawn together by bolts. The portion of the stock forming the flange protrudes above the dies and is bent over to the required angle with a soft-faced mallet. The buckles are worked out gradually along the protruding flange. A small spoon-shaped shrinkage tool of steel or maple is held under the flange while it is being hammered down and is of great help in removing buckles that form in the exposed flanges. A tool of this type is shown in Fig. 86.

FIG. 80.—A pneumatic planishing hammer being used to form contours in a piece of flat sheet.

A better understanding of the principles involved in this type of work may be acquired if you examine a small paper cup-shaped container in which chocolates are often packed in candy boxes or one type of paper drinking cup in which the bottom is flat and the sides are folded pleats. The corrugated sides of the candy container and the pleats in the drinking cup are there because the paper sides, when shaped in such forms, become smaller in diameter. Unlike metal, which can be hammered into shape by thickening, the paper must remain in folds.

You will discover these bending principles in the first attempt that you make in curving flanged material. After continued practice you should develop a fair degree of skill. The use of

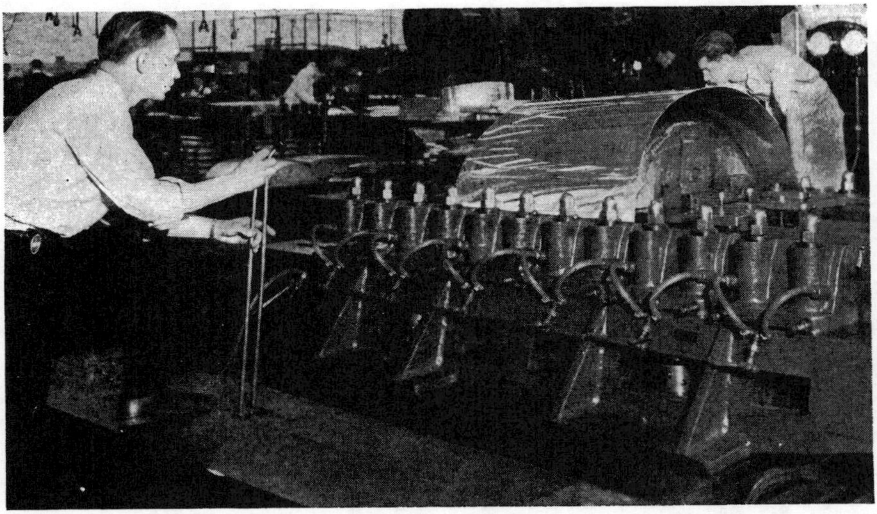

FIG. 81.—An Erco•stretching machine at the Martin plant. For certain kinds of deep formings, a stretcher will do work more efficiently than other types of equipment. The large sheet is firmly clamped down at each end. Then hydraulic power is turned on and the ram, fitted with a forming die, slowly rises. The ram may be stopped at critical periods for necessary adjustment if the stock has slipped. This picture shows the beginning of the stretching process. The man at the left controls the operation.

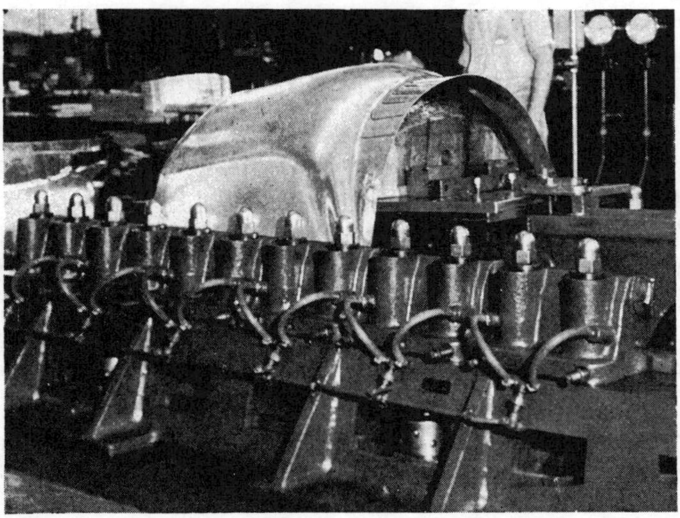

FIG. 82.—The same sheet at the end of the stretching operation. Note how the contour has been changed. It is sometimes necessary to influence the bends by hand bumping. The metal becomes thinner at the deepest point of stretching.

stringers and stiffeners throughout the airplane makes the forming operations described here a frequent occurrence.

The Hydraulic Stretching Machine.—For forming sheetmetal parts, such as cowling, wing tips, and wheel fairings, that are not highly stressed, a stretching machine may be used. This machine consists essentially of two rows of pneumatic hold-down clamps for retaining the sheet at opposite ends. A male die bolted to a hydraulic lifting table is elevated slowly from below the sheet. As the die rises, the sheet gradually conforms to the shape of the die. The sheet stretches and becomes thinner in gage in areas that correspond to the deepest draws in the die. The unstressed areas of the sheet retain their original thickness.

The dies may be castings of zinc, lead, or iron. They may also be made of laminated wood or fiber.

The sets of hold-down clamps can be loosened during the stretching process to allow the sheet to slip slightly, thus preventing tearing at the more highly stressed points (see Figs. 81 and 82).

The Sheetmetal Shrinker.—For further forming of curved or angular parts that would be distorted by rolling or turning machines, the sheetmetal shrinker is used. It produces faster and more uniform work than the methods of hand shrinking and stretching previously described.

The Erco sheetmetal shrinker is designed to reduce the length of metal in a localized area. Two pairs of identical interlocking jaws are used, the upper being attached to a reciprocating ram, the lower to a fixed post. The jaws are two wedge-shaped steel pieces resting on inclined anvils and held apart by springs. The working surfaces are roughened to aid in gripping the sheet. Stroke of the ram is so adjusted that after the work is gripped at two points the ram forces the jaws to slide down the inclined surfaces of the anvils, thereby compressing the work, *reducing the length, and increasing the thickness.* The working surfaces of the jaws remain parallel during the operation.

The Power Hammer.—Gathering and thickening locally may also be performed on a standard, high-speed percussion hammer, using a male die with a tapered spoonlike tongue and groove in the anvil, although primarily this type of power hammer forms by thinning the sheet and expanding the area, in the manner of a planishing hammer. Power hammers are now used chiefly for experimental work. Considerable skill, which can be gained only by experience and practice, is necessary for their operation. The uniformity of power-hammer work depends entirely on the ability of the operator. Consequently power-press forming is far more efficient for quantity production work.

FIG. 83.—Forming a joggle in the end of a stringer with the aid of a power press at Republic Aviation.

Joggling.—At intersections of angle stock and where riveted seams occur in the skin over stringers, the ends of the angle stock are joggled. This is a process of slightly offsetting both flanges of the angle material. The length of the offset, or joggle, depends on the width of the joint, and the depth must be equal to the combined thickness of the material at the joint.

Matching-steel joggling blocks, made to the exact dimensions of the offset, are used. The end of one flange of the angle is clamped between two blocks that are held together in a vise, or press. As the dies compress the flange that is clamped, the other flange spreads away from the blocks. Light blows of a smooth-faced plastic hammer bend the flange back in position before the angle is removed from the dies.

Joggle angles often require reworking for exact fits. The offset may be checked by holding the flat angle of the joggle on a steel surface plate, and then sliding a thickness gage or a piece of metal of the appropriate thickness under the joggle. If it is found impossible to insert the feeler gage under the offset, the joggle must be reworked to a greater depth. If, however, the clearance is too great, or the angle not true, the offset may be reduced by tapping the edge of either flange on the angle with a round-faced plastic hammer.

As illustrated in Fig. 83, presses fitted with joggle dies are used wherever warranted by quantity production. Airplane factories try to reduce the amount of handwork wherever possible. One man operating a joggling machine can turn out as much work in a day as many men making the joggles by hand.

FIG. 84.—Metal-forming blocks, as shown at the left, may be used to form sheetmetal parts. After the sheet has been cut to approximate size and drilled for centering pins, it is held on the block by a matching die which is not shown here. The flanges are formed by hammering. Compressing the dies in vise jaws or in a hydraulic press forms the channel depression.

Bumping.—Sheetmetal parts that require stretching and shrinking by hammering are said to be "bumped." The hand forming of such parts is no longer practical for factories that are doing production work, since it is much faster to form parts whenever possible by machine methods, such as hydraulic presses, drop hammers, and stamping. Sometimes machine-formed parts require a limited amount of hand bumping to ensure exact fitting. Such work may be done by using steel stretching or shrinking hammers on the original dies or with the aid of forming stakes. Rawhide or canvas bags filled with fine sand may also be used as a backing for bumping.

Power hammers, fitted with slightly convex dies, may be used in forming sheet stock to two dimensions. As the sheet is fed

Fig. 85.—Steel-faced forming dies. Sheets blanked to the stretch-out contour are hydraulically pressed between these two dies to form the small nose rib that is shown at the right. (*Curtiss-Wright, Buffalo, photograph.*)

between the reciprocating dies of the hammer, the metal is stretched, causing it to *dish up*. Skilled power-hammer operators can produce formed parts with great accuracy.

Forming blocks of steel, micarta, maple, or Masonite are used where hand bumping is required. The major requirements of such blocks are that they be accurately made, allowing for the thickness of the metal for the over-all dimensions of the finished part, that the die faces are smooth and clean, and that the dies are sufficiently durable for the run of the work.

For short runs of work or for practice in aviation schools, maple or Masonite blocks are generally used. If the shape of the forming block is concave, the material is blanked out somewhat larger than the die and a clamping block or steel washer plate holds the edges flat over the concave die. C clamps are generally used for this purpose. A round-faced plastic mallet or a steel planishing hammer is then used to draw the material down into the contours of the forming block. The material between the clamping plate and the die must be allowed to slip a little so the entire contour of the forming is not dependent on stretching and shrinking alone.

FIG. 86.—When metal is forced down around circular-shaped forming blocks, the edges tend to have many small bulges. To form smooth flanged surfaces it is necessary to shrink the metal. This is done by placing a pointed wood or steel shrinking tool under the flange as it is hammered against the block. The excess metal is allowed to flare out and is later trimmed off.

The material is worked down gradually all around the edge of the depression in the die. The deeper the draw, the thinner the material becomes. Consequently great care must be taken to prevent tearing through the material. Light blows should be struck in the direction that you want the metal to "flow," and the blows should be close to the sides of the forming block.

Only soft, or annealed, sheet can be bumped satisfactorily. It should be remembered that as in forging a metal, continued hammering will harden the material. Frequent annealing may be required during the bumping process.

Annealing requires the heating of the metal to the temperature range from 640 to 670°F. It should then be cooled to about 450°. Once the material has cooled below this temperature, the rate of cooling has little effect. For full annealing to produce a dead soft or "0" condition of aluminum alloy, the metal is brought up to 750 to 800°F., then gradually cooled in the furnace. The cooling rate must be controlled so that the material does not cool faster than 50° per hour until the metal has cooled to 500°. Below this temperature the cooling rate may be increased to open-air cooling. Most of the strengthening effects of heat-treating are removed by annealing.

HYDRAULIC PRESSING AND STAMPING

Each year an increasing amount of sheetmetal work in airplane factories is being done on presses. Although it is not possible for schools to install the giant types of presses now in use, mechanics who are going into factories should have a general idea of the kinds of parts turned out by these pressing and stamping machines. The material presented in this section is not intended to teach the use of presses, but to present an over-all picture that should familiarize the mechanic with press-forming operations.

DROP HAMMERS

The forerunner of hydraulic presses was the rope-lifted drop hammer. A concave die is secured by bolts to the lower bed of the drop hammer for formed sheetmetal-part production, and the aluminum-alloy sheet then placed on top of it. An upper punch die, bolted to the hammer head, drops down on the sheet, pressing it into the form of the lower die. Several blows may be necessary to finish the piece to the desired shape. The upper die is lifted by one or two ropes which are turned five or six times around a slowly revolving capstan drum at the top of the hammer. When the operator puts his weight on the free end of the rope, the die is hoisted between the two vertical guides of the machine. When the tension is released, the hammer drops down the guides of its own weight. The weight of the upper die and the hammer is sufficient to supply the necessary force. The amount of impact is determined by the height to which the hammer is lifted. If the part being hammered is shallow in form, the upper hammer hits directly on the aluminum-alloy sheet. When the curvatures in the metal are deep, which is called a *deep draw*, a steel draw ring made of boiler plate is first placed on top of the sheet. Over this, a number of 1/4 in. thick draw rings of plywood or fiber are used.

Fig. 87.—A Chambersburg hydraulic stamping machine. The receiving die is clamped to the lower bed of the press and the sheet placed on top. Then the upper die strikes a series of heavy blows that form the sheet to the required contour.

The draw rings are removed one at a time as the metal gradually assumes the desired shape. Rubber blankets are also used. They are piled on the sheet being stamped, and one thickness of rubber is removed after each blow until the upper die finally bottoms on the sheet in the lower die.

To absorb the terrific force of the impact, the bed, or impact blocks, of drop hammers are mounted on coil-spring supports carried over steel pilings.

Rope-lifted drop hammers are cumbersome to operate and are being replaced in most plants by drop hammers operated by compressed air.

In compressed-air hammers a driving rod raises and lowers the hammer, or ram, adding the much greater force of compressed air to the impact of gravity. The force of the blows of this machine can be much more closely controlled than on the rope-lifted drop hammer. With a slight pressure on a lever, the operator can move the ram as rapidly and with as much pressure as the work requires, usually beginning with light blows and then striking harder blows as the metal assumes the required shape. The action may also be set by the operator for automatic repetitive blows (see Fig. 87).

The dies for drop hammers are usually made of lead and zinc. The lower receiving die is of zinc, and the top punching die is of lead. They can be melted and used for casting new dies when no longer needed in making the part for which they were originally designed. Dies may be made of several different materials. Usually a pattern is first cast in plaster. The plaster form is then used as a pattern when the part is cast from zinc in a sand mold. Allowances for shrinking must be calculated. Some companies have made dural dies by melting scrap metal. If the punching die is to be of lead, this can be poured into the zinc die, and thus it is the exact reverse of the lower die. In long runs of drop-hammer work the punching die may be made of cast iron or steel with machine-polished surfaces.

Drop hammers can be dangerous machines. They should never be used without authority and then only after receiving specific instructions as to their safe operation. Safety latches, double controls, and steel foot guards cannot alone protect a careless worker.

HYDRAULIC PRESSES

When an aircraft plant goes into production on a large order, it must find a faster method for its stampings than the drop hammer. The solution to the problem is the large-size hydraulic press which can stamp out as many as 65 different parts in one motion. Over 3,000 different parts of Douglas planes, for example, are made on hydraulic presses. The majority of these "hydropresses" are of the vertical, downward-acting type having a spacious pedestal type of bed. The operating equipment is mounted overhead. The upper platen, or ram, ascends by means of oil-hydraulic mechanism.

Deep-drawn sheetmetal parts may be formed by the use of upper and lower matching dies made and mounted in a manner similar to that described for drop hammers (see Fig. 88). Deep-

FIG. 88.—This hydraulic press uses upper and lower dies of hardwood, faced with steel. The steel columns act as guides for the heavy upper platen which descends against the sheet and forces it into the lower die. Finished part is at the right. (*Curtiss-Wright, Buffalo, photograph.*)

drawing can be accomplished on hydro-presses without the use of expensively cast metal dies. Laminated wood or plywood, micarta, or tempered pressed wood are used successfully for many operations. The sheet stock is often greased to facilitate forming by lessening the tendency of the sheet to adhere to the dies. Unavoidable wrinkles are sometimes produced along the flanged edges of the formed part. They may be removed by handworking with a planishing hammer before they are trimmed and finished.

The most widely used method of forming shallow and medium draws on the hydraulic press is done by means of a single receiving die on the lower platen and a thick rubber pad attached to the upper or moving platen. When shallow parts are being cut or formed, the receiving dies are laid on the smooth steel bed of the press. The aluminum-alloy sheet is placed on top of the dies, and pressure exerted by the moving platen. The thick pad of live rubber mounted to the upper platen of the press moves down slowly. As it makes contact, the rubber blanket holds the parts and the press applies tremendous pressure.

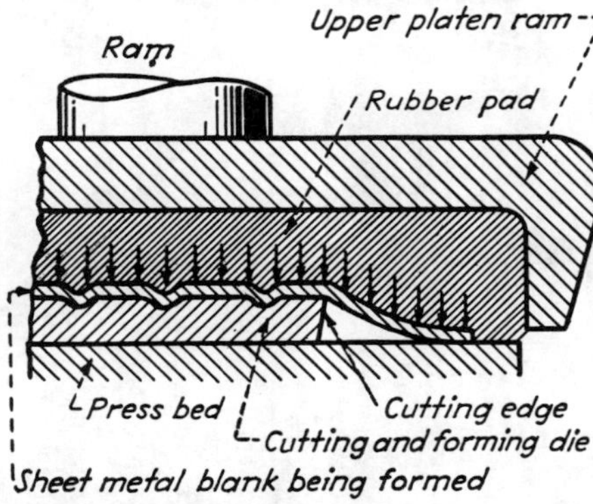

FIG. 89.—Drawing showing details of the Guerin process of blanking and forming. A heavy pad of live rubber is fastened to the upper platen ram. The sheet stock must extend sufficiently beyond the edge of the die to make contact with the bed of the press. This builds up tension in the unsupported area, causing a shearing action along the undercut lip of the die. The rubber pad produces a fluidlike pressure that is nearly uniform over the entire surface of the sheet being formed.

The largest presses exert 5,500 tons or more of pressure. By using the rubber-blanket method, it is not necessary to use two dies, and even the one die that is used is simpler to make than the usual type used in drop-hammer presses. Such great weight is put upon the live-rubber blanket that it becomes fluidlike and flows around the forming or cutting die, applying almost uniform pressure.

Cutting or blanking the parts is accomplished by using sharp-edged steel dies made in the outline of the required forms. The cutting dies may be placed anywhere on the bed of the press. They do not require fastening. Locating pins project from the upper faces of the dies to center the sheet stock, which is punched with matching holes by means of a simple drill template. Compression of the tough, abrasion-resisting rubber pad on the sheet causes tension in the unsupported portion between the die and the bed of the press. This results in a shearing or cutting action along the edges of the cutting die. The excess metal is forced downward against the press bed while the blank remains in place on top of the die (see Fig. 89).

FIG. 90.—A huge toggle press designed by engineers at North American Aviation for use in that factory. In the foreground, finished parts are being removed. This bed will then be reloaded and moved back under the press. Blanks are kept in place by centering pins in the forming dies as they are pressed in shape by the rubber pad fitted to the upper platen.

When cutting lightening holes, the rubber pad acts as its own stripper by breaking loose the excess, or waste, material. The method most commonly used today is called the *Guerin method*, and the patents are held by the Douglas Aircraft Co. One of the great advantages of the rubber-blanket method lies in the fact that many different kinds and shapes of parts can be stamped out at the same time by using a variety of dies to cover the entire lower platen. Large-size presses have a platen 186 in. long and

72 in. wide. The usual depth of parts formed by this method is rarely greater than 7 in. The thickness of the comparatively soft aluminum-alloy material formed ranges from 0.003 to 0.094 in., although it is possible to form narrow strips as thick as 0.125 in.

Hydraulic presses are controlled by hand levers or by electric push buttons for either manual or automatic operation. The ram travels rapidly to the work, changing to a slower and more powerful

FIG. 91.—A Birdsboro three-leg hydraulic press in use at Vultee. This press has a three-station rotary platen, or bed, which permits continuous pressing. The bed revolves under the press. As soon as one set of stampings is made, the platen is turned as the ram rises. Then the workers remove the stamped parts and a new section of the bed moves under the press. This permits continuous loading, pressing, and unloading.

pressing speed on contact so that the sheet will completely conform to all contours of the die. On reaching the bottom of the draw, the ram then returns to its "daylight" position with comparative rapidity.

To speed production, presses are built with several bolster or bed plates. While one set of stampings is being made in the press, another set is being laid out on an extra bolster plate mounted on a wheeled "buggy" running on tracks. When the first set is stamped, the plate on which it rests is slid out of the press and the new plate is slid in place. Thus one plate is being unloaded; another is being stamped; and a third and perhaps a fourth are being loaded. The press runs almost steadily, and in the course of a day literally thousands of parts can be made. The accompanying photographs give a clearer picture of the stampings than can be described in words.

Review Questions

1. How are bending blocks used?
2. Describe briefly the operation of a bending brake.
3. How should you mark a line that is to be bent?
4. What procedure is followed if metal cracks at the bend?
5. How does a bar folder differ from a bending brake?
6. For what kind of aircraft work is a press brake used?
7. How many dies are used in a press-brake operation?
8. Why are sheetmetal rolls used if a bending brake is available?
9. How can the radius of a bend be increased in sheetmetal roll operation?
10. Are the rolls always parallel?
11. How is a beading machine operated and what work will it perform?
12. Why are sheetmetal parts often flanged or beaded along the edges?
13. For what purpose is a draw bench used? How is it used?
14. What kind of aluminum alloy is used for spinning?
15. For what kind of work is an Erco sheetmetal former used?
16. Explain how sheetmetal can be shrunk.
17. For which kinds of parts is it necessary to shrink metal?
18. What shape is a hand shrinkage tool?
19. Why is it necessary to stretch sheetmetal?
20. Describe the operation of a machine shrinker.
21. What is a power hammer and how does it operate?
22. Describe joggling. Why is this process common on some airplane parts?
23. What tools are used in performing hand bumping operations?
24. Would you use 24S-T aluminum alloy for bumping?
25. How many dies are used in connection with drop hammers?
26. What is a deep draw? What is a draw ring?
27. How does a compressed-air drop hammer differ from other types of drop hammer?
28. Draw a diagram of how the rubber-blanket method is used with hydraulic presses.

Shop Work

In the making of the universal fitting, described in Project 2, several bending operations are required. The louver plate of Project 4 also requires bumping metal over a form. In Project 5 the two ends of the fairing are formed, and, in addition, slip rolls are used to form the cover. Other forming operations are required for making the parts shown in the drawings of Chap. 1.

CHAPTER 10

DRILLING AND HOW TO DO IT

Every sheetmetal man must know how to use the various types of drills that are found in aircraft plants. As holes must be drilled for some 80,000 rivets in an Army pursuit ship or a Navy fighter and for over 130,000 rivets in a medium-sized bomber—plus many additional holes for bolts—it is obvious that drilling is a frequent process.

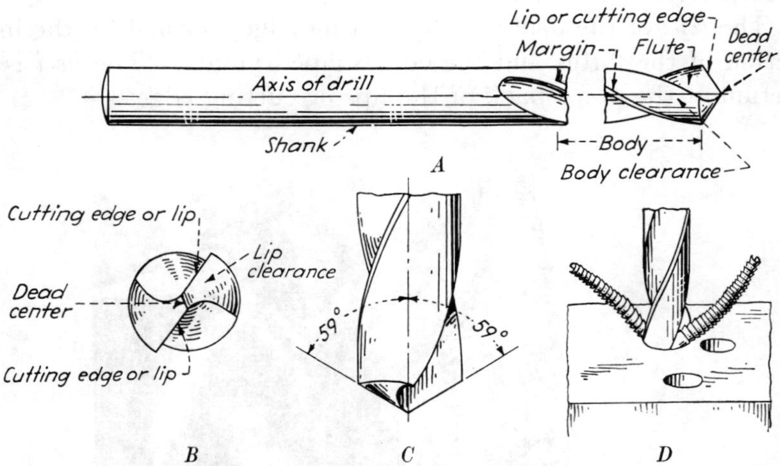

FIG. 92.—Parts of a twist drill are shown in drawings *A* and *B*. Drawing *C* shows lips of a drill correctly ground. Drills that are sharpened properly cause the chips to curl continuously, as in drawing *D*.

There are many types of drilling devices in airplane factories. In shop practice, it is common practice to refer to the entire drilling device as a *drill*. This includes the driving unit, either hand or power operated, as well as the twist-drill bit. It may mean a hand drill, a portable electric drill or a portable pneumatic drill. The *twist drill*, which is the tool that does the actual cutting, is also called a *drill*. For aircraft work, the twist drill is generally referred to by its *size number*, such as a No. 30 drill or a No. 50 drill.

The twist drill itself is made of steel and consists of three principal parts: the shank, the body, and the point. The *shank* is the portion that fits into the drill press on the end of the spindle. The *body* is the part from the shank to the point. The *Points* are the cone-shaped surfaces at the cutting end. *Flutes* are the spiral grooves formed on the side of a drill. Drills may have two, three, or four flutes. Chips are carried away from the tip through the flutes (see Fig. 92).

It should be noted that the extreme tip of the drill, called *dead center*, is not a point such as is found on an ice pick. It is a flat, sharp ridge formed by the intersection of two half-cone-shaped surfaces and is really the extreme end of the web. The failure of mechanics to understand this often leads them to handle a drill inefficiently.

The *lips* of the drill are the cutting edges formed by the intersection of the flutes and the cone-shaped points. The *heel* is the portion of the point back of the lips or cutting edges.

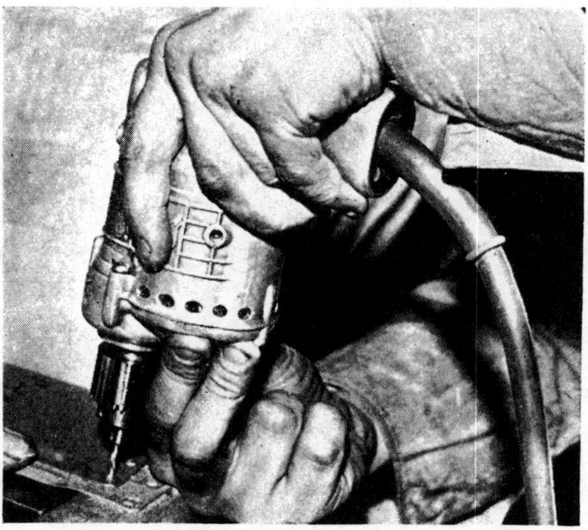

FIG. 93.—Small, compact, portable electric hand drills are used throughout aircraft plants. A key must be used to adjust this type of chuck.

Grades of Drill.—Twist drills are classified either as *carbon drills* or as *high-speed drills.* The carbon drills are not so durable as the high-speed variety and are used principally in hand drills for drilling softer metals at comparatively low speeds. As the name implies, high-speed drills are made to be used in power-driven drills turning at high speeds. They will not burn readily from friction as is the case with the less expensive and lower tempered carbon drills.

Drilling Devices.—The most simple kind of drilling device is the portable hand drill. A variation of this type is the breast drill, although the latter is rarely used for aircraft work. In the aircraft factory the most common types are the portable electric or the portable pneumatic drill. These are light in weight, easy to handle, and small enough so that they can be used in fairly close

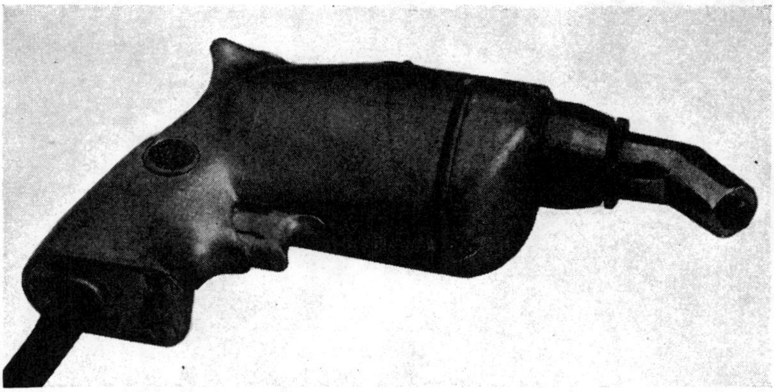

FIG. 94.—A midget hand drill with the chuck placed at an angle, which is an advantage when drilling in restricted areas. The switch is operated like the trigger on a pistol.

quarters (see Figs. 93–96). Lathes are often used for drilling machined fittings and parts where great accuracy is required. For benchwork, the drill press is used wherever possible.

Chucks.—Most of the smaller drilling devices for aircraft sheetmetal work use a similar method for holding the twist drill. A *chuck* attached to the end spindle or the drive shaft may be quickly tightened or loosened for gripping the drill. Two or more steel jaws, set radially in the chuck, center the drill shank and hold it firmly.

On larger portable drills and on drill presses, a key is required to adjust the chuck when changing drills. The key must be kept with the drill, and it is often secured to the drill handle with a rawhide thong or a metal chain. Care must be taken that the key does not become caught in the chuck.

Many of the larger drill presses retain the twist drill by means of a tapered socket at the end of the spindle instead of a chuck. The drills used with this device are of the tapered-shank type, having a flat *tang* at the end of the drill shank. The tapered shank of the twist drill fits in the spindle socket, which is slotted at

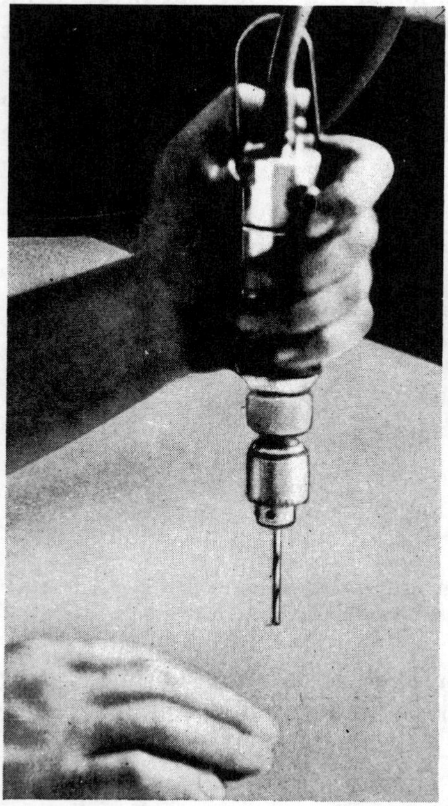

FIG. 95.—A light, pneumatic, portable drill. Air pressure and drill speed are controlled by a button valve, operated by the index finger.

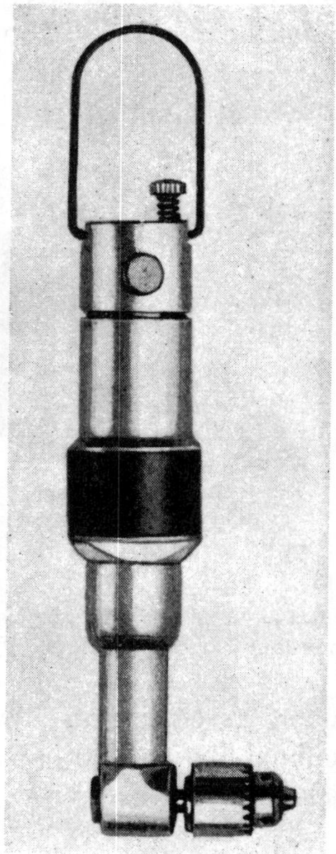

FIG. 96.—This pneumatic drill is fitted with a right-angle chuck. Its small size permits it to be used during assembly operations on parts that would otherwise require predrilling.

the extreme end to accommodate the tang. A small, flat, tapered driftpin is required to remove the drill from the socket. The drift is inserted through an opening in the side of the socket.

Portable drilling devices are usually described by the largest size drill that they can accommodate. For example, the chuck of a portable electric or a portable pneumatic drill that is made to hold any size drill up to ¼ in. is always called a *quarter-inch drill.* Likewise, a drill referred to as a *half-inch drill* will accommodate drills up to ½ in. in diameter. Drill presses are also classified by the largest size unit of work that may be centered under the spindle, such as a 22 in. drill press.

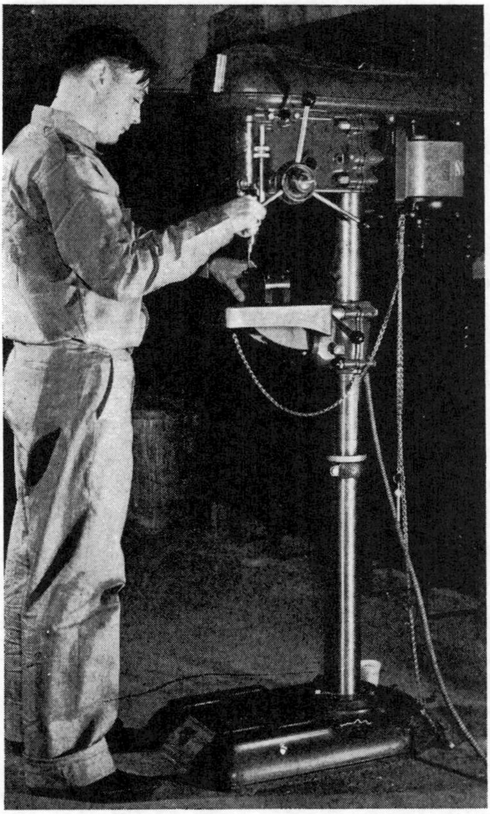

FIG. 97.—A Delta drill press being used in the LaGuardia Field shops of American Airlines. Batteries of light, sensitive drill presses of this type are used in aircraft production. The operator here is holding the work which is mounted in a drill-press vise. He controls the descent of the drill with the feed control in his right hand.

Drill Presses.—The drilling of fittings and subassemblies of a size that can be easily handled is done on a *drill press.* In all types, the work is held in a convenient position on a drill table while a power-driven drill descends on it. Greater drilling accuracy is obtained in a drill press than with a portable drill because of the fixed vertical path traveled by the descending drill. The large radial drills, which you may have seen in a machine shop, are equipped with automatic feeding devices, variable-speed spindles, and adjustable work tables. They are confined to heavy-duty work in the drilling of forgings, castings, and machined parts and are not regularly used for sheetmetal work.

Light, sensitive drill presses are used for most aircraft sheetmetal drill-press work. They are usually belt driven and may be adjusted for speeds up to 12,000 r.p.m. (see Fig. 97).

Portable drills may be mounted in bench stands and used as drill presses.

For production work on fittings or parts in which a number of holes must be drilled on the same surface, a *multiple* or *gang drill press* is used. These machines have a number of spindles so that several holes can be drilled simultaneously.

Tapping devices with reverse gearing may be attached to the spindles of drill presses for the production threading of fittings.

Securing Work for Drill Press.—All drill-press work, except for very large or heavy parts, should be secured to the drill-press table to prevent rotation. Work should never be held by hand against the force of the revolving drill. If the feed is too fast or, very often, when the drill breaks through, the penetration of the drill is abruptly reduced. When this happens, the drill has a tendency to lock or "hog in"; if the work is not secured, it will revolve. This may cause severe injury to the operator's hands, arms, or body.

The means of securing work to the adjustable drill table are termed *setups*. Drill-press vises, stops, C clamps, T bolts, and metal straps are used for setting up the work.

On the larger drill presses, the table is crossed with T slots so that inverted T-headed bolts can be used in the slots to hold the flat-base drill vises or metal straps. The T bolts can also be used to secure a steel block that acts as a *stop* to prevent the work from swinging around. The work must be centered directly below the drill, and the use of the stop has the advantage of allowing the work to move slightly and "find its own center." Jigs or drill templates should also be located against stops, if other means of securing are not used.

The devices used for clamping the work should be placed as close as possible to the drill. This is done to lessen vibration to reduce bending loads. Both dural and steel parts held in setups should be protected from marring by using soft aluminum vise faces or shims.

For drilling small fittings or parts of $\frac{3}{16}$ in. or less in thickness, it is often better to place them on a board and stop them with nails or to secure them to the drill-press table with C clamps.

Regardless of the type of drill setup used, be certain that the drill will clear as it goes through the work and not cut into any part of the setup or table.

FIG. 98.—When a considerable amount of drilling must be done, aircraft factories set up drill jigs. This is one type of jig in use in the Martin plant. The entire drill slides back and forth on two tracks. Guide holes have been lined up accurately in the cross members. When the drill is lowered through the guides, it drills a hole in the proper location in the sheet.

Drill Templates.—When a number of holes are being drilled in aluminum-alloy sheet, it is common practice to use a template, or jig, made of steel. The sheet is centered under the spindle in the usual way, and the jig is then secured over the work. Holes have previously been drilled through the template, or jig members, and the mechanic has only to use these holes for a guide. For drill-press operations rivet- and bolt-hole locations are often made oversize in a drill template to permit a hardened bushing, or sleevelike drill guide, to be inserted in the hole of the template. This prevents the drill from wearing or elongating the guide hole in the template. A single removable bushing is attached directly to the drill press by means of a fitting. It is automatically brought down into position as the drill descends on the work (see Fig. 98). In such instances the locations of the holes are not marked on the sheetmetal. The use of drill templates is explained in detail in the section on the Use of Templates.

There is much drilling, however, for which jigs or templates are not used. In such cases, the center of the hole may be marked by two crossed lines. A light prick punch is used to mark the exact center of the hole, which is the intersection of the cross. When the material comes to the driller marked in this manner, he should enlarge the prick-punch indentations by using a center punch. The center-punch marks serve to align the drill and guide the point.

Pilot Holes.—For holes that are to be 1/8 in. or larger, it is common practice to start the hole with a smaller size drill, which serves as a lead or pilot hole for the larger drill.

The pilot hole serves four purposes: (1) it prevents the drill from riding away from a center-punch mark; (2) it acts as a true guide for the larger drill; (3) it permits slight leeway for alignment when reaming to exact size during assembly; (4) harder metals are drilled with greater ease when pilot holes are used.

The length of the *dead center* or *point* at the tip of a drill depends upon the thickness of the *web* between the flutes. The larger the diameter of the drill the greater the thickness of the web and the wider the dead center. The dead center has an ineffective scraping action and does not cut cleanly. When a pilot hole is used, the ineffective scraping action is eliminated and more efficient drilling is accomplished. The drill chosen for the pilot hole should be no larger than necessary, or the finishing drill may drill out of round, chatter, or spoil the mouth of the hole. The size of the pilot drill should be slightly larger than the dead center of finishing drill point. When thick stock is drilled, care should be taken not to use excessive feeding pressure which would bend a small-diameter pilot drill, causing the pilot hole to be crooked. The larger drill will invariably follow the exact course of the pilot hole.

Extension Drills.—Where chuck interference with the work is a factor, standard twist drills may be extended by butt-brazing a length of drill rod to the end of the drill shank. The rod used for this purpose should be several thousandths of an inch less in thickness than the diameter of the drill. The brazed joint must also be ground down to drill diameter in order to prevent binding.

FIG. 99.—A light, sensitive drill-press head is shown mounted at the end of a tubular extension arm, which permits drilling at any point over a wide area. This device is usually used in connection with drill jigs. Here a steel drill template is clamped in place over a stack of blanked sheet stock. Fitted to the chuck of the drill is a drill guide so that holes in the template are protected from wear by a hardened steel bushing that descends into the template as each hole is drilled.

Angle Drilling.—In locations where the usual straight-shaft portable drills cannot be used, direct-drive angle drills can be used effectively. Portable drills can be obtained with the chuck set at right angles to the body of the drill. Small-angle adapters with separate collet chucks are also made in 30 and 90 deg. angles. They can be used by inserting them in the chuck of any ordinary straight-shaft portable drill.

Flexible-shaft Drilling.—There are numerous places in modern wing, fuselage, and float construction where drilling by means of extension, straight-shaft, or angled portable drills is impossible. In such close quarters, flexible-shaft drills are used. They are also known as *flexible-cable* or *snake* drills. In the larger types, a motor mounted on a portable stand drives a 6 ft. flexible shaft

FIG. 100.—In this picture a drill press mounted on a flexible arm is being used for countersinking to receive flush-type rivets. The sheet stock is held in place on the jig which rests on the drill table.

which is enclosed in a flexible housing. An ordinary drill chuck is fitted to the end of the flexible shaft. Angle-drill adapters can also be used with this type of drilling machine.

By brazing a twist drill to one end of a short length of tachometer or speedometer cable, many mechanics make their own snake drills. They are driven by securing the other end in the chuck of a portable drill. Snake drills of this type are efficient but dangerous, since they will whip around if the power is turned on when they are not held and guided.

Size of Drill.—Many different sizes of twist drills are manufactured for machine shop and other uses, but the aircraft sheet-metal man seldom uses more than a dozen different-sized drills. The most frequently used drills for riveting are listed on page 203. Drills are obtained in fractional sizes, wire-gage-number sizes, and letter sizes. Examine the table on page 184.

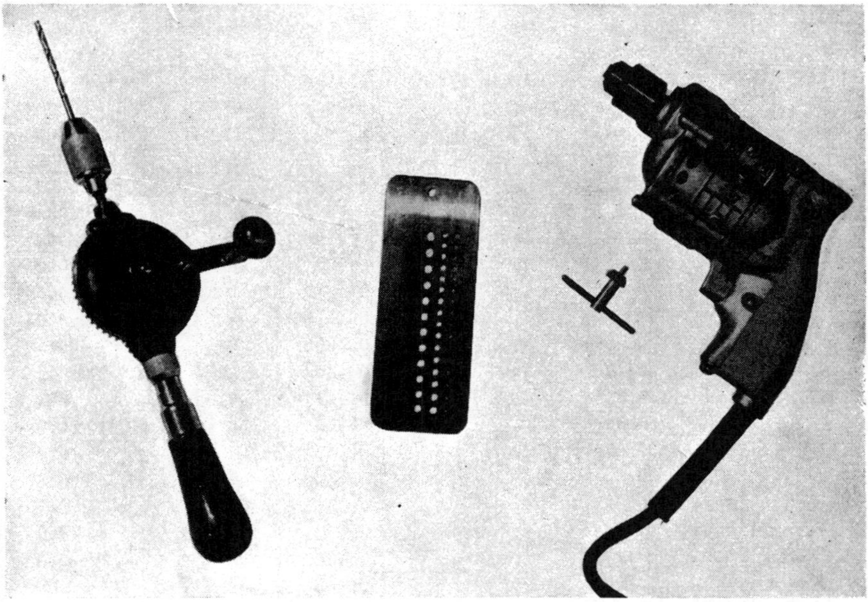

FIG. 101.—Left to right: a hand drill, a drill gage, and a light portable electric hand drill. The key tightens or loosens the chuck when drills are being changed. The size of a twist drill required for a job can be checked with a drill gage. The drill should make a snug fit when inserted into the hole.

Drills for rivet holes are identified by a number. A 1/8 in. rivet hole, for example, is drilled with a No. 30 drill. The rivet hole must have just a sufficient amount of clearance for the easy alignment of parts and the rapid insertion of rivets. A clearance of several thousandths of an inch is usually specified.

Drills used for most aircraft bolt holes are usually designated by the diameter of the bolt. A 1/4 in. bolt requires a 1/4 in. drill, and a 5/16 in. bolt requires a 5/16 in. drill.

TABLE OF DRILL SIZES

Letter size	Fractional size	Decimal equivalent	No. size	Fractional size	Decimal equivalent	No. size	Fractional size	Decimal equivalent
	1/2	0.500	1		0.228	40		0.098
	31/64	0.4843	2		0.221	41		0.096
	15/32	0.4687		7/32	0.2187		3/32	0.0937
	29/64	0.4531	3		0.213	42		0.0935
	7/16	0.4375	4		0.209	43		0.089
	27/64	0.4218	5		0.2055	44		0.086
Z		0.413	6		0.204	45		0.082
	13/32	0.4062		13/64	0.2031	46		0.081
Y		0.404	7		0.201	47		0.0785
X		0.397	8		0.199		5/64	0.0781
	25/64	0.3906	9		0.196	48		0.076
W		0.386	10		0.1935	49		0.073
V		0.377	11		0.191	50		0.070
	3/8	0.375	12		0.189	51		0.067
U		0.368		3/16	0.1875	52		0.0635
	23/64	0.3594	13		0.185		1/16	0.0625
T		0.358	14		0.182	53		0.0595
S		0.348	15		0.180	54		0.055
	11/32	0.3437	16		0.177	55		0.052
R		0.339	17		0.173		3/64	0.0468
Q		0.332		11/64	0.1718	56		0.0465
	21/64	0.3281	18		0.1695	57		0.043
P		0.323	19		0.166	58		0.042
O		0.316	20		0.161	59		0.041
	5/16	0.3125	21		0.159	60		0.040
N		0.302	22		0.157	61		0.039
	19/64	0.2968		5/32	0.1562	62		0.038
M		0.295	23		0.154	63		0.037
L		0.290	24		0.152	64		0.036
	9/32	0.2812	25		0.1495	65		0.035
K		0.281	26		0.147	66		0.033
J		0.277	27		0.144		1/32	0.032
I		0.272		9/64	0.1406	67		0.0313
H		0.266	28		0.1405	68		0.031
	17/64	0.2656	29		0.136	69		0.029
G		0.261	30		0.1285	70		0.028
F		0.257		1/8	0.125	71		0.026
E	1/4	0.250	31		0.120	72		0.025
D		0.246	32		0.116	73		0.024
C		0.242	33		0.113	74		0.0225
B		0.238	34		0.111	75		0.021
	15/64	0.2343	35		0.110	76		0.020
A		0.234		7/64	0.1093	77		0.018
			36		0.1065		1/64	0.016
			37		0.104	78		0.0156
			38		0.1015	79		0.0145
			39		0.0995	80		0.0135

The size of the drill should be checked before it is used. Drills that are not marked on the shank may be checked with a drill gage (see Fig. 101). A micrometer caliper may also be used for this purpose. Do not attempt to guess the size of a drill. In assembly work, if a hole is drilled oversize, the part is ruined.

Drilling Lubricants.—For the usual aircraft sheetmetal work with aluminum alloy, it is not necessary to use lubricants or cutting oils as an aid in drilling, as is common practice for drilling heavier machined parts. In drilling forged- and cast-aluminum-alloy parts and for steel fittings, it is more efficient to keep the drill saturated with a cutting oil.

The principal advantages of using lubricants in drilling aircraft parts are

1. The lubricant prevents the drill from burning due to friction caused by the high turning speeds.
2. Lubrication of the chips aids materially in chip clearance.
3. Pressure lubrication to the drill point clears the chips from the cutting edge and from the drill flutes.
4. A smoother machined finish results from proper lubrication.

LUBRICANTS RECOMMENDED FOR AIRCRAFT METALS

For aluminum and aluminum alloys—soluble oil, kerosene and lard oil compounds, light nonviscous neutral oils, soluble oil and kerosene mixtures.

For steel (1025, 4130)—soluble oil, sulfurized oil.

For steel (18-8 *stainless*)—2 parts sulfurized cutting oil and 1 part carbon tetrachloride.

Drill Points.—The angle of the cutting edge varies for different kinds of metals. Drills for cutting hard steels have a flatter cutting angle than drills used for aluminum alloys. The extra material resulting from the flatter angles strengthens the cutting lip of the drill. Drills used for aircraft sheetmetal are generally an exception to this practice. Since comparatively thin materials are used, speed in drilling is not a controlling factor. Drills that are sharpened to a normal angle suitable for steel are used for most sheet stock, since they drill a cleaner hole. It is possible, however, to increase the speed on some types of work if a steeper point is used on aluminum alloys.

Bent Drills.—Drills of the smaller gages are frequently bent during drilling operations. This is generally due to forcing the drill or is the result of the drill's striking a hard object, such as a bucking iron, as it penetrates the sheet.

Small-diameter drills that are bent can be straightened by placing them flat on a surface plate or an anvil and striking the shank lightly with a plastic hammer as they are slowly rotated by hand. This is an emergency measure and is not an efficient mechanical practice, since often the flutes are damaged by hammer blows and perfect straightening is difficult to obtain. Then, too, high-speed drills that are more than a few degrees out of true will often break on straightening.

Drills that are broken in the shank area can be salvaged if there is a sufficient amount of the shank remaining to permit rounding of the jagged end on a grinder. Drills that have become shortened in this manner are less apt to bend or break because of the greater rigidity and strength resulting from their shortened length.

Use of Portable Drills.—The most common error made by beginners is to hold a portable drill at an incorrect angle. The drill should be held at right angles to the work. If the drill is in a horizontal position, the mechanic can see if it is too far to the left or right, but he cannot tell if the rear of the drill is too high or too low. When learning to drill, a mechanic often needs the services of a helper to sight the angle that he cannot see. After a certain amount of practice, the driller learns to hold the drill at the proper angle.

In starting to drill, if the drill has a tendency to travel away from the center, this condition can be corrected by aiming the point of the drill in the opposite direction and gradually bringing the drill back to a position at right angles to the work. This is a common practice in drilling out rivets, because of the difficulty in keeping the drill centered on a rivet head. In drilling thin sheet, however, this method may elongate holes and should not be used except by an experienced driller.

Another common mistake is to put too much pressure on the drill. Most dural sheet is not thick and is soft compared with steel or iron. If the mechanic pushes or crowds a drill with too much force, he may break the drill point. He is almost sure to plunge the drill through the far side of the sheet, so that rough edges form around the hole like those in a tin can when a nail is driven through. The speed of pneumatic-powered drills is regulated by pressure on the trigger. Pressure should be decreased just before the drill cuts through the far side of the sheet.

When the drill penetrates a fitting or a part, it should not be stopped immediately on breaking through, but should be inserted for approximately half of its length while still running, and then withdrawn. This operation requires judgment and skill since it is very easy to ream the hole oversize; but if this is done properly, cleaner holes will result. Portable drills must always be held in a balanced position, otherwise the weight of the drilling device will be transmitted to the twist drill and bear against the side of the hole, causing possible elongation of the holes.

Approved Procedures for Portable-drill Operation

1. Arrange the electric cord or the air-hose lead to the drill so that you or anyone else will not trip over it. If the lead wire is damaged, don't use the drill.

2. Determine the exact size of the hole to be drilled by carefully checking the blueprint or by getting definite information from your leadman.

3. Select the drill and determine its size by examining markings, by checking with the drill gage, or by using a micrometer.

4. Examine the drill to see that it is properly ground and not distorted or bent. Regrind if it appears to be at all dull. Discard it if it is distorted. It can be straightened if it is only slightly bent.

5. Wipe the drill clean with a rag.

6. Make certain that the power is off; then secure the drill firmly in the chuck, always holding the chuck away from your face. Pliers should never be used for this operation.

7. It is dangerous to wear loose clothing, neckties, gloves, or long sleeves during drilling operations. Sleeves should be cut off above the elbow rather than rolled up. Not the least hazard is hair, which should be kept short if a cap is not worn.

8. Before you start to drill, be sure that your fellow workers in the immediate vicinity are clear. If you cannot see the other side of the work, shout a warning or signal by tapping before drilling.

9. See that the work to be drilled is held securely in the jig or the vise. When drilling skin or parts that tend to bend, a helper using a suitable hardwood bucking block is required.

10. Take firm stance and brace yourself, but do not bear your full weight on the drill. Ease the pressure just before the drill breaks through. Do not use sufficient force to "bow" the drill. Always hold the portable drill in a manner that would not cause you to fall or damage the skin if the drill should break.

11. For overhead work or where chips are flying, wear goggles.

12. When drilling rivet holes, keep the drill at right angles to the work, regardless of the contour.

13. Keep your finger on the trigger or switch at all times.

14. Turn the drill on for a moment before drilling to be sure that the drill is running true, but don't play with the drill.

15. Touch the drill point to the center-punch mark, or pilot hole, before turning power on. When the power is on, hold the drill firmly to keep it centered and to prevent it from riding away from the hole.

16. When the drill penetrates, allow it to run approximately half its length through the hole before withdrawing, but it must be held in a balanced position to prevent the hole from becoming elongated.

17. Do not underestimate the power of large, ½ in. portable drills. The auxiliary handle should be kept in place and used. Unless the work is very large and heavy, it should be securely stopped or clamped. If the drill hogs in the work so that it becomes jammed, it may dangerously spin light work or in heavy work pull out of the operator's hands and cause the body of the drill itself to spin.

18. Extension drills should be steadied near the fluted end and not removed from the hole until they have stopped revolving. Flexible-cable drills should be used only if they have handles. They should not be used at all if the cable is kinked.

19. Do not use a drill that has become overheated. At any sign of a short circuit, return the drill to the tool crib and report the trouble.

20. On small portable drills it is a common but often dangerous practice to stop the drill by hand pressure on the revolving chuck. Try to avoid this, if possible. If finger rings are worn, they are apt to jam in the chuck.

21. Do not attempt to remove a drill from the chuck unless the power is turned off. If the chuck jams and cannot be loosened by hand, tapping it lightly all the way around with a plastic hammer or a block of wood will usually break it loose.

22. Drill chips should be brushed away from the work. Do not use compressed air, rags, or cotton waste.

23. If you put a portable drill down temporarily, be sure that it is placed in such a way that it cannot fall or otherwise injure anyone

Approved Procedure for Drill-press Operation

1. Carefully check the drill template or the blueprint for the exact size of the hole to be drilled.

2. Select the drill and determine its size by examining markings, by checking with the drill gage, or by using a micrometer. To avoid mistakes, do not have more than one drill in the immediate vicinity of the work at one time.

3. Examine the drill to see that it is properly ground. Don't hesitate to resharpen the drill if necessary.

4. Wipe the shank of the drill clean, and insert it properly in the chuck; then tighten the chuck with the key.

5. Start the drill-press motor for a moment to see that the drill is running true.

6. Arrange the work in an appropriate setup on the drill table. The work should always be either stopped or clamped. Don't depend on holding it by hand.

7. Set the depth gage to prevent the drill from cutting the jig, the template, the clamps, or the table. Use a hardwood block on the drill table if the stock is light gage.

8. Without turning on the power, bring the drill down to the work to see that the center-punch mark, pilot hole, or guide hole is centered directly under the drill.

9. Make adjustments for proper spindle speeds. The highest speed that will maintain drilling efficiency should be used. As a general rule, the softer the work, the higher the speed. When using small drills for aircraft work, it is better to lean toward too much speed rather than toward not enough.

10. Set the feed adjustment or adjust the hand-feed lever for convenience. Use a light or a slow feed if you are not sure of the proper feed setting.

11. For starting the drill, turn on the power and then bring the drill slowly down to the work by hand feed until you are sure that it is centered. Experience is required for the most efficient use of speeds and feeds. The drill should show signs of clean cutting immediately. Take it easy until you see how it is going, and keep your hand on the feeding lever.

12. When drilling thick stock, if the hole is rough or irregular, recheck the drill for proper grinding.

13. Try to maintain a continuous, compactly rolled chip curl, as this will aid in chip clearance, but feeding too fast is apt to result in hogging or in drill breakage. Never remove chips by hand or with air pressure.

14. Turn on pressure lubrication on heavy stock when required. In any event, lubricate the drill frequently with oil either during or between drilling operations.

15. When successive holes are being drilled and it is necessary to shift clamps or hold-down devices, turn off the power each time the position of the work is shifted on the drill table.

16. Remove burrs by hand, using an oversize drill.

17. When drilling operations are completed, remove and return the drill to proper place. Clean the cutting compound and the chips off the drill table. An expert airplane mechanic is neat and orderly.

Why Drills Break.—Beginners in sheetmetal work often break a number of drills before they learn to handle a drill properly. The drill is brittle; and because it turns rapidly for most aircraft sheetmetal work, it will break if undue strain is put upon it.

Drills break for several reasons. They may be pushed through a sheet with so much pressure that the point strikes a hard object at an angle on the opposite side. Failure to center the work or an incorrect drilling angle puts strain on the drill, especially if a template or a jig is being used. Drills may be broken if a drill that is too large is forced through the hole in a drill template or jig. Any play or spring between the spindle and the setup on the drill table is likely to cause breakage.

One of the most common causes of broken drills is improper grinding. If the lip clearance angle is not correct, the edges of the cutting lips may break down because of insufficient support. If the drill has insufficient lip clearance, there may cease to be any cutting edge and as a result the drill may split up the center. There is also a tendency on the part of an inexperienced drill-press operator to apply excessive feeding pressure on a dull drill.

A First Aid for Drill-press Operators*

Symptoms	Probable cause	Remedy
Breaking of drill	Spring or back lash in press or work. Too little lip clearance. Too low speed in proportion to the feed. Dull drill	Test press and work for rigidity and alignment. Regrind properly. Increase speed or decrease feed. Sharpen drill
Breaking down of outer corners of cutting edges	Material being drilled has hard spots, scale, or sand inclusions. Too much speed. Improper cutting compound. No lubricant at point of drill	Reduce speed. Use proper cutting compound and correct application
Breaking of drill when drilling brass or wood	Chips clog up flutes	Increase speed. Use drills designed for these materials
Broken tang	Imperfect fit of taper shank in the socket—due to nicks, dirt, burrs, or worn-out socket	Get a new socket or ream old one to prevent recurrence
Chipping of margin	Oversize jig bushing	Use proper size bushing
Chipping of lip or cutting edges	Too much feed. Too much lip clearance	Reduce feed. Regrind properly
Chipping or checking of a high-speed drill	Heated and cooled too quickly while grinding or while drilling. Too much feed	Warm slowly before using. Do not throw cold water on hot drill while grinding or drilling. Reduce feed
Hole too large	Unequal angle or length of the cutting edges or both. Loose spindle	Regrind properly. Test spindle for rigidity
Only one lip cutting	Unequal length or angle of cutting lips or both	Regrind drill properly
Splitting up center	Too little lip clearance. Too much feed	Regrind with proper lip clearance. Reduce feed
Rough hole	Dull or improperly ground drill. Lack of lubricant or wrong lubricant. Improper setup. Too much feed	Regrind properly. Lubricate or change lubricant. Reduce feed

* Courtesy of the Cleveland Twist Drill Co.

BURRING

The process of removing metal burrs from a sheet or a part after drilling is known as *burring*. Small burrs or chips usually adhere to the far edges of holes drilled in metal parts. This is a regular occurrence when drilling aluminum alloys. The burr must be removed to ensure proper joining or fitting on assembly.

Burring can be easily accomplished on the softer metals by placing a twist drill several sizes larger than the drilled hole and simply twisting it by hand. Only drills that are ground to a fairly flat point should be used. Care must be taken that the burring drill is perpendicular to the work and that it is turned in a clockwise direction. Only slight pressure is required, and one revolution is usually sufficient. *Avoid cutting into the stock.*

The squared-off tip of a fine file may also be used for burring, but care must be exercised to avoid scratching the surrounding surface.

Burrs can be eliminated during drilling whenever it is possible to clamp a piece of scrap metal as a backing plate against the part being drilled. The drill is then run through the work and through the back plate. It will be found that the burr occurs only on the scrap-metal back plate if the pieces have been tightly clamped.

DRILL GRINDING

All airplane mechanics must be able to sharpen a drill properly. Electric bench-type and pedestal grinders are located at accessible points in most factories to enable the mechanic to renew the drill points quickly when drills become dull or broken. Sharpening is best accomplished on the face of a smooth emery wheel. If the emery wheel is grooved or chipped, it can be refaced by using a refacing tool. If this is necessary, the operator should wear goggles even though the grinder may be equipped with an eye shield. The precaution of wearing goggles cannot be overemphasized, since there is great danger from emery chips and dust during this operation.

The side of an emery wheel can also be used for sharpening drills and is often preferred by mechanics, since it generally offers a smoother surface. The tool rest, however, cannot be readily used for this work at the side of the wheel; it is safer to use the face of the wheel.

A broken drill usually splinters raggedly, and it is necessary to grind off the broken portion so that it is square with the shank before attempting to resharpen the tip. This can be quickly accomplished on the rough emery wheel. The actual sharpening should be done on the fine emery wheel.

Three major points must be considered in grinding a drill:

1. To make the cutting lips the same length.
2. To provide proper lip clearance.
3. To make the angle of the cutting lips in proper relation to the longitudinal axis of the drill.

How To Grind a Drill

1. In grinding a drill, the mechanic should hold the drill shank in his right hand and support the point end with his left hand resting on the tool rest. The cutting edge should be placed in a nearly horizontal plane and parallel to the face of the grinding wheel. In this position the drill will form an angle of about 60 deg. with the face of the wheel. The right hand should be slightly lower than the left hand.

2. The cutting edge is then pressed lightly against the face of the wheel, and the shank end is moved downward in a slightly curving motion. Do not twist the drill during this operation but maintain the pivot with your left hand.

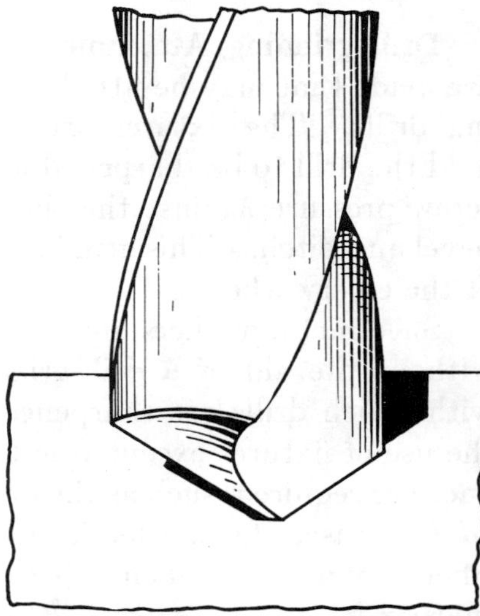

Fig. 102.—This shows a drill that has been ground incorrectly. The angles of the lips are equal, but their lengths are different. Here the hole is larger than the drill and the interior surfaces will be scored.

3. The direction of grinding should be from the cutting edge toward the heel, that is, on the downstroke only. As the drill is brought up from each cutting stroke, it should not be raised above a horizontal position to prevent the pitch or clearance from becoming too shallow. The grinding should be continued only long enough to renew the cutting edges and angled clearance. Excessive grinding is needless.

4. Care should be taken to avoid overheating the drill during grinding. This precaution is essential when carbon drills are ground. Using only light pressure against the emery wheel and the frequent immersing of the drill in the water pot will prevent burning the drill tip. Burning can be detected by the discoloring or turning blue of the drill tip. When a drill is burned, it loses its

hardness, or temper, and consequently its usefulness as a production tool, unless the burned area is ground away. High-speed drills should never be dipped in water to cool them during grinding, as this is very likely to crack the lips.

5. The grinding of both cutting lips should progress together. Don't grind too much off one lip before starting on the other. The grinding should be continued alternately until both lips are ground to an equal, accurate, and smooth finish.

Drill-grinding Attachments.—Fixtures known as *drill holders* are made that may be fitted to grinding wheels for use in sharpening drills. The fixtures are attached to the grinding rest and hold the drill to be sharpened in a viselike grip by means of thumbscrew pressure against the shank. They are adjustable for both bevel and pitch. This grinding is usually accomplished at the side of the emery wheel

Sheetmetal workers must know how to sharpen drills, however, without the aid of a drill-grinding attachment. The frequency with which drills are sharpened for production riveting prohibits the use of fixtures except where extreme accuracy and close tolerance are required, such as the drilling of forged or extruded fittings. In any case, the mechanic will be able to handle a drill more efficiently and tell when it is cutting properly if he knows how to sharpen it.

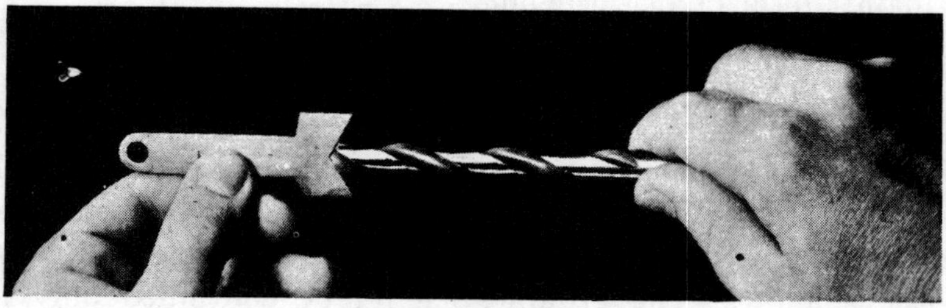

FIG. 103.—A gage of the type shown may be used to determine the correct angle of the lips after the drill has been ground.

Checking Drill Tips.—Lip clearance for general work should be from 12 to 15 deg., the smaller angle being for hard metals and the 15 deg. angle for the light dural. This angle may be checked by using a drill gage (see Fig. 103), or a gage may be improvised by using a rectangular sheet of paper 3 by 8½ in. Place a mark on the margin of the left end of the strip 1¾ in. from the lower side.

Fold the strip around the drill with its right upper corner on the marginal mark. Then compare the clearance angle with the diagonal formed by the edge of the strip. A clearance angle under 12 deg. will result in possible breakage, whereas an angle over 15 deg. may result in chipping of the leading edges. The length of the cutting edges must be the same. The angle of the cutting edges may also be checked with a protractor or a drill-grinding gage.

Review Questions

1. Describe the parts of a twist drill.

2. Distinguish between carbon drills and high-speed drills.

3. What is the largest size drill that should be used in a ½ in. drill press?

4. What is a chuck and what purpose does it serve?

5. What is a gang drill?

6. Give four methods of securing work to the table of a drill press.

7. How is a drill template used to speed production work?

8. Give four reasons for the use of pilot holes when drilling.

9. Name three attachments that may be used for drilling deep, blind, or angular holes.

10. How do you distinguish between different drill sizes?

11. What number drills are generally used for the following size of holes: ½; ⅜; ¼; $\frac{3}{16}$; ⅛? Give the decimal equivalent of the following size drills: No. 30, No. 50, No. 10.

12. Is it necessary to lubricate a drill when working with aluminum-alloy sheet?

13. Why is burring an important operation? How is burring performed?

14. List the precautions you would take before using a portable drill.

15. Can bent drills be salvaged?

16. What are some of the common errors made by beginning drillers?

17. State three common causes of drill breakage.

18. When must goggles be worn during drilling?

19. When the drill point penetrates the far side of the metal is the drill immediately withdrawn?

20. In drilling small parts on a drill press, is it permissible to hold the work in your hand?

21. What may be the cause of breaking down the outer corners of the cutting edges of a drill?

22. If drilled holes are found to be too large, what may be the trouble?

23. Are cutting lips on a perfectly ground drill the same length?

24. What causes a drilled hole to be rough and irregular?

25. Describe how to grind a drill.

Shop Work

Drilling is a skill that requires considerable practice. It is suggested that aluminum-alloy sheet, properly secured in a vise, be used for drilling practice. Rivet and bolt holes of various sizes should be marked and drilled until the student can do a clean, accurate job. All the projects of Chap. 15 call for drilling, but the student should have some preliminary practice before starting on the projects.

CHAPTER 11

HOW TO RIVET

Every sheetmetal mechanic should be a skilled riveter. The fact that there are 78,000 rivets in a Curtiss P-40, over 130,000 in a Martin bomber, and about 250,000 in a Flying Fortress is an indication of how important riveting is in modern airplane plants. A glance at even the exterior of any all-metal airplane will disclose the thousands of rivets of different types that are used.

Airplane structures are welded together by various methods, but the most common means of joining aluminum-alloy sheets is by riveting. In addition to the riveted skin, rivets are also used for joining spar sections, for holding ribs in place, for securing dural fittings to various parts of the airplane, and for fastening innumerable bracing members and other parts together. Rivets are installed both by portable hand-tool methods and by powered stationary riveting devices.

KINDS OF RIVETS

Rivets are classified by their *head shape*, by the *material* of which they are made, and by their *size*. Types of rivet heads will be explained first. The four most common types are *round head*, *brazier head*, *flat head*, and *flush or countersunk head*. They are shown in Fig. 104.

The choice of rivet head depends upon the part of the airplane that is being riveted. On external parts, where the least possible resistance is desired, *countersunk* or *flush*-type rivets are used. In appearance, the head is similar to that of a flat wood screw without the slot. On some airplanes, all external surfaces are flush-riveted. Others use flush rivets only on the leading edge of the wings. On wing surfaces, control surfaces, and fuselages, where flush rivets are not used, brazier heads are installed. Next to flush rivets, they have less area protruding than any other type. A variety known as *shallow brazier-head rivets* has even less exposed area than the regular brazier-head type. Round heads are seldom used externally, because of their large heads. The trend in combat and transport planes is definitely to the flush rivets because they offer less parasite drag than other rivets. Flat heads are not used except for the riveting of internal parts. As indicated in Fig. 104, their flat head is unlike the flat head of a wood screw, as the top of the rivet head is raised above the surface and resembles the formed head made on rivet shanks during the riveting process.

A number of different types of rivets may be used in the fabrication of a single airplane. Their selection is based on their strength and working or driving properties. For example, 2S and

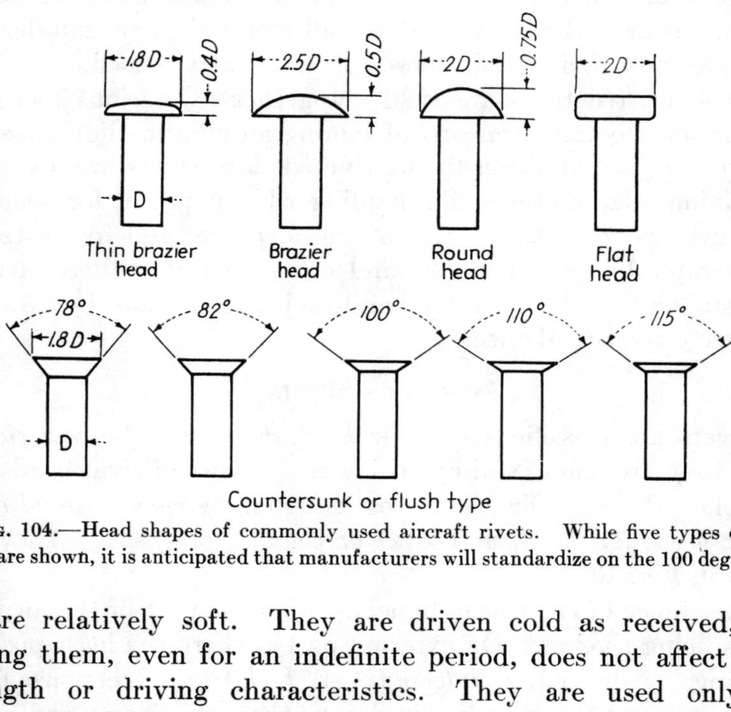

FIG. 104.—Head shapes of commonly used aircraft rivets. While five types of flush rivets are shown, it is anticipated that manufacturers will standardize on the 100 deg. head.

3S are relatively soft. They are driven cold as received, and storing them, even for an indefinite period, does not affect their strength or driving characteristics. They are used only for nonstructural parts that are lightly stressed, such as for the riveting of pyralin or Plexiglas windshield frames and other parts on which great stress is not applied.

Two commonly used rivets are 17S and 17S-T. The "T" in the identification symbol indicates that the rivet has been fully heat-treated. Rivets of 17S must always be heat-treated to obtain maximum strength. Rivets of 17S-T reach the aircraft factory in a fully hardened state. They are too hard to work with easily, and they must be re-heat-treated, or annealed, in the factory before being used. Heat-treatment consists of holding the rivets at a temperature of 930 to 950°F. for 5 to 30 min., depending on the size and quantity. Rivets are then quenched in cold water. The heating is done in an electric or a gas furnace, and a pyrometer is used to indicate furnace temperature.

Rivets of this type either must be used within 15 or 20 min. after heat-treating or must be stored in refrigerators. The refrigeration process keeps them soft. They are commonly called *icebox rivets.* If not kept in a refrigerator they gradually harden in room temperature, reaching their full strength about four days after being driven.

Where strength higher than that of 17S-T is required, 24S-T rivets are used. Driven immediately after being heated to a temperature range of 910 to 930°F. and then quenched, they develop their ultimate shear strength in about 1 day. Since the rate of age hardening of 24S-T rivets is more rapid than that of 17S-T rivets, it is necessary to drive them sooner after quenching. Ideally they should be driven within 5 min. of the time that they are quenched. In actual practice they are put immediately into refrigerators or dry-ice containers and stored until used. At temperatures of $-50°$ rivets remain soft enough for driving for a period of several weeks.

Rivets of A17S-T (designated as AD, or dimple head, in the rivet code on page 58) are always furnished in the heat-treated condition. They require no further preparation and are driven in the as-received condition. They are used principally as a substitute for 17S rivets. The strength of A17S-T rivets is not so great as that of 17S rivets that are heat-treated in the aircraft factory, but they are so nearly alike that they have been found satisfactory for most aircraft work. Their use eliminates the heat-treating and cold-storage processes. They can be stored indefinitely with no change of properties. They drive as easily as 17S-T rivets and more easily than 24S-T rivets.

To guard against the use of nonheat-treated material, 17S rivets are sometimes ordered in the fully heat-treated condition, 17S-T. If some of these escape reheat treatment, they can be detected immediately by the fact that they can be driven only with difficulty.

Rivets of 53S-W and 53S-T are increasingly popular for certain types of construction. They do not require heat-treating in the aircraft factory. The 53S-T rivets are simply 53S-W rivets that have been aged for about 6 hr. at 355°F. They are stronger than 53S-W rivets but are somewhat harder to drive; consequently they are not used so frequently as 53S-W. The 53S-T type can be stored indefinitely at room temperature without change in strength or driving characteristics, but the 53S-W type becomes

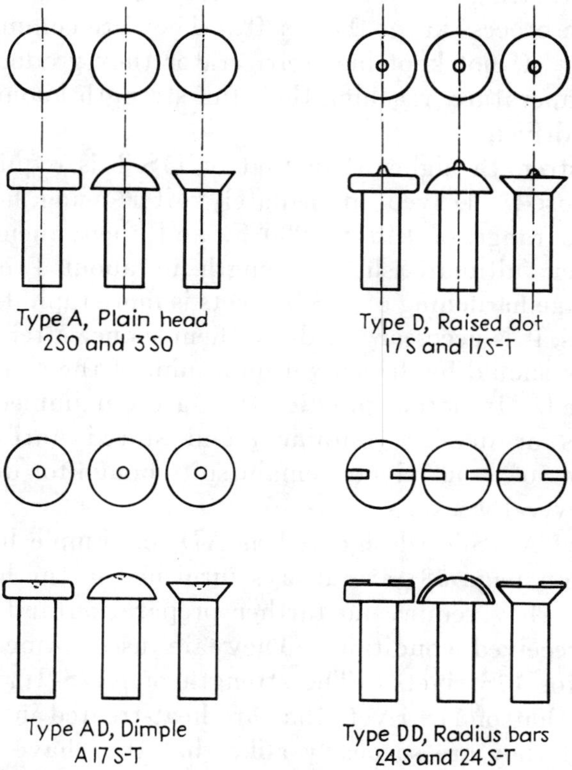

FIG. 105.—Identification marks on the heads of the four most commonly used rivet alloys.

hard after several months. Their ease of driving can be restored by heat-treating, temperatures being in the range of 960 to 980°F. Rivets of 53S-W and 53S-T have excellent properties and are better in this respect than 17S-T, 24S-T, or A17S-T rivets.

Identification of Rivets.—Riveters working in a factory must be able to identify rivets so that the proper rivet will be used. It is easy to distinguish among the various types of heads, but a special system had to be worked out to tell the kind of alloy.

In addition to the rivet code, printed on page 58, every airplane mechanic must be familiar with the identifying symbols on rivet heads. Regardless of the type of rivet head the symbols shown in Fig. 105 are in use.

Rivet Sizes.—The size of rivets to be used is specified by the engineers, and the mechanic must follow directions carefully. Rivets that may be quite satisfactory for one part are often unsatisfactory for another part.

All rivets except flush rivets are measured from the lower side of the head to the extreme end of the shank. Flush rivets are measured from the top of the head to the end of the shank. For most aircraft construction the range in length is from 1/8 to 2 in. Diameters of rivet shanks range in size from 1/16 in., which are used for instruments and delicate parts, to 1/2 in., used on plate stock of heavy bombers. For automatic riveting, the rivets used have a shank with an end that is slightly rounded for more rapid insertion. They are known as *chamfered shanks.*

In general when a large-diameter rivet is used in thin sheet, the pressure required to drive the rivet frequently causes an undesirable bulging of the thin material around the rivet head. The diameter of the rivet shank, therefore, should not exceed two and one-half to three times the thickness of the sheet being riveted. On the other hand, the rivet should not be smaller in diameter than the thickest sheet through which it is driven. Where possible, rivets having about the same properties as the parts being riveted should be used.

Rivet Spacing.—The spacing of rivets depends upon the thickness of the sheets being joined and upon the amount of stress that they will receive. Three times the rivet diameter is the minimum spacing. Rivets should not be placed closer to the edge of the material than twice the diameter of the rivet hole. Rivets that are too close to the edge tend to bulge the sheet. If they are too far from the edge, the sheet may curl or dish up. The mechanic should follow the rivet spacing exactly as indicated on the blueprints.

Rivet Holes.—Holes for rivets can be laid out and drilled or punched before or during assembly. If the holes are made before assembly, the process is known as *predrilling*. Small pilot holes may be made before assembly, then reamed to proper size with a larger drill during assembly so that the holes in the two sheets will exactly coincide. Rivets should fit snugly. The best clearance is the smallest one that will permit the rivet to be inserted

FIG. 106.—After rivets are heat-treated in an airplane factory they are stored in refrigerators until used. These are dry-ice containers in the Boeing plant. Each container is kept stocked with various types and sizes.

easily and without delay. If rivets are too loose, they are apt to shear or to cause eccentrically shaped heads when driven.

As the chapters on drilling and jigs emphasize, production assembly work is speeded if as many rivet holes as possible are predrilled.

The following table of drill sizes has almost become a national standard in aircraft factories, but the mechanic should consult his leadman or carefully check the blueprints before any drilling is started.

Drill-size No.	Decimal equivalent of drill No., inches	Common rivet sizes, inches
50	0.0700	1/16
40	0.0980	3/32
30	0.1285	1/8
21	0.1590	5/32
12	0.1890	3/16

RIVETING PROCEDURE

There are several methods of riveting, but regardless of the equipment used the effect is the same. The rivet is originally

FIG. 107.—A bucking bar, shown at the right, is held firmly against the shank of the rivet. The die or set of the riveting gun is pushed against the rivet head. The gunner then exerts pressure on the trigger and starts riveting. On small parts one man is able to both drive and buck rivets.

made with one head, and in the riveting process a second head is formed on the shank. This is accomplished by the hammering pressure of a die placed against the head while a heavy bucking, or dolly bar is held against the shank. The vibration from the blows on the head cause the shank to become flattened.

In starting a riveting job the parts to be fastened together are held by clamps, sheetmetal screws, speed fasteners, or machine screws or by clamping in a smooth-jawed vise. If the parts have not been predrilled, rivet holes may now be drilled or reamed to size if they have pilot holes. If drilling is necessary, the parts should be removed later from the temporary clamping and the chips and burrs cleaned from around the holes. The means of clamping should then be replaced. Rivet holes tend to get out of alignment during the driving operation because of slippage, swelling, or stretching of the metal. For this reason the work should be firmly assembled before the driving is started. The temporary fasteners should not mar the metal parts but should be tight enough to prevent the rivets from squeezing out, or flashing, between the parts of the joint.

The vast majority of rivets are driven by portable, pneumatic riveting hammers, commonly called *riveting guns*. These are fitted with dies of various sizes, to accommodate the different sizes and types of rivets. For driving flush rivets the driving end of the die is flat, but dies used for other rivet-head types are indented to fit over the rivet head.

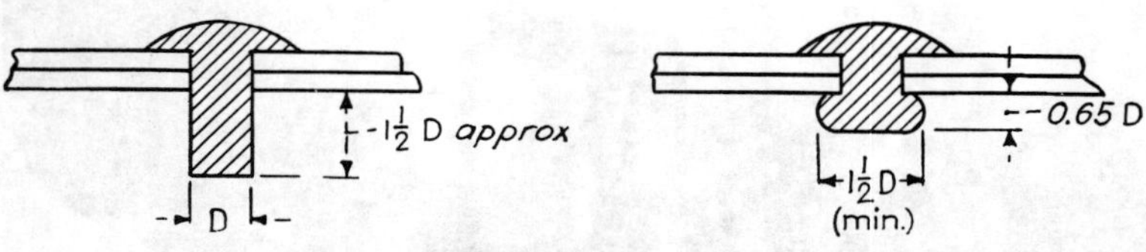

FIG. 108.—A rivet before and after being driven.

The first step is to put the rivet in the hole, pushed down so that the head is tightly against the sheet. It is important that the sheets be held firmly together in the immediate area of the rivet. If there is a tendency for the sheets to bulge apart, it is common practice for the bucker to hold the bucking bar against his sheet alongside the rivet shank. At the same time the riveting gun is pushed against the rivet head. When the rivet is pushed into proper position, the bucking bar is held firmly and squarely against the protruding rivet shank, as shown in Fig. 107. While the bucking bar is in this position, the die in the rivet gun must rest in a similar position on the head of the rivet. The gunner then exerts pressure on the trigger and starts driving. A small, flat head is formed on the rivet shank under the bucking iron because of the hammering of the gun on the original head of the rivet. The bucker removes the bar and examines the new head, which should be one and one-half times the original diameter of the rivet shank in width and about one-half the diameter of the original shank in height (see Fig. 108). If the head thus formed is narrower and higher than the dimensions given, more driving is necessary. If it is wider and shallower, it must be removed and replaced.

It is important that the rivet die and the bucking bar be held in a straight line, or the head may not form evenly. Both rivet heads should be tight against the work when the rivet is completed.

FIG. 109.—A group of bucking bars or bucking dollies. Different shapes are required for different locations. The end of the bar that forms the rivet head must be polished and have slightly chamfered edges to prevent marring the work.

The bucking dolly, or bucking iron, is made of steel. Its size and shape depend on the size of the rivets being headed and the space available for holding the dolly. A piece of inch-square cold-rolled-steel bar stock is generally used. The end that is held against the rivet shank should be flat and smooth and have rounded corners to prevent marring the material. Dolly bars of several shapes are available in aircraft factories to permit the mechanic doing the bucking to reach into various spaces.

Riveting Devices.—Several types of pneumatic riveting guns and compression riveting machines are in general use. All of them work on the same general principle. The one-shot gun, the slow-hitting hammer, the vibrating hammer, and the squeeze-type

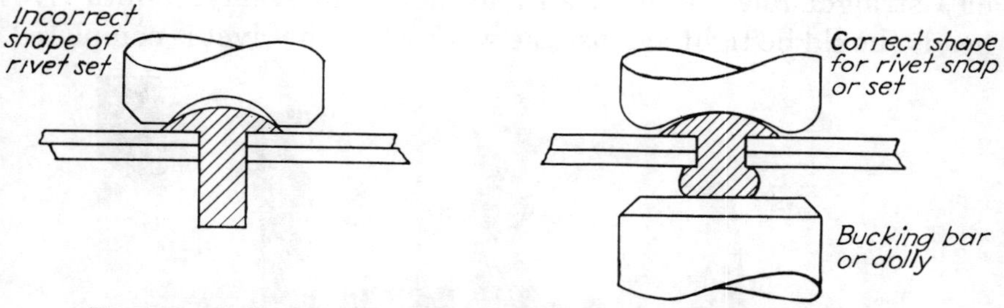

FIG. 110.—A rivet set must conform to the type of rivet head being used.

riveter are all used both as portable riveting tools or as fixed riveting machines. Both large and small parts, including subassemblies, can be riveted by one man if a fixed, or stationary,

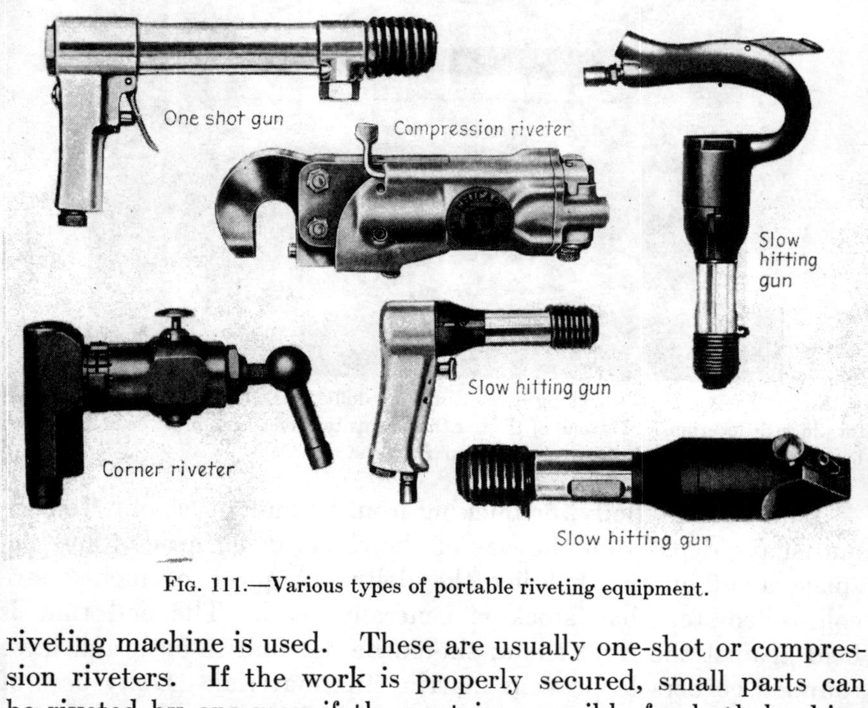

FIG. 111.—Various types of portable riveting equipment.

riveting machine is used. These are usually one-shot or compression riveters. If the work is properly secured, small parts can be riveted by one man if the part is accessible for both bucking and riveting. The greater part of riveted work, however, requires a two-man team, composed of one riveter, or gunner, and one bucker. For example, in fuselage construction, the gunner works on the outside and the bucker works on the inside.

The size of the gun used for a particular job depends upon the size of the rivets being driven and the accessibility of the rivet. The larger the rivet, the greater the air pressure that is required. Air pressure reaches the gun through a long, flexible rubber hose. An air regulator is usually fitted to the handle of the gun. Approximate air pressures for four of the most common rivet sizes are given in the table below. Conditions may vary slightly with different alloys.

Approximate Air Pressure for Rivet Guns

Rivet Size	Air Pressure, Pounds Per Square Inch
3/32	25
1/8	40
5/32	60
3/16	90

One-shot Gun.—The one-shot gun is designed to drive the rivet with just one blow. It is a larger and heavier gun than other types and is generally used for heavy riveting. The trigger must be depressed for each action of the gun. It is sometimes difficult to control when being used for riveting light-gage materials. Under suitable conditions it is the fastest method of riveting.

Slow-hitting Gun.—This gun strikes several blows to form the rivet. It is widely used for driving medium-sized rivets and can be well controlled. The die continues to strike the rivet head as long as the trigger is depressed.

Fast-hitting or Vibrating Hammer.—This hammer heads the rivet with a number of comparatively lightweight blows. Like the slow-hitting hammer it continues to strike the head while the trigger is depressed. It is generally used with the softer rivets. It strikes about 5,000 blows per minute.

Corner Riveter.—This is so named because it can be used in corners and in close quarters where there is not enough space for a vibrator. The chief difference between this hammer and the other types described lies in the fact that in this type the die is set at right angles to the gun. Blows are short and light.

Compression Riveters.—The compression riveter differs in action from the riveting guns in that it forms the rivet head by means of squeezing or compression instead of distinct blows. Once it is adjusted for a particular type of work, it will form rivet heads of much greater uniformity than the riveting hammers. It is made both as a portable unit and as a stationary riveting machine. As a portable unit it is larger and more unwieldy than

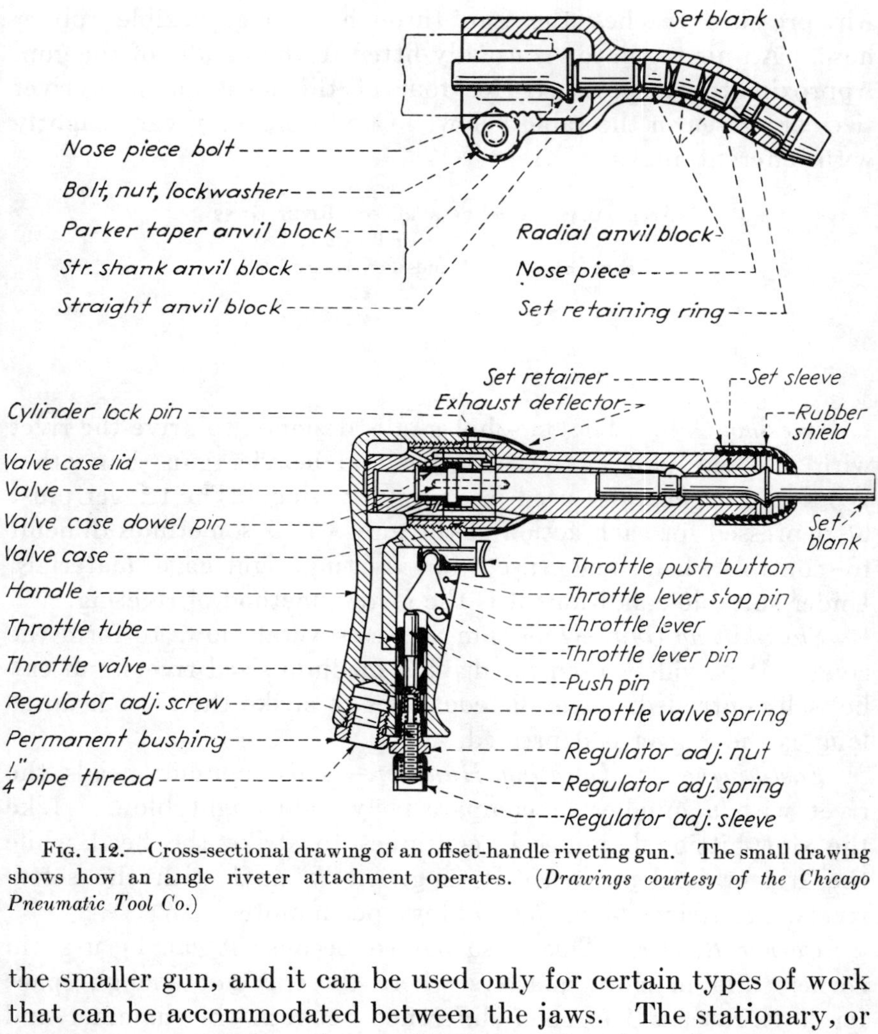

FIG. 112.—Cross-sectional drawing of an offset-handle riveting gun. The small drawing shows how an angle riveter attachment operates. (*Drawings courtesy of the Chicago Pneumatic Tool Co.*)

the smaller gun, and it can be used only for certain types of work that can be accommodated between the jaws. The stationary, or fixed jaw, containing the anvil die, is placed against the head of the rivet. Compression riveters may be fitted with dimpling dies and used for dimpling the material in preparation for flush riveting.

Handles.—Several styles of handle are in popular use on riveting guns. The names differ slightly with different manu-

Fig. 113.—A portable compression riveter is here being used in riveting the trailing edge of an American Airlines DC-3. (*Photograph by Independent Pneumatic Tool Co.*)

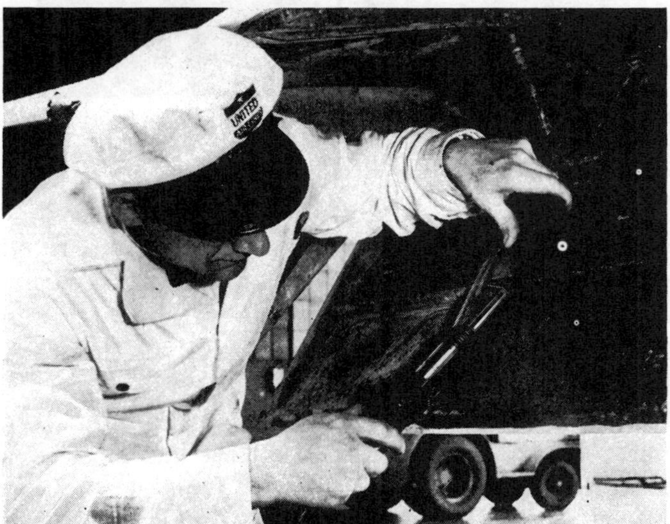

Fig. 114.—A Thor pneumatic riveting hammer in use. The mechanic does both riveting and bucking. A bent-angle rivet die is in this gun.

facturers, but the more commonly used types are the pistol grip, the offset handle, the revolver, and the push button. A lever, trigger, or push button is used to operate the gun. The control may be depressed either by the thumb or by the index finger.

Fig. 115.—A slow-hitting hammer of the push-button type is being used in riveting the stiffener on the web of a Martin wing spar. It is the responsibility of the riveter to insert the rivets and signal the bucker when he is ready to drive.

Rivet Dies or Sets.—As previously pointed out, riveting guns have removable dies so that several types of dies can be used with the same gun. Dies are held in the gun by a retaining spring which is unscrewed to remove the die. Rivet sets used for the same size rivet are manufactured in several different lengths. The choice of the proper length to use depends upon the driving conditions. Where it is possible to get the gun close to the work, a short, straight set is most efficient. Long sets are sometimes necessary when the gun cannot be brought close to the work because of structural interference. The offset die is a bent-rivet set and may be obtained in several different angles. It is used for corner riveting and to reach rivets that are inaccessible to a straight die.

Flush sets are different from other rivet sets in that they have flat or convex ends. Edges are also rounded slightly to prevent marring the material. One type of flush set is known as the *mushroom set*. It is bell-shaped at the driving end so that it is considerably larger than the rivet head. A swiveling device is sometimes used with a flush set to permit greater freedom of action for restricted driving conditions.

FIG. 116.—A riveting team driving flat-head rivets with a one-shot gun at the Martin plant.

Hand rivet sets are used to a limited extent where pneumatic riveting hammers are not practicable or where greater accuracy is desired than can be obtained by power tools. They are made to be driven with a hammer. The rivet set has a concave die as well as a hole drilled in the same end to fit the diameter of the rivet shank in order to act as a draw set in pulling the material together before riveting.

Rivet sets should be kept clean and should be recut or replaced when worn. The cupped end should be slightly larger in its concave diameter than the curve forming the head of the rivet. If it is smaller, it will tend to make a ring around the head of the rivet. The edges of the die should be slightly rounded to prevent marring the metal around the rivet.

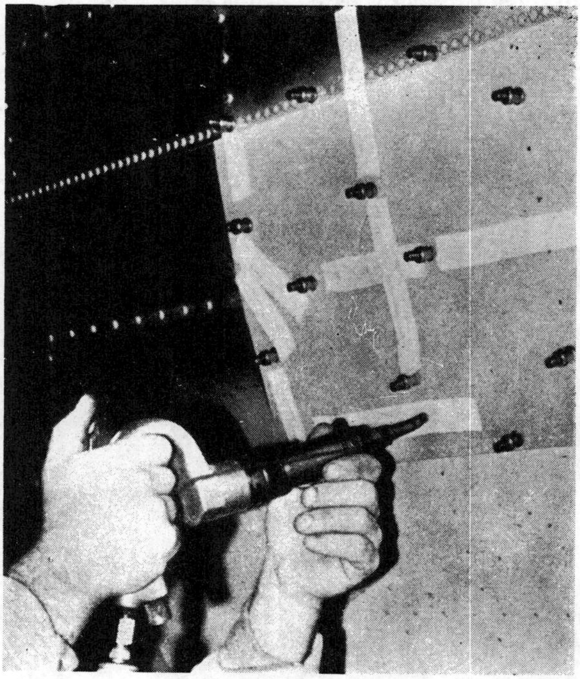

FIG. 117.—Rivets will often fall out of rivet holes unless held in place by masking tape or commercial-grade adhesive tape. The tape also helps to keep the skin from being marred by the die in the gun. Cleco skin fasteners hold the sheet in place until the rivets are driven.

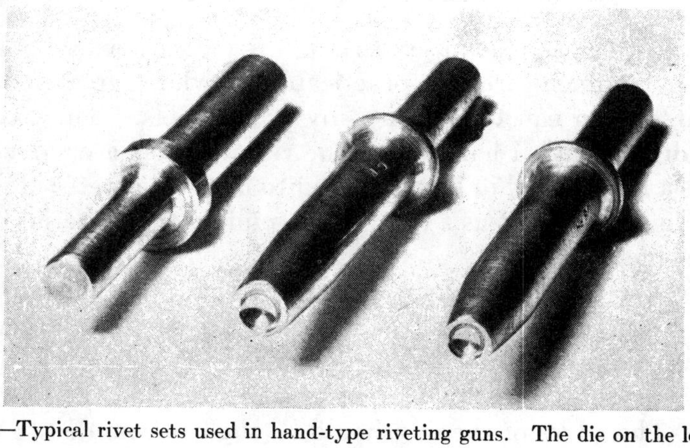

FIG. 118.—Typical rivet sets used in hand-type riveting guns. The die on the left is for flush rivets.

Masking tape or commercial adhesive tape is often put over the end of the rivet set to protect the rivet.

Flush Riveting.—Because of the demand for increased speed being placed upon all combat airplanes, engineers have overcome drag wherever possible by using flush rivets in exterior surfaces. Flush rivets are more difficult to install, since the parts being riveted must be either dimpled or countersunk, which is one extra operation following drilling. An additional hazard is the close proximity of the rivet die to the material during riveting. If considerable skill is not used, the material will be damaged by the

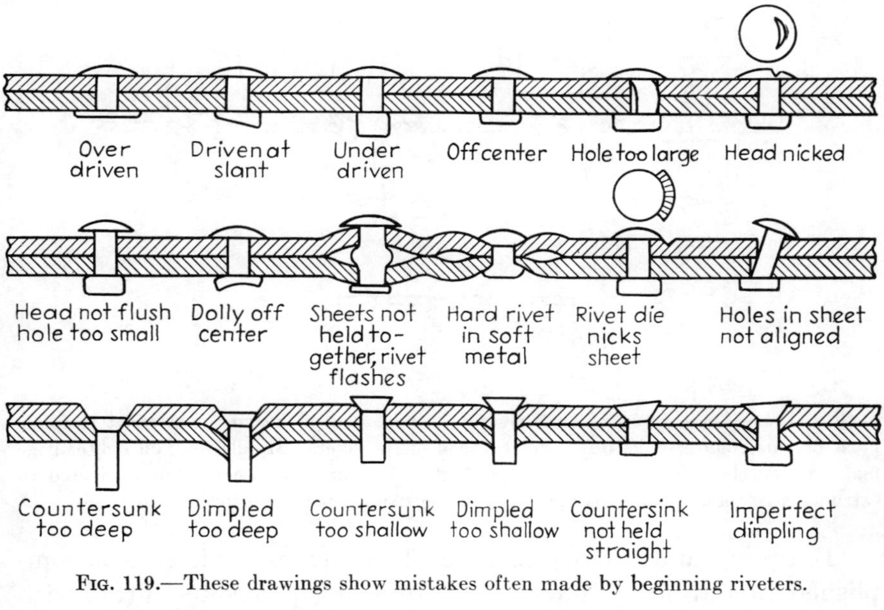

FIG. 119.—These drawings show mistakes often made by beginning riveters.

die. Flush rivets are made with heads of several different angles. The industry is standardizing on the 100 deg. rivet, but rivets of 78, 115, and 120 deg. are also used.

For heavy-gage sheet or extruded material the rivet hole is countersunk to afford a stopperlike fit for the rivet. A countersinking tool has a cutting face beveled to the angle of the rivet head and is kept centered by a pilot shaft inserted in the rivet hole. A stopping device automatically acts as a depth gage so that the hole will not become too deep.

Where light-gage material is used, a depression, or dimple, is made around the hole by press countersinking in the sheet before assembly. The rivet is seated in this depression. Whenever possible, the sheet is dimpled rather than countersunk, as dimpling is considerably faster.

In both methods the assembly head of the rivet is formed in the same way with a bucking bar, and a smooth-faced die is used in the gun. Rows of rivets are inserted and held in place by masking tape or adhesive tape. The tape protects the sheet and also prevents rivets from falling out of the holes owing to vibration.

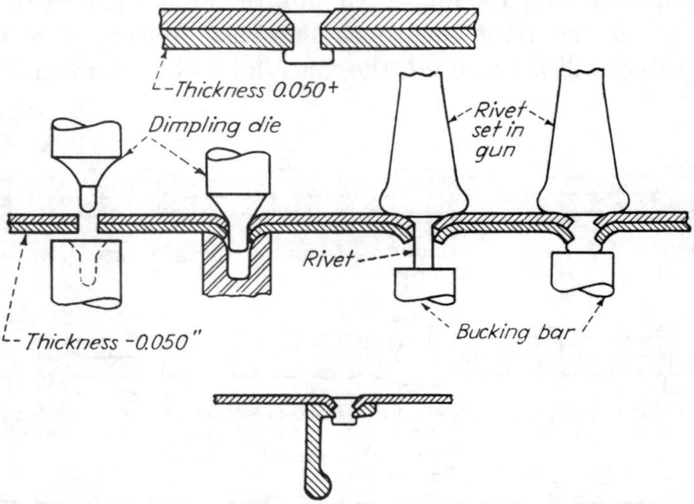

FIG. 120.—Three types of flush riveting. Top line: on heavier gage sheet the hole must first be countersunk to receive the head of the rivet. Middle row: on lighter gage material the sheet is dimpled before riveting. Bottom line: where skin is riveted to extruded stringers, the sheet is dimpled and the stringer is countersunk.

Dimpling and often punching of lighter gage sheet is accomplished on stationary, pneumatic, squeeze-type riveters fitted with dimpling dies. Some machines use the rivet itself as a dimpling die after the hole has been punched. This method can be used only if the sheet is less than 0.025 in. thick. Where riveted assemblies are readily portable, as many as eight or ten rivets can be driven at one time by a compression riveter equipped with a long flat die. The development of gang-riveting machines of this type has done much to further quantity production.

Automatic Riveting Machines.—Machines that produce riveting operations automatically are used wherever possible in production work. They produce more uniform riveting, five to ten times as fast as any other method. Without previous marking, holes are punched, the sheets dimpled, if for flush rivets, and the rivets inserted and headed, all automatically. Foot-operated

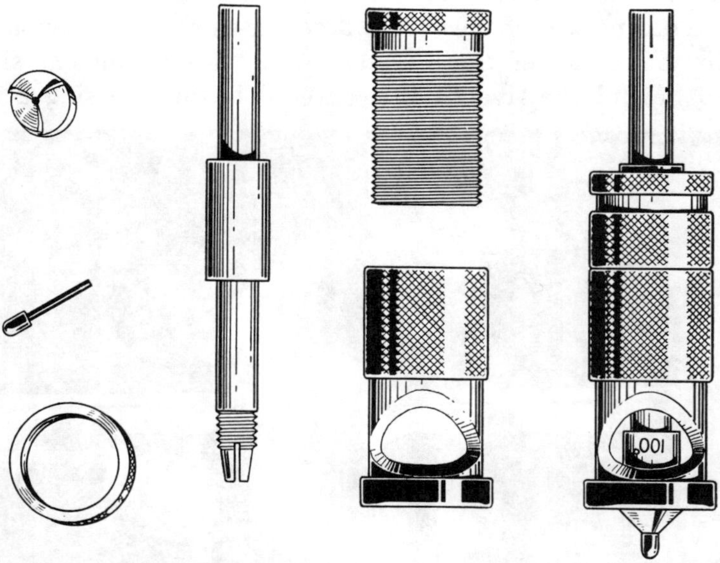

FIG. 121.—A stop countersink prevents the countersink from penetrating too far into the sheet.

lever controls permit the operator to keep his hands free to shift the parts being riveted (see Fig. 123).

Removing Rivets.—If, after close inspection, rivets show even the slightest deformity or lack of alignment, they must be removed and replaced. This is an unvarying law of aircraft sheetmetal

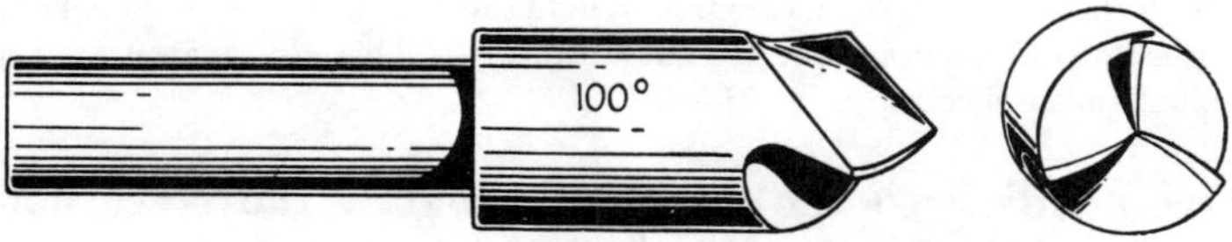

FIG. 122.—A 100 deg. spiral-fluted countersink.

construction. The drawings of Fig. 119 show several ways in which rivets have been incorrectly driven. Among the reasons for replacing rivets are the following: rivet marred by dolly bar or rivet set; rivet driven at slant, or shank bent over; rivet too short, causing head to be shallow; rivet pancaked too flat from overdriving; sheets spread apart, and rivet flashed between sheets; rivet driven too tightly, causing sheets to buckle; two rivet heads not in alignment; and head of countersunk rivet not flush with outside surface or driven below the surface.

To removed a damaged rivet a center-punch mark should be made in the *center* of the original head. A bucking bar should be used behind the rivet if the material is thin. Using a twist

FIG. 123.—An Erco automatic riveter in use at Vultee. On parts where this machine can be used it saves a great amount of time and labor. The machine is operated by a foot pedal and both the operator's hands are free to hold the work. Holes are punched through the sheets of metal and rivets are inserted automatically. This ensures accurate alignment. This machine handles sheet up to 96 in. wide.

drill corresponding to the size used to drill the rivet hole, the mechanic should drill through the head but no farther. A small drift punch is then inserted diagonally in the drilled hole, and the rivet head is knocked off when the drift punch is hit lightly with a hammer. The shank is then driven out by the drift punch.

Occasionally cold chisels of a width close to the diameter of the rivet are used to shear off the heads of rivets. If the chisel has had its corners ground off, the material will not be marred. While the head is being sheared off, the material should always be bucked up.

If during the removal of a rivet the skin is damaged, a mechanic must not insert a larger size of rivet without the permission of his supervisor and the Army or Navy inspector.

The removal of flush rivets requires slightly more skill. If the assembly head on the interior is accessible and has been formed

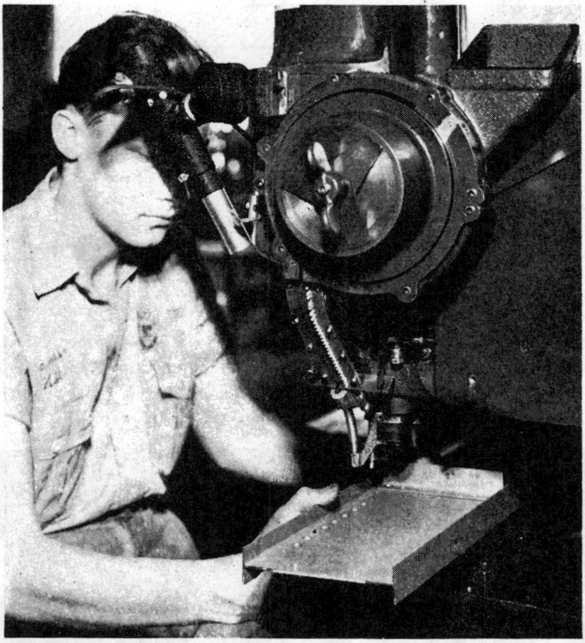

FIG. 124.—Another type of Erco punching and riveting machine, used by Glenn L. Martin Co. It is a deep, open-throat riveter which punches the hole, puts the rivet in place, and finally heads the rivet shank. Chamfered-shank rivets are used to make insertion easier.

over heavy material such as an extrusion, the formed head can be drilled through, as mentioned above, and then sheared off. If the material is thin, it may be necessary to drill completely through the shank of the rivet and then cut the assembly head with diagonal cutting pliers. Then the remainder of the rivet is drifted out from the inside.

GOOD RIVETING PRACTICE

Check your gun to make sure that the rivet set is the right size. If you pick up a gun that someone else has been using, the set may

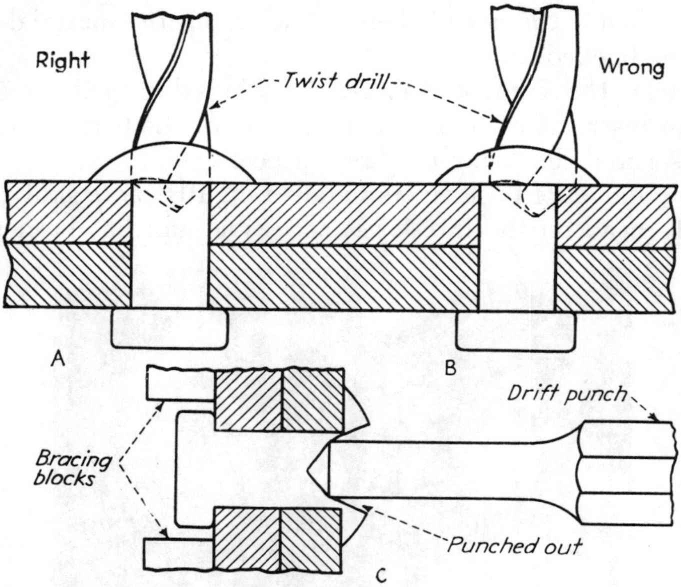

FIG. 125.—Steps in removing defective rivets. (*A*) Drill through head only. (*B*) Incorrect method; if drill is started off center due to inaccurate center punching, it tends to cut into the sheet. (*C*) Fragments of rivet head will shear off as shank is driven out with a drift punch.

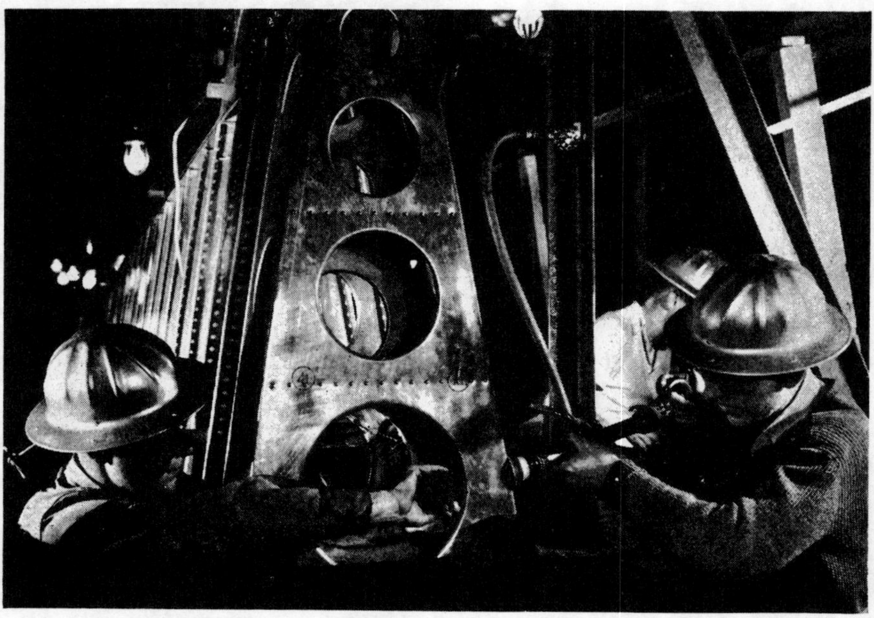

FIG. 126.—Douglas sheetmetal workers riveting an aileron section of the B-19 bomber. Note the heavy rivet gun being used and the rubber flange that protects the skin from the end of the rivet die.

be too large or too small for your purpose. Also check the adjusting screw on the gun to make certain that the pressure is right for your purpose. Remove your finger from the trigger as soon as a rivet is driven.

If two sheets of different thicknesses are being fastened together, the original head of the rivet is usually placed so that it will be next to the thinner sheet. The rivet is invariably inserted from the outside of the airplane when skin is being riveted. The bucking is done from the inside.

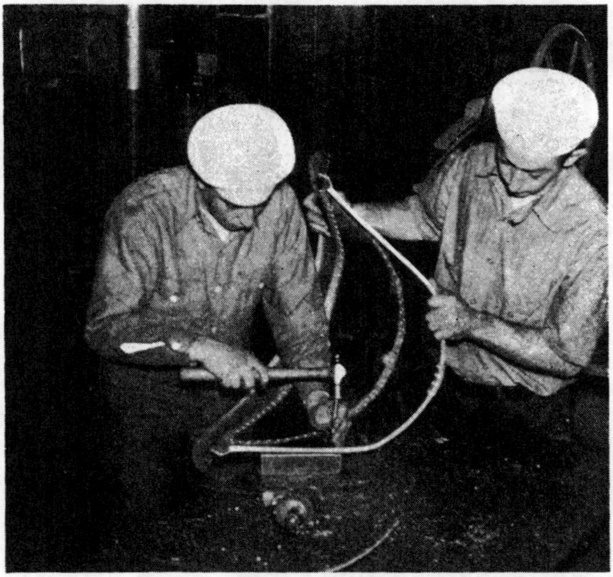

FIG. 127.—On parts that cannot be easily handled with rivet guns, hand rivet sets are used. The usual practice is to insert the rivet from below and head the shank with a concave hand die. The head is bucked by a metal block. These are enlisted men at the U. S. Naval Air Station, New York.

What the Bucker Does.—The rivet bucker has a job that may be more difficult than that of the riveter. He has to squirm around in small, interior surfaces. Often he must lie down, and holding the bucking iron in cramped quarters is often tiring. The first lesson that a bucker needs to learn is to hold the dolly bar tightly against the rivet. If the bucker does not work smoothly with his partner, whom he often cannot see, the heads of the rivets will not be formed properly. If the gunner drives a rivet when the bucking bar is not held tightly, the rivet set may be driven right through the sheet; or if not, the sheet may be seriously damaged.

Consequently, if the gunner drives a rivet too hard and the bucker sees that the formed head will be too flat, the bucker should not raise the bucking iron. The flat rivet head can be removed, and a new rivet inserted later.

The gunner needs to hold the gun tightly against the head of the rivet and not pull it away until he has released the trigger.

FIG. 128.—Every rivet is inspected. Inspector at upper right has a phano pencil and is encircling an imperfect rivet which must be replaced. Inspector on inside of nacelle is using a flashlight to examine formed rivet heads. Rivets that require further driving are marked with two parallel lines. This is the Douglas B-19.

Otherwise there will be marks on the rivet head, and the set may jump off. If the rivet is gunned too long, it may crystallize. Experience will bring a skill that enables you to make a formed head one and one-half times the diameter of the original shank. That is the correct size.

Watch for "oilcans" as you rivet. If the parts are not fitted together properly, there will be slight bulges between rivets. You can detect these by pushing lightly against the surface, and you can discover any feeling that is like the bottom of an oilcan. When learning to rivet, study each formed head, and make sure that you do not make heads like the incorrect ones in Fig. 119.

Keep the air hose clean and free from kinks. Do not put a riveting gun down in any position where it might fall.

Signals for Riveting Teams.—Success in athletics or in military maneuvers depends upon coordinated teamwork. To maintain

FIG. 129.—This is flush riveting on the Bell P-39 Airacobra fuselage. A mushroom-type rivet die is used in these slow-hitting hammers. Skin is being held temporarily in place with Cleco fasteners.

the high standard of efficiency required in aircraft riveting, good teamwork is also essential. It does not matter which side of the rivet you are on; the *gunner* and the *bucker* of the riveting team must work efficiently together without loss of motion or time.

Most aircraft riveting is carried on under conditions where it is impossible, because of noise or obstructions, for the gunner or the bucker to communicate with each other by verbal or visual means. Consequently sound signals must be used, which are transmitted by pressure or by tapping on the rivet with the bucking bar.

Riveting signals or codes are not standardized throughout the aircraft industry. They vary somewhat even in the same plant. They are generally originated and agreed upon by each riveting team.

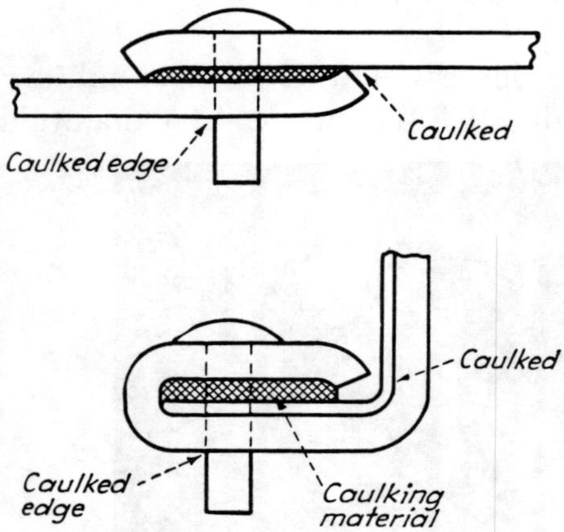

FIG. 130.—Gas- or liquidtight joints require a sealing medium such as rubber or Neoprene tape, Bakelite varnish, or soybean compound. Often rivets are driven wet with zinc chromate primer. In the above illustration the joint will become compressed when the rivets are driven.

The following signals are most frequently used; although some variations may occur, signals in general are based on this code:

One tap by bucker, or slight pressure on rivet—"Go ahead and rivet."

Two successive taps—"Stop, enough, rivet headed."

One light tap—"Just a little more driving."

One heavy tap—"Considerably more driving."

Three taps—"Rivet is bad, must be removed."

In the event that the signal for a *bad* rivet is given, the gunner usually draws a ring around the rivet with a red metal-marking pencil. Rivets so marked are removed and replaced later.

Be sure to check your signals with your partner before you start your first riveting job.

Review Questions

1. How are rivets classified?
2. Name the four most commonly used types of rivet head.
3. What is the advantage of countersunk rivets?
4. What determines the choice of rivet heads?
5. Which are stronger, 17S-T rivets or 24S-T rivets?
6. What operations are included in the heat-treatment of rivets?
7. How soon after heat-treatment must 17S-T and 24S-T rivets be used?
8. In connection with rivets, what do these letters signify: A, AD, D, DD?
9. Describe the markings on the heads of rivets and identify them.

10. How is the length of brazier-head and flush-type rivets measured?

11. What is a chamfered shank?

12. What rule is generally followed for rivet spacing?

13. How much larger should the rivet hole be than the rivet it accommodates?

14. How are sheets held together while rivets are being driven?

15. Are most rivet guns electrically or pneumatically operated?

16. What approximate dimensions should the formed head have?

17. How are bucking irons used?

18. Name several kinds of rivet gun and describe how they drive the rivet.

19. What air pressure is used for the following rivet sizes: $\frac{3}{32}$, $\frac{1}{8}$, $\frac{5}{32}$, $\frac{3}{16}$?

20. Why are rivet dies removable?

21. What is a hand rivet set?

22. Describe the various steps necessary in flush riveting.

23. How should rivets be removed?

24. Draw a sketch of a number of imperfectly driven rivets.

25. Describe the signaling system between members of a rivet team.

Shop Work

The shock-absorber fairing of Project 5 requires riveting. Most schools have developed their own practice work for riveting, based on available sheetmetal and tools. It should be emphasized that projects are most valuable which approach the methods of factory production work as closely as possible. Practice in handling countersunk rivets is especially valuable. Scrap aluminum-alloy material may be utilized to good advantage for riveting practice.

CHAPTER 12

JIG ASSEMBLY IN MODERN AIRCRAFT FACTORIES

A *jig* is a frame for holding parts during construction. Jigs vary in size from the small type that rests on a bench to the monster jigs used in building our larger bombers and flying boats. They are used because they speed production and make work easier for both the construction mechanics and the assembly mechanics.

Jigs are often classified according to the part of the airplane that is being made in the jig, such as a wing jig, a fuselage jig, or a rudder jig. They are further described according to the material from which they are made, such as wooden jig, steel jig, tubular jig, L-angle jig.

There are several qualities that airplane jigs must have. First, they must be extremely accurate. Some of the photographs in this chapter may lead you to believe that jigs are heavy, crude structures similar to the framework that holds up an electric sign on a roof. This is not so. Jigs are often set in concrete and lined up with a surveyor's transit. They are measured accurately, and the tolerances in a wing jig, for example, may be only $\frac{1}{100}$ in. Unless a jig is accurately made, the parts constructed in it cannot be accurate.

A second desirable quality is what might be called facility. Parts must fit into the jig easily and come out easily and quickly when the part is finished. A few years ago, jigs had a tendency to be cumbersome, and sometimes one hour or more was required to unfasten all the bolts in removing a major part from the jig. Now wing nuts, spring clamps, and other simple fastening devices are used to save time wherever possible.

Accessibility is also desirable. Whenever possible, a mechanic should be able to stand on the floor, rather than on a platform or scaffold. If he can reach all parts of the jig, he can work more rapidly and with greater safety. For this reason, many jigs are made so that they can be rotated and locked in two or more positions. On such jigs a mechanic changes the position of the work to the point where it is most accessible.

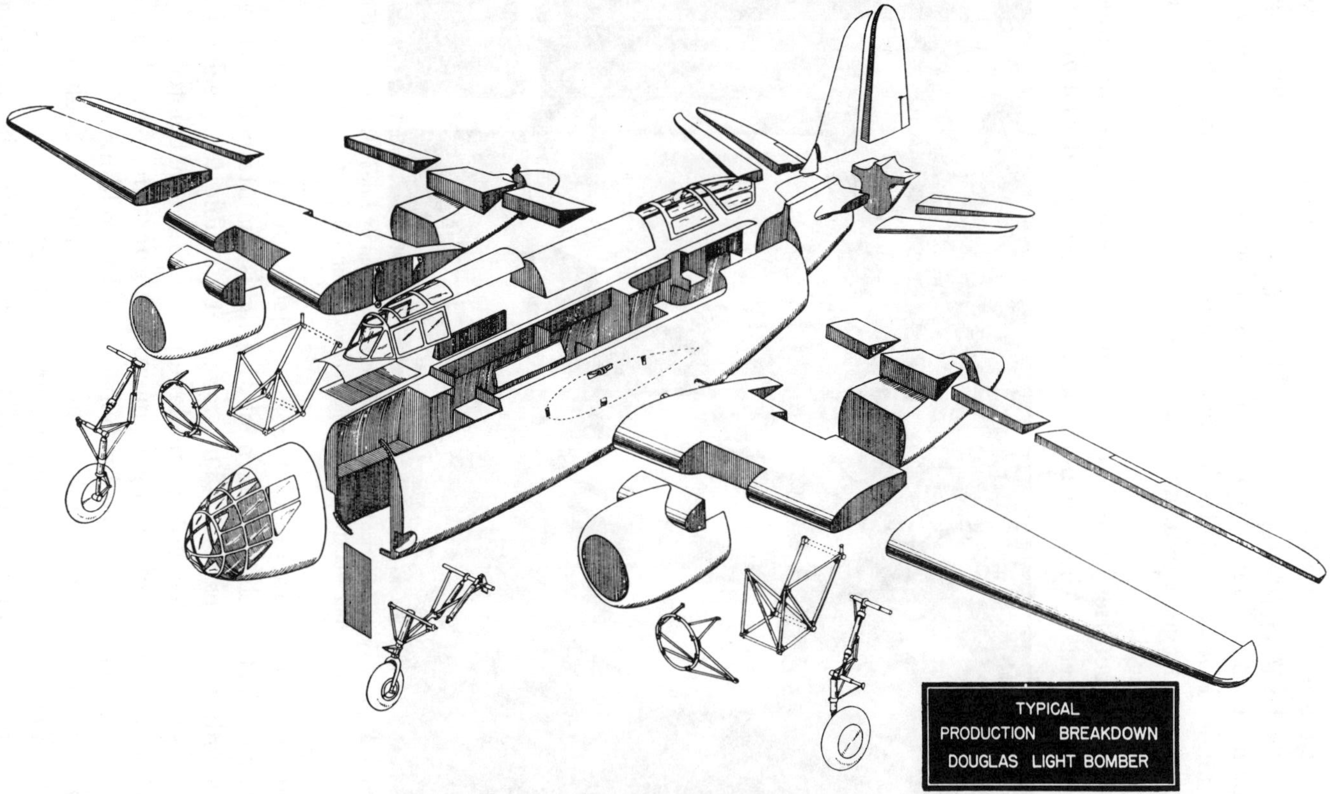

FIG. 131.—This shows how a military airplane is divided into many different subassemblies to speed production. There is at least one jig for each subassembly.

Sturdiness is another necessary characteristic when many parts are to pass through a jig. This accounts for many large jigs being anchored securely in concrete and for the heavy, tubular, steel-angle I-beam and U-channel supports. As a jig must be used over and over again, a weak, flimsy jig would soon be forced out of alignment.

Aircraft factories have jig departments where jigs are designed and constructed. Airplane methods of design are usually employed

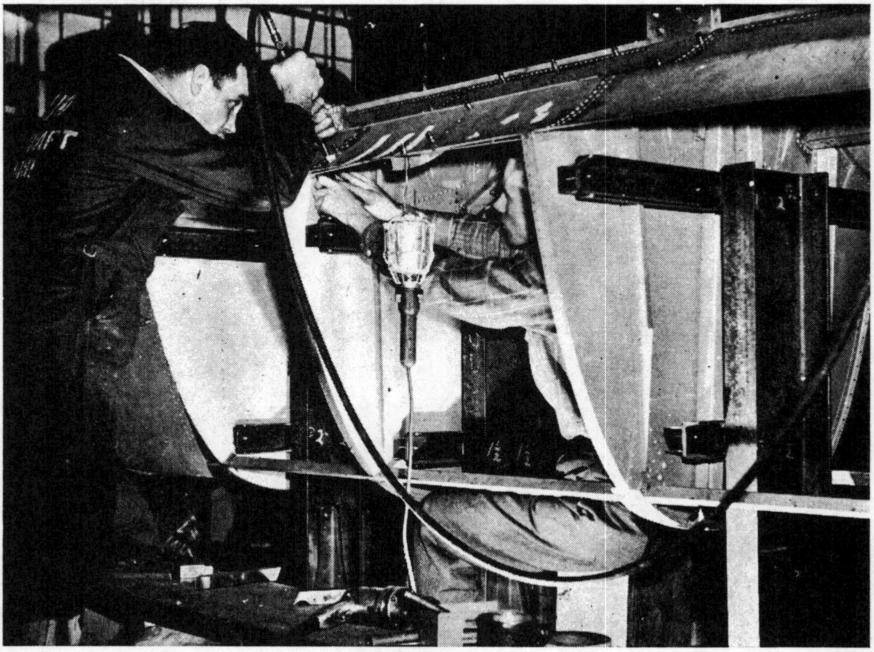

FIG. 132.—A simple type of vertical jig with two cross arms used by Edo in the construction of seaplane floats. In this jig the float is upside down.

in the structural bracing of the jig. Although weight is not an important factor, the strength of the jig is maintained with as few members as possible. This makes it possible for mechanics to have greater access to the airplane part being constructed.

The main parts of the jig framework are fastened together as securely as possible either by bolting or by welding. Most of the heavier structural members such as steel angles, U channels, and I beams are joined by electric-arc welding.

Iron pipe in diameters up to 12 in. is also used for the principal stanchions by several manufacturers because of the unusual strength of the tubular shape. The pipe is also cut and welded by the electric-arc method.

FIG. 133.—Fuselage jigs at Republic Aviation Corporation. Two halves which will be joined together are in each jig. The section on the right forms the right half, and that on the left forms the left half. A jig of this type gives the mechanics great freedom of action as they can quickly get to all parts.

FIG. 134.—Jigs in which the fuselage is made in two halves have also been used at Martin. A number of subassemblies are installed within this section before the other half is bolted in place, simplifying installation, as working space is limited when the two halves are fastened together.

The lighter jig-bracing and attachment fittings are usually made of steel bar stock or steel angle and oxygen-acetylene welded.

Extreme accuracy of measurement is required at and between the points where the airplane parts are attached to the jig. The attachment fittings usually need accurate drilling and careful machining. They are generally oxygen-acetylene welded or brazed in place but may be bolted for adjustment if expansion and contraction, due to temperature change, is a factor.

A

FIG. 135.—These three photographs show how different jigs are used to build the leading edge of wings for Martin bombers. In the picture above, nose ribs are clamped in a vertical jig, each against a steel tongue. In photograph *B*, skin which has been cut and formed to shape in another department is placed over the nose ribs. Over the whole assembly a drill jig is lowered. The mechanics use the drill guides in the jig to drill rivet holes. Then the drill jig is lifted, the skin is held temporarily in place, and the entire unit is lifted from this jig and moved to the revolving jig shown in photograph *C*. Flush rivets are used to complete this subassembly.

Some jigs are made portable by use of castors that can be locked in position; others have permanent foundations.

FUSELAGE JIGS

There is no standard type of fuselage jig. Production engineers have designed a variety of jigs in which to build fuselages,

B

C

Fig. 135.—For descriptive legend see opposite page.

and each is constructed for the particular airplane to be built. In one type the entire fuselage is built. The jig holds the former rings or bulkheads and the longerons or stringers. Then sheet-metal skin is riveted to the framework members.

In another type the fuselage is made in two halves, usually being split vertically down through the center. This makes it possible for more men to work on both the outside and the inside

FIG. 136.—Jigs for nacelle doors which open to allow lowering and retracting of main landing wheels in a Martin B-26 bomber. The aluminum-alloy framework is put in place and then the clamping crossmembers of the jig are swung up into place and locked into position. Locking devices of various types are fastened to chains so they cannot become lost. After the frame is riveted together, it will be removed to another jig where skin will be riveted in place.

at the same time. A great deal of handwork is required for installation of controls and armament. As soon as the skin is riveted in place, installations of cables, wires, and pipe lines and other interior work may be done. The two halves are bolted together afterward.

Still another type of fuselage jig is made in several sections. The nose is made in one jig; the central section of the fuselage is a second; and the tail section in a third. Then all three sections are bolted and riveted together.

The hulls of flying boats and seaplane floats are started upside down in jigs. When the keel, all the bulkheads, and the stringers are in place and the bottom sheets riveted together, the hull is lifted out of the jig, turned right side up, and put in a new jig, where the work is continued.

WING JIGS

The style of the wing jig depends on how large the wing is. The simplest type for small airplanes consists of two upright

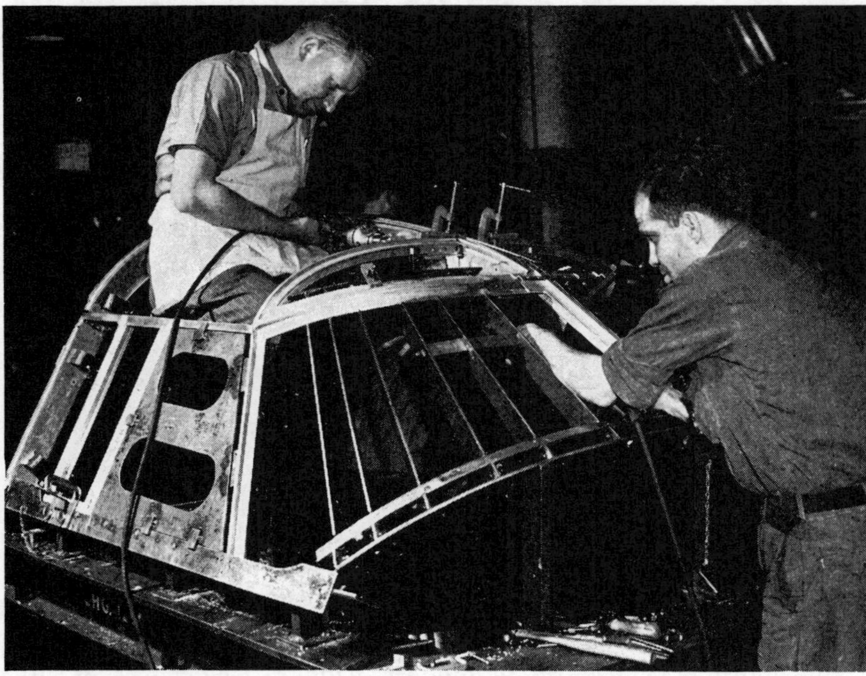

FIG. 137.—Pilot-cabin assembly jig for a B-26. Parts that have been cut and formed to exact shape are assembled here. Light parts such as these must be held rigidly in place to prevent distortion.

members with a crosspiece forming a T at the top of each post, like a telephone pole, and another cross member below it. The front spar is laid across the top, and the rear spar is laid on the bottom cross member. Ribs are slid down the spars to locations marked on the spars, usually indicated by assembly holes drilled previously for fittings. Then tie rods, bracing members, compression members, and other parts of the wing are installed.

In small planes, such as trainers, wings are made in one entire panel, either right or left. They are built in a horizontal position and usually can be rotated around their longitudinal axis. In many of the larger ships, wings are made in several different sections and then bolted together, as shown in some of the photographs in this chapter.

Large wings of this type are usually assembled in a vertical position. This allows mechanics to work on both sides of the wing at the same time. Scaffolding is ordinarily required, because

FIG. 138.—Most wings are made in vertical jigs. Here three subassemblies for a Bell Airacobra wing are brought together at this stage.

of the depth of the chord in modern wings. Regardless of the type of wing jig used, the main longitudinal members, which constitute the spars, are put in place first. Next, the ribs or the chord members that form the honeycomb sections are installed.

It is often necessary to remove parts of the jig bracing as the work on the panel progresses. The main jig-attachment points are on the spar hinge fittings at the root and on the ends of the spars at the wing tips. Sometimes a section of the skin covering must be left off until after the wing has been removed from the jig, because of additional mounting points on the interior of the framework.

Some airplanes, such as the Curtiss pursuits, have a wing made in two sections that are bolted together before final assembly. The fuselage is lowered over the wing section and bolted directly to it.

CONTROL SURFACE JIGS

Jigs for ailerons, elevators, and stabilizers are similar to small wing jigs. The jig for the rudder of a large bomber or a flying

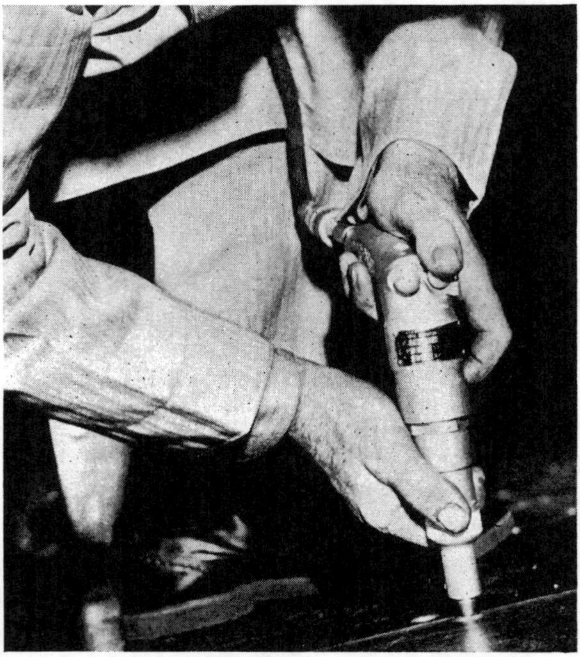

Fig. 139.—A Thor pneumatic reversible screw driver. When many sheetmetal screws need to be driven, a power screw driver helps to speed the work.

boat may be larger and more complex than the entire wing jig for a small plane.

Control-surface jigs are usually built in a vertical position. Since the structural members of the panels are smaller and more closely spaced than in wings, the jigs are designed to permit a maximum of working area.

HOW JIGS ARE USED

The easiest way to understand the use of jigs is to study the photographs in this chapter. Most of the jigs shown here are assembly jigs, used either for subassembly or for final assembly of a major unit. There are also fabricating jigs, which are used in holding material during a punching, drilling, or cutting operation. Sometimes fabricating jigs are called *fixtures*, as is usually the case when parts are held securely during a drilling operation. Actually, there is no hard and fast distinction between jigs and fixtures. In some plants, such a unit may be called a jig, whereas in another plant, it might be called a fixture.

Assembly jigs hold the framework of a part, a subassembly, or a complete unit, while cross members and skin are being riveted, welded, or bolted together. After the frame is secure, the same jig holds the frame while the skin is being attached and while wires, cables, tubing, controls, and fittings are installed. Parts are held in a jig by bolts, wing nuts, C clamps, specially designed fast-locking arrangements, and various other fastening devices. The engineers designing the jig try to make the fastenings as simple and as easy to operate as possible. It is also necessary to construct jigs so that parts can be removed when work is completed. This problem often affects the design of the entire jig.

JIG SERVICE FACILITIES

The larger jigs must have safe scaffolds and sufficient space on working platforms. Stairways or ladders must also be convenient. Chain hoists or monorails are located at points where heavy materials or completed parts may be put in place or removed.

Electric-power and compressed-air outlets must be accessible for drilling and riveting operations. Where possible, this is done by means of overhead conduits and hoses with drop connections spaced at appropriate points. This helps in reducing the hazard of having electric cables and hose lines cluttering the floors and decks.

Suitable lighting facilities must be provided. In addition to the stationary fixtures designed to reduce glare, many portable extension lights must be used for interior work.

Review Questions

1. Name a few different purposes for which aircraft jigs are used.
2. What features do well-constructed jigs have?
3. Why are surveyor's transits used to line up jigs?
4. If some fuselage jigs are set solidly in the concrete floor, why is it that in other plants fuselages are assembled in movable jigs and pushed along the assembly floor?

5. Describe several kinds of fuselage jig.
6. What different methods of building wings are used?
7. Why are parts of the framework of jigs made removable?
8. How are parts secured in the jig?
9. Explain the difference between a jig and a fixture.
10. What is the advantage in rotating jigs?

NOTE:—Students who have time for a more lengthy study of aircraft construction methods are referred to the authors' "The Aviation Mechanic," published by the McGraw-Hill Book Company, Inc., New York, in 1941. In this 563-page book, 224 pages are devoted to describing how airplanes are built, and 241 photographs and drawings illustrate all phases of aircraft construction.

CHAPTER 13

SKIN FITTING

The frameworks of fuselages, hulls, wings, tail groups, and control surfaces are covered with sheetmetal, generally referred to as the *skin*, or *covering*. The job of fitting the skin sections in place on these framework assemblies is done by *skin fitters*. A considerable amount of handwork is performed by the skin fitter that is generally beyond the scope of engineering drawings. Consequently, experience, judgment, and mechanical skill are prerequisites of his work. He is definitely classed as a skilled mechanic in an airplane factory.

The skin fitter must be thoroughly familiar with the working characteristics of all types of aircraft sheetmetal stock used for skins. Often sections of coverings are but 0.020 in. in thickness, and they must be handled carefully. Valuable material and irreplaceable time may easily be wasted through lack of ability or knowledge.

Grain of Sheetmetal.—It is a commonly known fact that in the use of wood the direction in which the grain runs has a definite bearing on the strength of the member. The grain in sheetmetal, although less obvious, is definitely present and is an important strength factor from a structural viewpoint. The grain in wood runs up and down the trunk of the tree and follows the various limbs, or branches. The grain in sheetmetal stock results from compressing and stretching the granular molecules of metal under the tremendous pressure of the rolls in the rolling mill where it is produced. The grain will usually be found to run the long way of the sheet, because it forms parallel to the direction of rolling at the aluminum mills.

If the grain in a sheet is not readily apparent, it can be determined by wiping the sheet off with a little nitrate dope thinner which will bring into view the fine lines or grain produced by the rolls.

Like wood, the greatest strength of sheet stock is developed when it is bent at right angles to the direction of the grain, although somewhat greater resistance is encountered in bending. The grain of the sheet covering a fuselage or a hull should run longitudinally, that is, fore and aft. On wings and control surfaces such as ailerons, flaps, and horizontal stabilizers, the grain in the skin should run laterally, from tip to tip. The process of forming

FIG. 140.—Cleco fasteners being used to hold sheets of skin in place at Republic Aviation Co. To eliminate wrinkles, more than the usual number of fasteners are used on this canopy. Fasteners are removed as rivets are driven.

aluminum-alloy sheet stock imparts great strength to the finished parts. It is important that the skin fitter check the direction of the grain in the parts that he installs even though he may not have been responsible for their fabrication.

Fitting Skin Sections.—There are many variations in the work that the skin fitter is called on to do. Different structures present a variety of situations. The tip section at the top of the vertical fin may require slight additional stretching after it has been hydraulically pressed to shape. This the skin fitter may do on a bumping anvil with the aid of a planishing hammer. In fitting a fairing along a wing root some slight eccentricity of forming may require a small amount of shrinking to prevent the part from wrinkling or buckling as it is drawn tightly into place by the rivets. This condition must be determined and corrected by the skin

FIG. 141.—This photograph shows how the skin has been fitted around the nose of a Boeing Stratoliner. Upper sheets lap over lower sheets, and front sheets lap over successive sheets to the rear. Sheets are held by double rows of staggered rivets. Sealing compound is used between the sheets.

fitter before assembly. He may find it necessary to bolt the fairing in place several times, removing it to the shrinking blocks between fittings for additional forming, before it is finally turned over to the riveters. Brake cables may rub against edges of the skin on the landing-gear fairings. Again, this is a job for the skin fitter. He may find it necessary to remove additional material around the opening in the fairing through which the cable passes. If the hole is small and oval in shape, which is usually the case, he will probably use both left and right aircraft snips for enlarging and a half-round second-cut file and an emery cloth for finishing the edges.

The framework, or skeleton, of the fuselage is mounted on a steel jig. It consists principally of formers to which longitudinal stringers have been riveted. Pilot rivet holes have been drilled in the stringers to receive the skin. This drilling is done during primary assembly using a No. 50 drill. A permanent or a temporary floor is often installed in the fuselage by the time it reaches the external skin-fitting stage on the assembly line. The entire

FIG. 142.—Fastening skin to the lower side of the center section of a Douglas DC-3 wing. There are more than 100,000 rivets in this transport airplane.

framework is generally held in place by easily removable bolts that secure the formers to the jig.

There are many individual sections of skin on a fuselage. When they are received for assembly, they are already numbered as to installation position and marked left, right, top, or bottom. Airfoil sections are similarly marked with the addition of leading edge, trailing edge, or tip. The skin fitter, however, must be able to read the assembly blueprints to determine their exact location and method of attachment. In the hull construction of a wooden surf boat, a number of narrow planks are bent to conformity. Similarly, a number of skin sections are used in the covering of an airplane because of the compound curvatures essential to aerodynamic efficiency. Single small sections of covering can be formed more easily to shape than can large sections. Large sections of skin have a tendency to wrinkle and require a greater amount of shrinking and stretching.

Joining Sheet.—Because of the number of sections of skin that make up the covering, there must be many joints. The skin

FIG. 143.—It is desirable that the fairing, which covers the joint between the wing root and the fuselage, be easily removable for inspection of wing fittings. Consequently it is often installed with machine screws which cut their own threads and which are self-locking. (*Curtiss-Wright photograph.*)

is joined in two ways, either by butting the adjacent edges of the sheet together or by lapping one sheet over the other to form the joint. In either case, the sheets are usually joined at formers or at stringers. If a flush-butt joint is employed, it is designed to fall along the center line of the stringer to which two rows of rivets are used to secure the edge of the sheet. In unusual situations where this is not possible, a narrow strip of sheet stock is used on the inside of the skin along the seam to form the butt joint. When a lap joint is used, it is usually designed so that both sheets overlap the width of the flange on the former ring and are centered for riveting on that flange.

Skin sections are lapped for much the same reason that houses are shingled—to keep out the weather. In addition, however, the joint must be protected from the air stream. Skin sections, therefore, are assembled so that they extend over, or lap, one another, from the top down and from the front to the rear. On a fuselage, it would seem necessary to put on the bottom and the rear sections first. This is not always the case, since often sections of skin can be assembled in place by sliding one section under the

FIG. 144.—Many sections of skin on pursuit ships are not installed until well along in the assembly process, as it is necessary to make numerous installations in the interior of the fuselage. This Bell Airacobra fuselage is tipped on its side for greater accessibility.

edge of another where the joint has been left unfastened for this purpose.

Modern machine-production methods of cutting, forming, and drilling have speeded assembly operations tremendously, but hand fitting of skin sections is still required, although kept to a minimum in most airplane factories. The skin fitter usually receives the blanked-out skin sections in a partly curved or formed condition. Sometimes as much as 3 in. of waste material is left to be trimmed from the edges of the sheet. This is not the result of carelessness, but because it is often possible to "jockey" a straight curved sheet around to secure a better fit.

The skin fitter starts the assembly of a section of covering on a fuselage by first checking the number of the section with the assembly print for location, the direction of the grain, and the accuracy of the forming. The conformity of the section is tested by holding it tightly in place on the fuselage. He may find it necessary to increase the curvature slightly. This can be done by again running the sheet through the slip rolls. Again he may find that additional bumping is required for a better fit, necessitating the use of rawhide or rubber mallets or plastic hammers.

FIG. 145.—Canopy subassemblies require careful fitting. This is a cockpit cover for a Republic pursuit. Plexiglas windows have been installed and protected with wrapping paper and scotch tape. This entire subassembly must be watertight.

For the next operation the skin fitter requires the services of a helper who takes his position inside the fuselage. The skin fitter works on the outside, holding the section of skin in place with the aid of padded wood blocks. The helper, using the pilot rivet holes in the stringers and former flanges as guides, then drills through the central portion of the sheet. If $\frac{1}{8}$ in. rivets are specified, he uses a No. 30 drill, thus reaming the No. 50 pilot holes and putting rivet holes in the skin.

The skin is then tacked in position in the central portion by using either skin fasteners that are applied with a special plierlike tool or No. 540 1/8 in. machine screws with fiber washers under the heads and nuts to protect the skin. In some instances self-threading sheetmetal screws may be used with fiber washers under the heads, but only when both the holes in the framework as well as in the skin are pilot holes. The use of sheetmetal screws in

FIG. 146.—Conveyer systems are used in most plants. This is a point in the Vultee plant where the complete fuselage and the tail section of a trainer are joined. The mechanic in the foreground can raise or lower the fuselage so that it may be held in exact position for bolting it to the tail assembly.

holes that have been reamed to rivet size tends to make the rivet holes irregular in shape.

The fastening of the skin section is continued, working alternately in four directions from the middle, that is, up and down along the flange of the former and fore and aft along the stringer. This method secures the skin to the fuselage framework in the shape of a cross. The temporary fastenings are spaced at approximately every six holes.

All wrinkles must be worked out toward the outside edges of the sheet as the work progresses. Wrinkles are referred to as *oilcans* because of the tendency of the buckled sheet to react in the same way as the bottom of an oilcan when pressure is applied. The skin fitter uses thumb pressure to test for oilcans.

Fig. 147.—Mechanics are shown fitting sections of skin on the belly of a fuselage. Parker-Kalon sheetmetal screws are used as temporary fastenings, spaced every 2 or 3 in. A fiber washer is used under the head of each screw to prevent marring the sheet.

After all rivet holes have been drilled, the temporary fastenings are taken out and the skin section is removed from the framework. The burrs left by drilling must be removed from both sides of all holes in the skin, the stringers, and the former flanges. *Burring* is accomplished with a few light turns of a countersinker or a larger drill. In this way particles of metal left around the edges of the drilled holes are eliminated. If they were not removed, the joint would not be tight and rivets might expand, or *flash*, between the parts being riveted. Care must be exercised during the burring operation to prevent actually countersinking the edges of the holes.

If the skin is to be flush-riveted, dimpling the sheet is the next operation. The skin fitter can do this by holding the sheet between the dimpling dies, which may be fitted to the jaws of a compression riveting machine. A small pilot plug passes through the rivet hole in the skin to keep it centered during the depressing, or dimpling, operation. If the contours of some sections of the skin are so formed that they cannot be dimpled by machine, hand-dimpling dies can be used. These dies resemble a grommet punch, and the top die is struck a light blow with a hammer in a similar manner. Usually only comparatively thin sheet is dimpled, although aluminum-alloy sheet can be dimpled up to 0.072 in. in thickness. Heavier gage material must be countersunk to receive the head of the rivet or, in the case of stringers or the flanges on formers, to receive the dimpled skin.

After all points on the framework and skin have been prepared to receive the dimpled rivets, the skin may again be temporarily fitted in position to see that no distortions have occurred.

The next step consists of trimming the sheet to the exact size. Accuracy of measurement at this point is essential. Cutting lines are scribed on the skin parallel to the center lines of the rivet holes along the edges of the sheet. The distance of the edge away from the center line of rivet holes might be, for example, $\frac{5}{8}$ in., or any distance governed by the specifications set according to the width of the stringers or the width of the flanges on the formers. The edges of the skin section are very slightly bent down or crimped all around after cutting. This is done so that, when the skin is riveted in place, the material between the line of rivets and the edge of the sheet does not curl or *dish up*. Because of this, the section of skin should be marked very slightly oversize for cutting if a butt joint is to be used.

If an edge of the skin section is to be cut in a straight line, a power shear may best be used. If the edge to be cut is curved and the sheet is of thin material, aircraft hand snips may be used. For cutting curves on heavier gage material, portable rotary shears or a Doall machine can be employed. Routers are excellent for cutting irregularly shaped sections if the sheet is flat but are not suitable for cutting curved or formed sheets.

The final finishing of the edges of the skin may require the use of a vixen file, since there is often a risk of spoiling the sheet by cutting too close with power cutting machines. Sanding disks or belt sanders may also be used for smoothing the edges. If hand filing is unnecessary, a hand burring tool of the V-slot or knife-sharpener type should be used along the edges of the skin.

The skin section is now ready to be riveted in its location by the riveters.

The preceding operations listed may be followed in the order given for almost any type of skin-fitting job. On curved surfaces the mechanic should remember to start to fit the sheet from the highest point of the curve and work downward.

The skin fitter should be able to make serviceable many of the machine-made parts that would otherwise be rejected owing to their lack of coincidence or exact fit. A capable skin fitter should possess the ability to make almost any part with hand forming and cutting tools that can be accomplished by machine production methods.

Review Questions

1. Explain how sheetmetal can have a grain.
2. Is greater strength developed if bends are parallel to the grain or at right angles to the grain?
3. What are some of the jobs a skin fitter performs?
4. What is a flush-butt joint and how is it made?
5. How is skin tacked in place?
6. In what order is skin generally applied for joggled or overlapped joints?
7. What is an oilcan, as applied to skin fitting?
8. How is dimpling performed?
9. What is the heaviest gage of sheet that is usually dimpled?
10. Why are the edges of sheet cut by skin fitters rather than by previous workers?

CHAPTER 14

SPOT WELDING

In a textbook on aircraft sheetmetal work it may be necessary to explain why machine welding is included when there is no discussion of oxyacetylene or gas welding. Gas welding is a separate subject which requires a textbook devoted solely to its technique. Several good books are on the market.[1]

Sheetmetal workers in airplane factories do not handle gas-welding equipment. Gas welding is a specialized trade and requires considerable skill. It is used on steel-tubing engine mounts and tubular fuselages and for other parts, especially steel fittings.

It should be emphasized here that sheetmetal workers who have not had thorough instruction in gas welding may get into trouble if they tinker with oxyacetylene equipment. Gas-welding equipment is distinctly dangerous if you do not know how to handle it.

Machine welding, on the other hand, is a subassembly operation done in the sheetmetal department of a factory. Once the welding machine is set up, its operation is relatively simple, although there is a definite skill required to get perfect welds. A sheetmetal man might be shifted on short notice to do machine welding, and consequently he should know the general principles on which the machines operate.

This type of welding is known as *resistance welding.* It is usually referred to as *spot welding.* Metal sheets are joined together by passing an electric current of low voltage and extremely high amperage through the sheets. The two sheets are held together under slight pressure between two electrodes, and the current produces an intense heat. The resistance set up causes the metal to melt locally. When the metal is molten, the current is automatically shut off. The weld is finished when a heavy pressure fuses the two metals together. The usual practice is to

[1] See L. S. Elzea, "Aircraft Welding," McGraw-Hill Book Company, Inc., New York, 1942.

use one dome-shaped electrode on the upper, or movable arm and one flat electrode on the lower, or fixed arm.

This method is playing an increasingly important part in airplane production. Nearly every factory in the country is carrying on experiments to improve the technique. Not only are new welding machines being developed, but aeronautical engineers

FIG. 148.—A Taylor-Winfield spot-welding machine in operation at Vought-Sikorsky. This aircraft firm has been one of the pioneers in building airplanes with welded parts. This panel is typical of many subassemblies that are welded.

are designing parts especially for spot welding. Cowling, fairing, air scoops, ducts, tunnels, and many other parts are being made more rapidly today because of spot welding. On some airplanes stiffeners are spot welded to the metal skin that they help to support.

The great advantage of spot welding is its speed. Riveting is essentially a one-at-a-time operation on most airplane parts, even though gang riveters are used on some parts. Spot welding is much faster than riveting. Aircraft production men hope that a greater use of spot welding will be one of the factors that will help the United States to build military planes at a more rapid rate.

The chief disadvantage of spot welding is that until recently it was not approved for structural parts that must stand great stress. Now, with improved methods, an increasing amount of

FIG. 149.—A close-up view of the electrodes of a Sciaky spot welder. Notice how the U-channel stiffener is welded to the skin and to other stiffeners. This is a subassembly for a Bell Airacobra.

spot welding is being approved for military ships. In the future, spot welding is destined to be an important factor in sheetmetal fabrication, and some engineers believe that it will replace riveting for many major structural parts.

Engineers at Bell Aircraft, where extensive research has been done, estimate that a spot-welded joint is about 60 per cent stronger than a riveted joint made up of rivets of the same diameter and spacing as the spot welds. Spot welding is more economical than riveting and eliminates the more lengthy process of flush riveting. The same streamlined effect is produced, as the spots in welding do not protrude. Another advantage of welding is that the weight of rivet heads is dispensed with. This may appear to be a small item, but a medium-sized bomber has some 130,000 rivets, and with rivet heads on both ends of the rivets

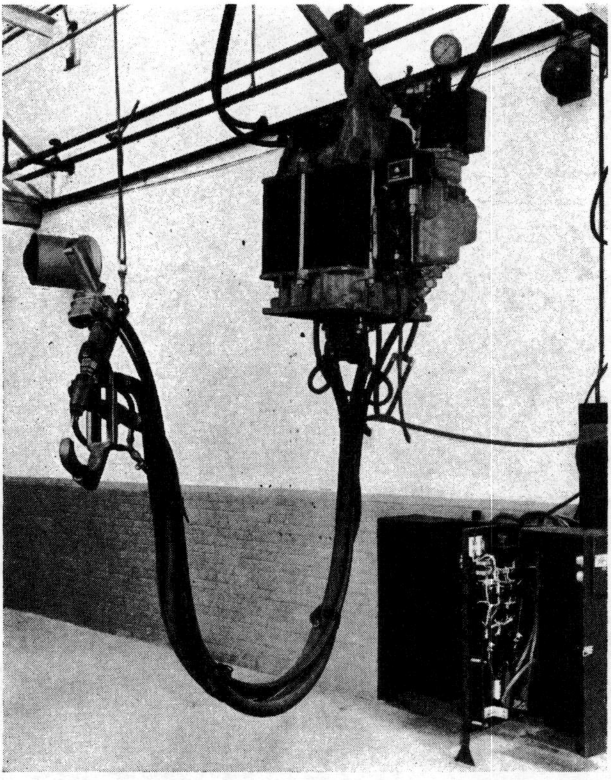

FIG. 150.—A portable, gun-type spot welder made by Progressive Welding Co. On certain parts of the airplane a gun-type welder has an advantage over the larger, fixed welding machines. (*Bell Aircraft photograph.*)

this means 260,000 heads, the weight of which is worth saving. However, if a rivet is improperly placed, it can be removed without much difficulty, but a spot weld is fixed. Repairs of riveted structures are generally easier to make than repairs of welded sheet.

On aircraft blueprints, the asterisk (*) is the symbol of spot welding in most plants.

Spot welding of steel has been done for many years, for which work a current of approximately 7,000 amp. was sufficient. But light aluminum alloys have much greater conductivity and require two or three times as much current as do steels. Currents as high as 35,000 amp. are being used for aircraft parts.

To turn out successful welds the machine process must be controlled exactly. The amount of current, the time that it is allowed to flow, and the pressure of the electrodes must be con-

FIG. 151.—At the Lockheed plant, preference is given to this type of welding machine. Note that the electrodes are circular disks. The upper wheel is power-driven, while the lower wheel is a follower. Once the timing is set, the work moves through the rollers at a fixed rate of speed and the welding impulses are automatically timed. An increasing amount of welding is done in this factory. The machine is a 450 kva. Federal combination spot and roll welder with G.E. controls.

sidered as well as the electrical and the thermal conductivity, the plastic range, and the oxide resistance of the metals. As mentioned above, the two electrodes press against the outsides of the metal; the current flows through; and a resistance is set up. As the resistance occurs, the metal is melted and a "nugget" is formed. The nugget penetrates the two inner surfaces of the sheets being joined but should never completely penetrate the sheets.

As the current is applied, pressure is also exerted to reduce the contact resistance between the sheets as well as between the sheets and the electrodes. The pressure also helps to obtain proper and controlled solidification of the molten metal that forms the nugget. After considerable research it was discovered that a second pressure impulse following the first discharge produced a nugget of much finer grain structure which was free from cracks and pores. Consequently the weld was stronger and more fatigue resistant.

Welding and "forging" pressures are obtained from one double-acting arm or from a pair of air cylinders applied as a squeezing action, not by impact. This secondary pressure is given various terms by manufacturers of welding equipment: *forged action*, *recompression*, or *second-pressure impulse*. At this writing it is limited to aluminum alloys and to sheet of 0.032 in. and slightly more in thickness.

The time that the current is left on is measured in cycles, or frequency, of power supply. One cycle of a 60 cycle frequency is equal to $\frac{1}{60}$ sec.; 3 cycles are equal to $\frac{1}{20}$ sec.; and so on. For aluminum alloys, when welded on the foregoing type of equipment, the timing range is from 4 to 15 cycles, increasing in direct relation to the thickness of the material. On some of the new machines, weld timing is measured in hundredths of a second, as the welding energy is converted to direct current. One machine is capable of producing spot welds of a quality to be compared favorably with those made on an energy-storage welder by using less than half-cycle timing, thus obtaining unidirectional current flow.

The strength of the spot weld is relative to the diameter of the nugget, just as the strength of a rivet is related to the diameter of its shank. The nugget in a weld is controlled by the size of the smaller electrode, so that with constant current and pressure, strength values may be easily determined.

The only evidence of a good weld is a slight impression of the smaller of the two electrodes. If the weld is poor, there may be cracks in sheet, excessive denting, penetration, or porosity of the metal surrounding the weld.

TYPES OF EQUIPMENT

Spot-welding machines are of three types: the rocker-arm type, the press type, and the roll type. The rocker-arm type consists of two horns of a length and a diameter to suit the throat depth and the secondary current. The upper arm is movable and is actuated by air or hydraulic means and applies pressure to the electrodes to a preset value and time. Such machines can weld a piece approximately 38 in. wide.

The press-type welder operates in a similar manner but applies pressure by the axial movement of a vertical plunger, or quill. It can take a piece of material about 34 in. wide.

In the roll spot welder, a pair of large, water-cooled copper-alloy wheels is substituted for the fixed electrodes of the ordinary spot welder. The upper wheel is driven; the lower one idles. The work is fed between the wheels and the automatic electrical control passes current at fixed intervals.

Electrically, spot-welding machines may be divided into two classes: standard alternating-current machines and accumulation-of-energy machines. The alternating-current welders pass *alternating* current at low voltage through the joint. The accumulation-of-energy machines are of two types: the condenser and the reactor, which discharge *direct* current through the material.

Materials.—Any of the existing aluminum alloys can be spot welded. Alloys of different physical and mechanical analysis can be welded to each other. Certain combinations, however, give better results. According to Charles W. Dodge, spot-welding engineer at Vought-Sikorsky Aircraft, the following combinations are in order of preference.

24S-T Alclad and 24S-RT Alclad.
17S-T Alclad and 17S-RT Alclad.
3S-H and 3S-½H.
52S-H and 52S-½H.
53S-W or T.
24S-O Alclad.
17S-O Alclad.
3S-O.
52S-O.
53S-O.
2S-O or H.

The use of soft alloys, such as 3S-O, 52S-O, and 24S-O Alclad are not recommended. Satisfactory results with these alloys are seldom obtained because the high welding pressures necessary are likely to create badly deformed surfaces on these materials.

Rolling after Spot Welding.—Large flat panels containing many spot welds are subject to warping. They must often be rolled after welding in order to straighten the sheet. The rolling process irons out any buckles produced by the welding and also increases the strength of the welds. All necessary rolling must be done within 1 hr. after welding is finished.

SEAM WELDING

There is no basic difference between spot welding and seam welding. In some aircraft parts, such as gasoline tanks and oil tanks, it is necessary to have leakproof seams. In such instances, the joint is made by a continuous row of welded spots that overlap one another.

The electrodes in seam welding are rollers, made of the same type of material as used for spot-welding electrodes. They are given a curved or a V-shaped contour corresponding to the conical contour of the spot-welding electrodes. A motor is used to drive one roller, and the other roll is an idler. A pressure mechanism brings the electrodes together.

POKE WELDING

Poke welding is another form of spot welding. In this process only one electrode needs to be in direct contact with the local spot to be welded. The second electrode, or lead, is clamped to any part of the material. This method is used to weld places on the airplane that are inaccessible to welding machines. The movable electrode is operated by hand like a rivet gun. The operator exerts pressure against the sheet, and the current is turned on from a pressure switch. The current is not shut off automatically, and the operator must use judgment as to the time that the current is left on.

CLEANING SURFACES BEFORE WELDING

On aluminum alloys there is a thin oxide coating that must be removed along the line to be welded. This prevents "surface heating" and also reduces the amount of aluminum that is picked up by the electrode. If electrodes pick up aluminum, they must be changed or cleaned, which adds to the cost of the spot-welding process.

Sheetmetal is cleaned for spot welding in several ways. The cheapest method is to clean the surface where welds will occur with a fine grade of abrasive cloth, fine steel wool, or a fine scratch brush. Some aircraft plants clean with an etching solution applied with a paint brush. The solution consists of 3 lb. of gum tragacanth, 10 gal. of hot water, and 30 lb. of 30 per cent hydrofluoric acid. Mechanics working with such a mixture wear both goggles and gloves. The etch is left on the metal for a period of 15 sec. to 1 min. Then it is washed off in running water. Cold water is satisfactory, but hot water is better.

Review Questions

1. Why is spot welding done in the sheetmetal department when gas welding is usually done elsewhere?
2. What is the difference between resistance welding and spot welding?
3. Describe what occurs during the spot-welding operation.
4. Why is spot welding finding an increased use in aircraft plants?
5. What are its advantages and its disadvantages?
6. Is a spot-welded joint as strong as a riveted joint?
7. Name two electric welding machines.
8. Why are sheets rolled after spot welding?
9. On what parts is seam welding used?
10. Must sheetmetal always be cleaned following welding?

CHAPTER 15

SHOP PROJECTS

This chapter contains five shop projects that bring into use the skills and tools described previously. The blueprints in Chap. 1 can also be utilized for the making of some of the simpler parts and fittings.

These are suggestions only. A number of aviation schools have developed their own series of projects over a period of years, which may fit their needs better than do these projects. It is emphasized that these are simple and elementary projects. If there is time, more difficult sheetmetal parts should be made by students.

If sufficient room is available in the school shop, it is recommended that a fuselage jig be constructed and that practice be given the students in building bulkheads, stringers, and fittings and in riveting skin in place. The same can be done in building wing sections or parts of the tail assembly.

Project 1. A Drill-grinding Gage

(A photograph of this gage is on page 194.)

Tools and Materials

One piece of sheet steel 2¾ by 1⅛ by 1/16 in.; a 6 in. steel rule; a pair of dividers; a scriber; a prick punch; a hammer; a machinist's square and a protractor; soft vise jaws; a hack saw; smooth, flat, and triangular files; a ¼ in. drill.

Operations

1. True up one edge of the metal (line *A*, Fig. 1).
2. With dividers set to ½ in., lay out two points locating center line *C*.
3. Repeat operations with dividers set at 1 in., locating line *E*.
4. Divide each of two spaces *A*-*C* and *C*-*E* in half, scribing in lines *B* and *D*, making four ¼ in. spaces, as in Fig. 1.

5. Using the square, scribe in perpendicular lines 1, 2, 3, and 4, using the measurements given in Fig. 1. Start line 1 about ⅛ in. from the left edge.

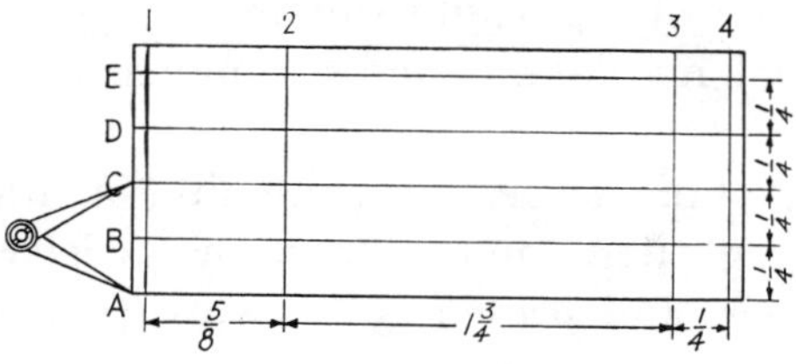

FIG. 1.

6. At the intersection of center line C and perpendicular line 3, prick-punch lightly. Set dividers to ¼ in., and scribe the radius as shown in Fig. 2.

7. Set the protractor to 59 deg.; and taking the true edge as a base, scribe in lines F and H, beginning at line E. Reset the protractor to 59 deg. on the opposite side, and scribe in line G. Once again reset the protractor, this time to 78 deg. (12 deg. from vertical), and scribe in line I. The last two lines should be begun at line A, Fig. 2.

8. The gage is now ready to be cut out. Using a hack saw, cut outside the lines outlined in Fig. 2. File exactly to size using a smooth file for the finishing cut.

9. Drill a ¼ in. hole at point J, and the gage will now appear as in Fig. 3.

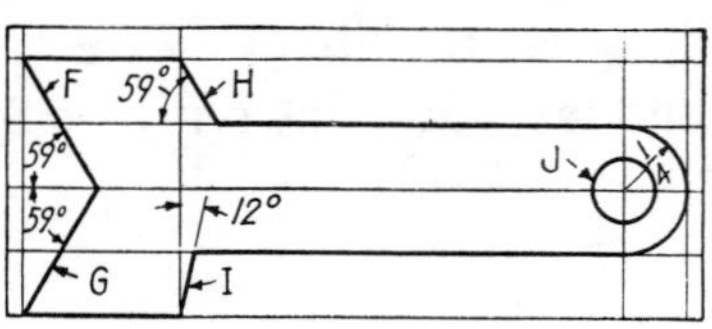

FIG. 2.

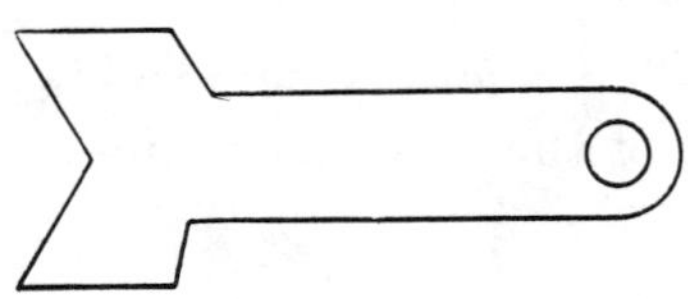

FIG. 3.

10. Draw-file the surfaces smooth, removing all scriber marks, and then polish all over with emery cloth and oil. Be sure to keep the edges square. A final polish with steel wool and oil will produce a high luster.

STANDARD OF ACHIEVEMENT

Check your gage on the following points:

1. Are all measurements exactly to size?
2. Are all angles correct?

3. Are all corners sharp as laid out originally?

4. Is the radius exactly ¼ in. from the center at all points?

5. Is the ¼ in. hole centered?

6. Are all edges straight and square?

7. Are all tool marks and burrs removed from the edges and the surfaces?

8. Is the gage finished in a workmanlike manner?

After checking these points to your satisfaction, stamp on your shop number, and present your work to your instructor for examination and rating.

Project 2. Universal Fitting

Operations

1. Obtain a blank of 0.065 in. 24S-O material 2 by 4 in.

2. Coat one side with layout dye, and pencil a light center line 11/16 in. from and parallel to one 4 in. side.

3. Lay out another center line at a right angle to the first, 2 in. from one edge. All further layout work will be done from these two lines.

4. Set dividers to 21/32 in., and lay out a line parallel to the long center line.

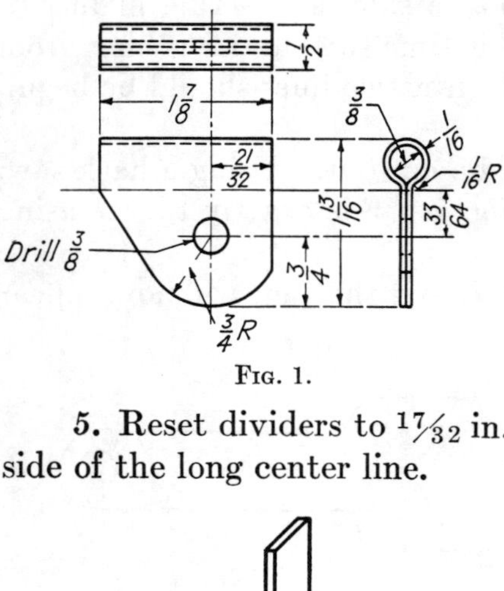

Fig. 1.

5. Reset dividers to 17/32 in., and lay out a line on the opposite side of the long center line.

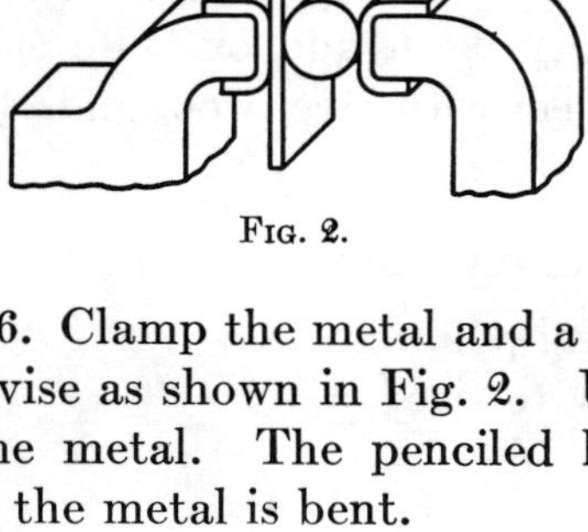

Fig. 2.

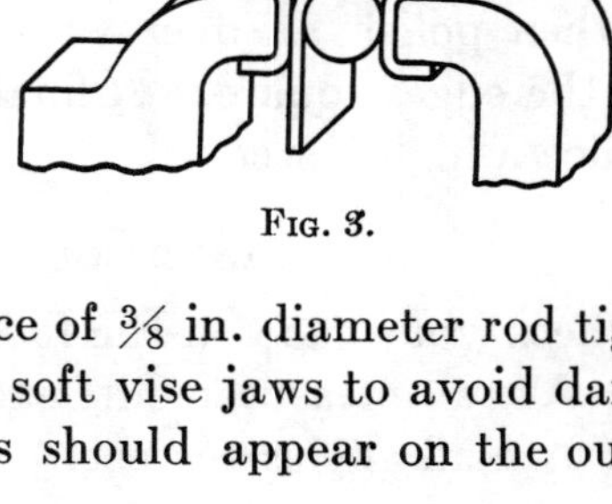

Fig. 3.

6. Clamp the metal and a piece of ⅜ in. diameter rod tightly in a vise as shown in Fig. 2. Use soft vise jaws to avoid damage to the metal. The penciled lines should appear on the outside after the metal is bent.

7. Hammer the metal with a mallet or a hard block of wood and a hammer so that it folds around the rod until it touches the vise jaw. The short center line should be exactly over the center of the rod as shown in Fig. 3.

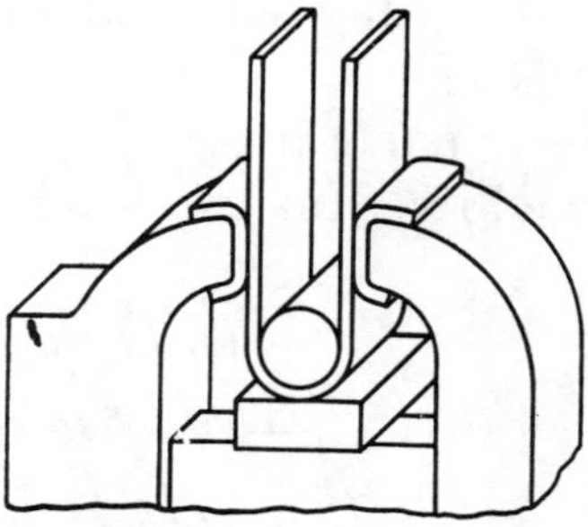

FIG. 4.

8. Remove the metal from the vise, invert, and clamp the two ends between the vise jaws. Slowly close the vise until the metal takes a U shape as in Fig. 4.

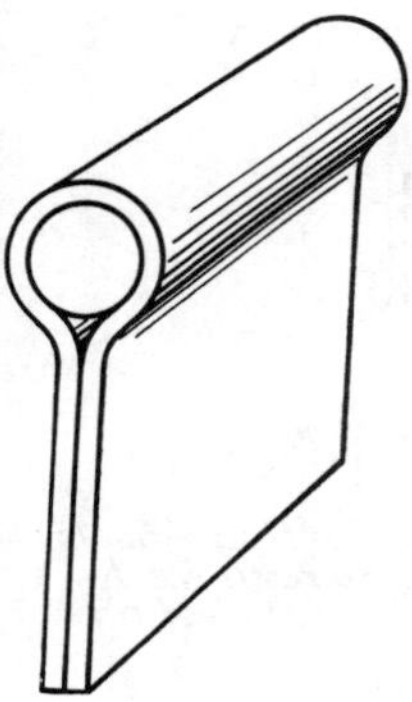

FIG. 5.

9. With the 3/8 in. rod lying in the lower part of the U, and with a suitable metal block under the fitting to prevent its sliding down, slowly close the vise until the fitting takes the shape shown in Fig. 5. Use soft jaws on the vise to avoid damaging the material during this operation.

10. On each end, measure from the top of the curve a distance of 1 1/16 in. (1 13/16 minus 3/4 in.), and scribe a light line across the metal at right angles to the long center line. Prick-punch the intersection of these two lines lightly.

11. Set dividers to 3/4 in., and scribe a circle using the prick-punch mark as a center.

12. On the edge of the wide side of the fitting locate a point 3 3/64 in. above the center line of the hole. Scribe a line from this point tangent to the 3/4 in. radius arc.

13. Drill the hole, first with a pilot drill, then with a 3/8 in. drill.

14. Hack saw and file the fitting to the contour line. Finish with fine emery cloth. Figure 6 shows the completed fitting.

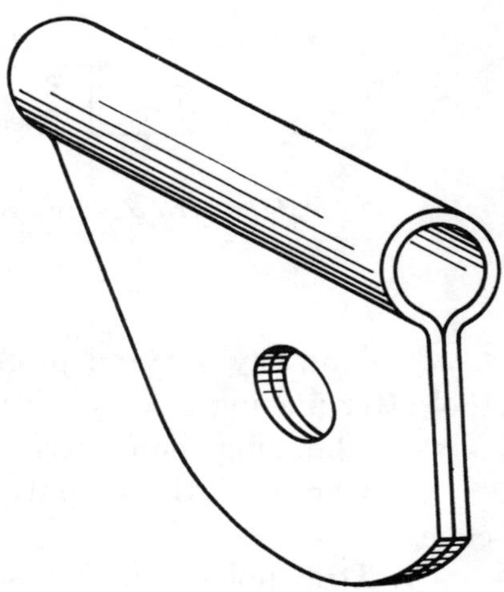

FIG. 6.

Project 3. Edge-burring Tool

OPERATIONS

1. Obtain two blanks of 0.049 in. chrome-molybdenum steel 6 1/4 by 2 in., and coat one side of one blank with layout dye.

2. Scribe a center line longitudinally across the metal.

3. Joggle the two pieces 3/32 in. off center at a point 4 in. from one end.

4. Locate, prick-punch, drill, and countersink holes 1 and 4, and rivet the two blanks together.

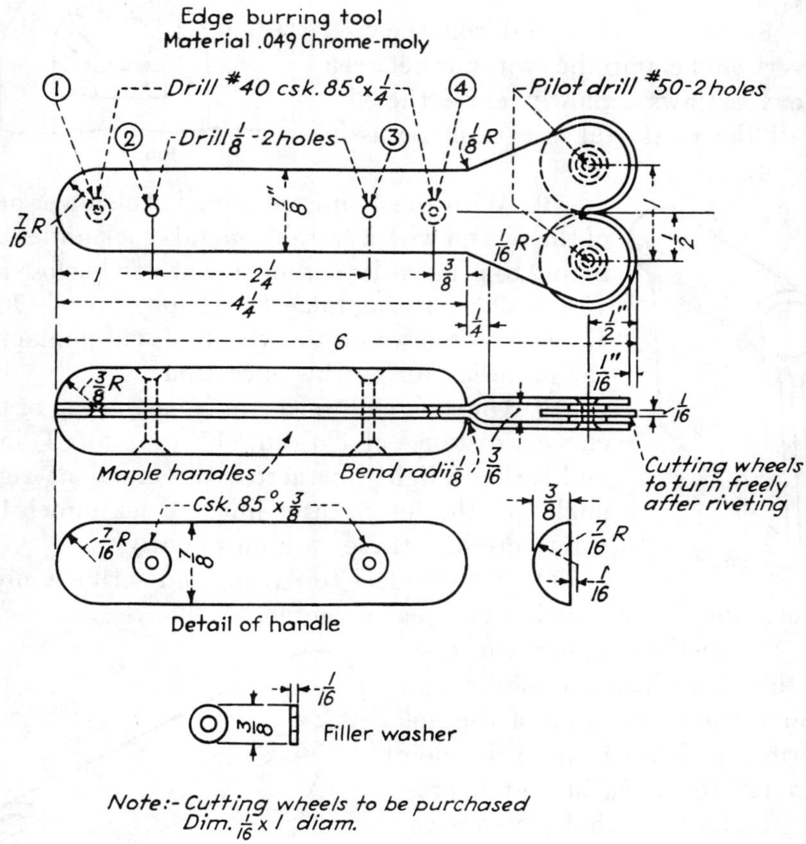

Fig. 1.

5. Now lay out and prick-punch the other four holes on the tool after placing a scrap piece of 3/16 in. metal in the forked end to avoid bending the material.

6. Complete the layout, cut to the contour, and finish the edges.

7. Drill holes 2 and 3 with a No. 40 drill and the cutting-wheel bearing holes with a No. 50 pilot drill.

8. Obtain two pieces of maple 1/2 by 1 by 4 in.

9. Clamp one piece to the metal handle, and draw the outline of the tool on the wood. Before removing the clamp, drill through for the rivets. Repeat the operation on the other piece of maple.

10. Cut the wood to the outline, countersink, and finish to shape.

11. Rivet the two pieces to the handle with 1/8 by 1 in., flat, countersunk-head 2S rivets and finish with sandpaper and two coats of shellac.

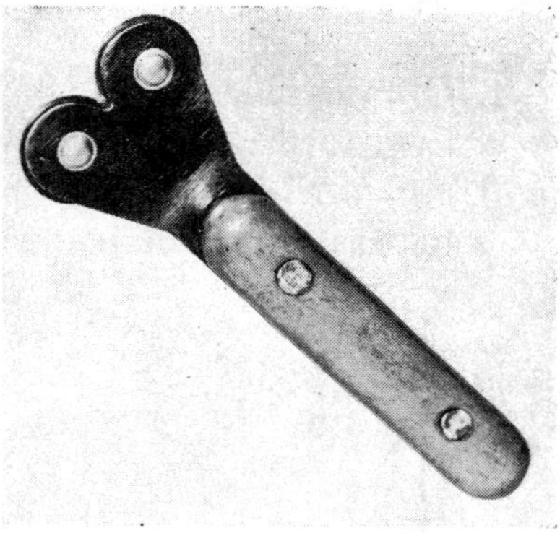

Fig. 2.

NOTE: The cutting wheels may be obtained from a knife sharpener which can be purchased at any 5 and 10 cent store. Select one with 1 in. diameter wheels. Any commercial spacer washers can be used, or they can be made of 1/16 in. steel. No dimensions are

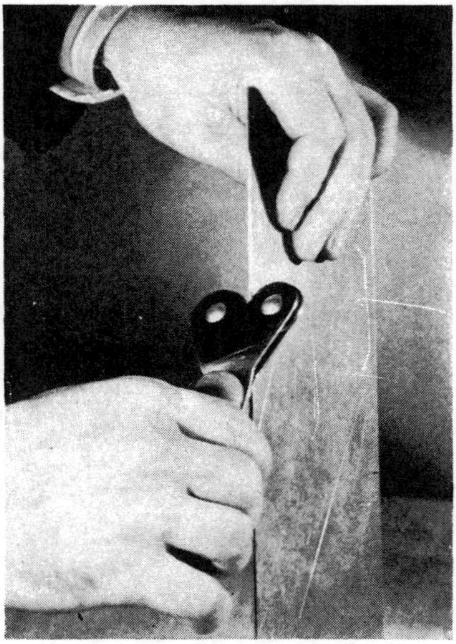

Fig. 3.

given for the bearing hole, as this will vary with the make of knife sharpener purchased. After the wheels have been riveted in place, the space between them should not be greater than 0.005 in.

Project 4. Louver Plate

Operations

1. Obtain a blank of 2S-¼H aluminum 0.041 by 4¾ by 4¼ in.

2. Lay out the points at which the four ⅛ in. relief holes will be drilled. All layout work must be done with a soft lead pencil to avoid scratching the material.

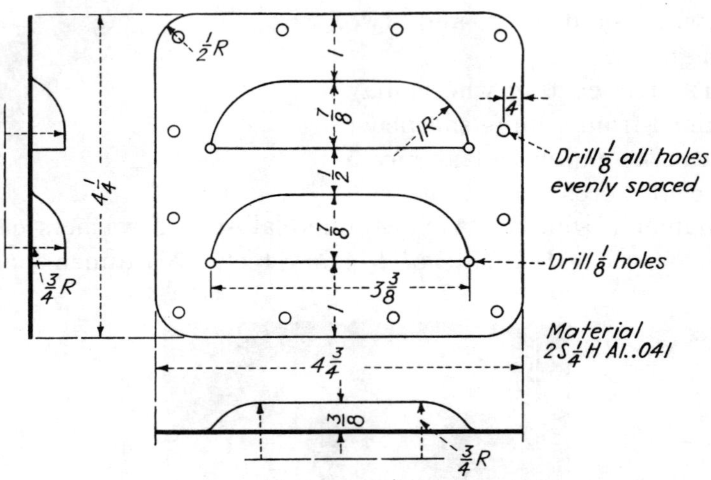

Louver plate

Fig. 1.

3. Draw two lines connecting these four holes to serve as cutting lines.

4. Prick-punch the metal, and drill the holes.

5. Cut on connecting lines with a metal-cutting coping saw.

6. Attach a blank to the forming block with a clamp faced with masking tape to avoid scratches.

7. Bump the metal into form with a maple punch and a hammer. This work must be done carefully so that the metal will not be cracked.

8. Remove the work from the form, and finish the surface with fine emery cloth and oil. If desired, a highly polished finish may be obtained with a cloth buffing wheel and rouge.

9. Locate and drill rivet holes along edge.

Project 5. Shock-absorber Fairing

The first drawing in this group shows the flat layout for all four parts. In an aircraft plant this drawing would not be shown, but it is included here as an aid to school classes. Note that on

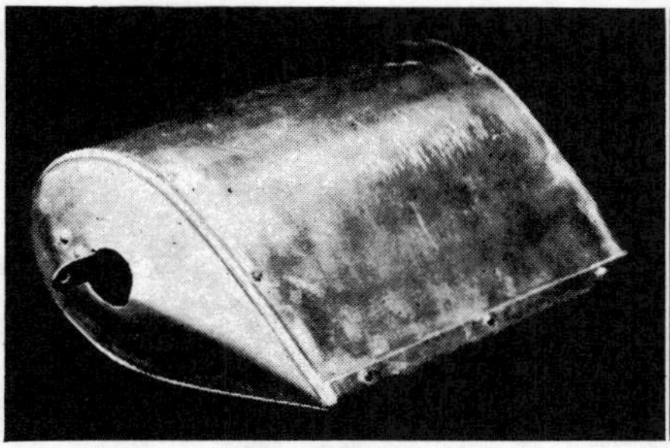

FIG. 1.

FIG. 2.

These are two views of a streamlined fairing cover that may be used as a shock-absorber housing on a Piper Cub. The following drawings are presented in order that this may be used as a school project. It will be found that a great variety of typical sheetmetal practices are involved in this project.

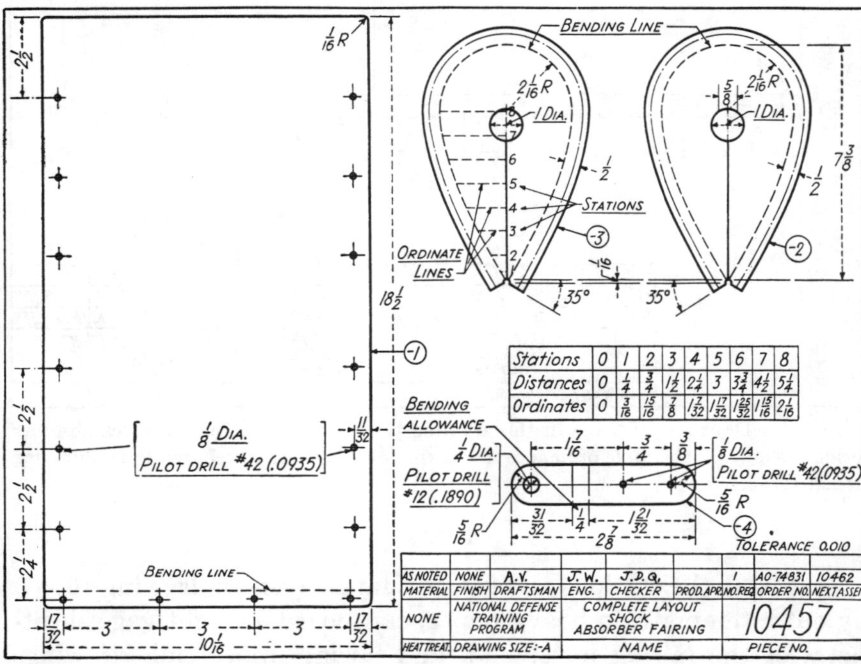

FIG. 3.—Drawing #10457. This drawing shows the complete flat layout of all parts of the shock absorber fairing. These measurements must be developed by the mechanic for each of the various parts and may be obtained from the detailed drawings.

drawing #10457 the parts are given dash numbers, —1, —2, —3 and —4. Yet on subsequent drawings these parts have numbers of their own. Thus the cover, shown in drawing #10458, is the same as that shown in the flat layout as part 10457-1.

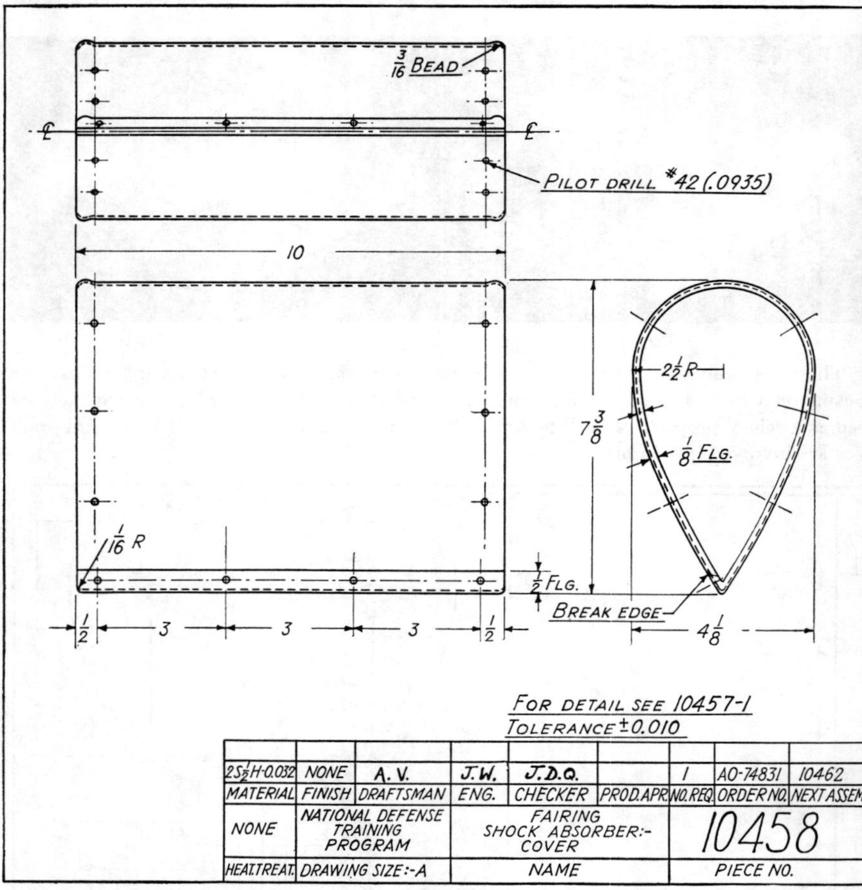

FIG. 4.—Drawing #10458. In this drawing the skin or cover for the shock-absorber fairing is shown. The table ordinance in drawing #10457 must be referred to in obtaining the flat layout.

Ends

1. Using the stations and the ordinates given on drawing 10457, lay out a template on heavy paper, cardboard, or light-gage sheet-metal of the fairing lower end, and fairing upper end, drawings 10459 and 10460, respectively. Carefully cut a template to the exact contour.

2. Transfer the outline to two blanks of 0.032 in. 2S-0 (dead-soft aluminum) sheet material.

3. Place one blank between the upper and the lower portions of the forming blocks, and clamp the blocks together slowly.

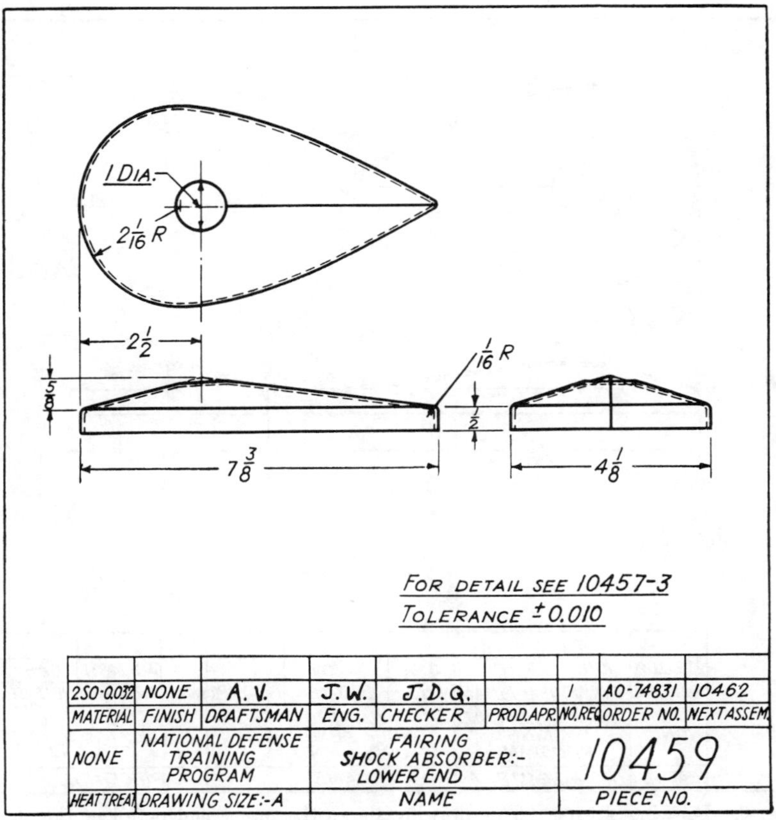

Fig. 5.—Drawing #10459. This drawing shows three views of the lower end of the shock-absorber fairing. This part may be made over maple, masonite, or steel forming blocks.

A large vise or a press may be used for this operation. Before clamping make sure that the metal is centered on the blocks and that a uniform amount of metal extends on the sides (see Fig. 86 in Chap. 9).

4. Using a mallet and a maple forming tool draw the material down evenly until a flange of at least ½ in. depth is obtained.

5. Mark off a line ½ in. below the bending line, and cut away the surplus material. Dress the edges smooth and true.

6. Locate the center of 1 in. hole, and cut and dress the edge to a smooth finish.

7. Repeat operations 3 to 6 on the second blank. In addition, cut out the notch for the clip as shown in drawing 10460.

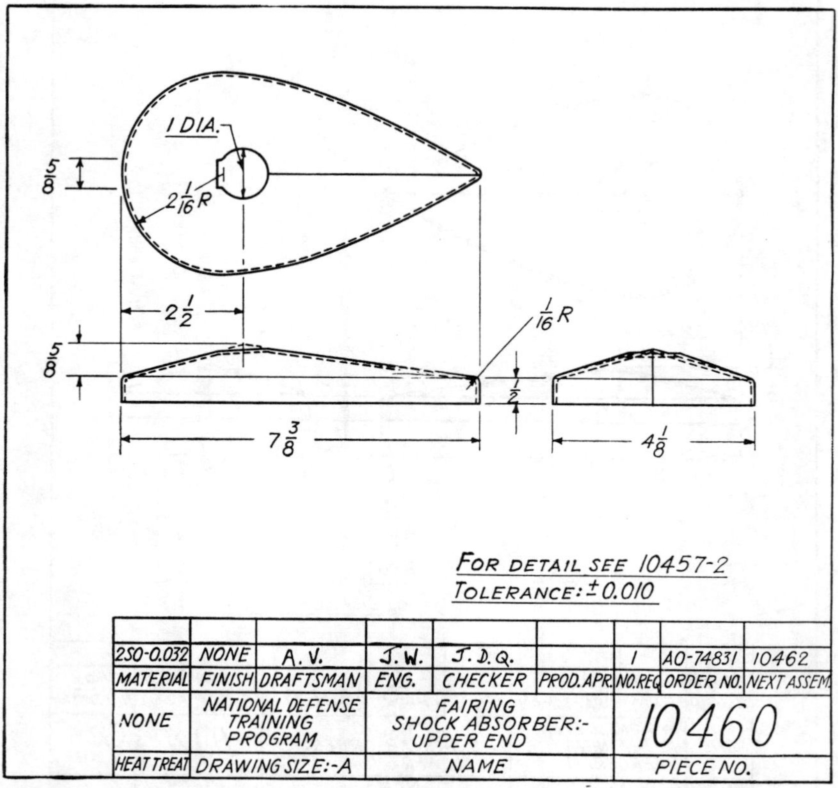

Fig. 6.—Drawing #10460. This drawing shows the upper end detail of the shock-absorber fairing. It is made in a similar manner to the lower end with the exception of the notch for the clip in the center hole.

8. Lay out the attachment clip shown in drawing 10461 (flat layout on drawing 10457-4). Cut to the contour, drill, bend, and rivet to the upper end as shown in assembly drawing 10462.

Cover

1. Lay out the cover (drawing 10458) on a piece of 0.032 in. 2S-½H sheet material. The flat layout of this part is given on drawing 10457.

2. Cut the material to size on a squaring shear, and finish the corners with a small radius as shown.

3. Locate and drill all pilot holes.

4. Form the cover to the shape of the end pieces on slip rolls.

5. Fold the end over on the bending line using a bending brake or a bar folder.

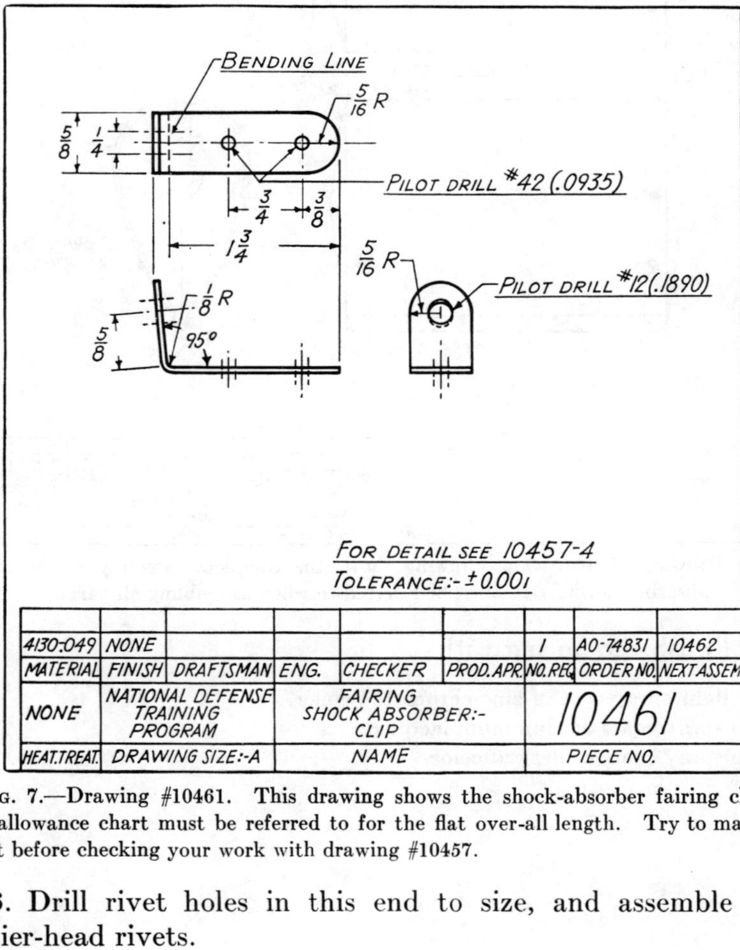

Fig. 7.—Drawing #10461. This drawing shows the shock-absorber fairing clip. A bend-allowance chart must be referred to for the flat over-all length. Try to make this layout before checking your work with drawing #10457.

6. Drill rivet holes in this end to size, and assemble with brazier-head rivets.

Assembly

1. Assemble the upper end to the cover, using brazier-head rivets.

2. Assemble the lower end to the cover, using Parker-Kalon sheetmetal screws. A No. 39 drill must be used for these holes.

3. Install rubber grommets in the ends. The one for the upper end must be modified to fit around the clip as shown in drawing 10462.

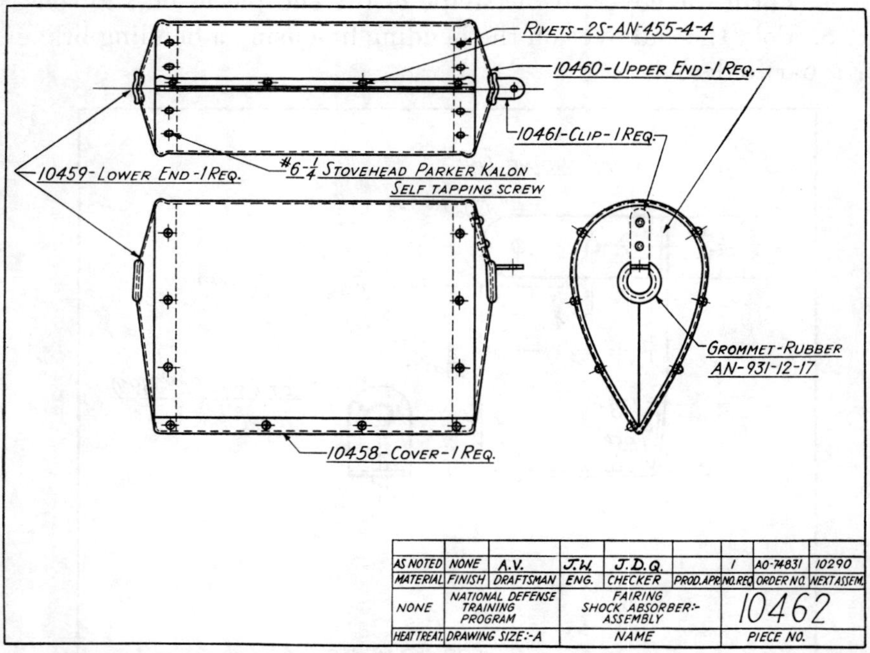

FIG. 8.—Drawing #10462. This drawing shows the complete assembly of the shock-absorber fairing. It must be referred to when assembling all parts.

4. Finish the fairing with

One light spray coat of zinc chromate primer.
Two spray coats of aluminum lacquer.
Two spray coats of desired color.

APPENDIX I

NOMENCLATURE

The following definitions should be known by all mechanics. They are taken from Report 474, National Advisory Committee for Aeronautics, and are the official terms used in this country.

aileron. A hinged or movable portion of an airplane wing, the primary function of which is to impress a rolling motion on the airplane. It is usually part of the trailing edge of a wing.

aircraft. Any weight-carrying device designed to be supported by the air, either by buoyancy or by dynamic action.

airfoil. Any surface, such as an airplane wing, aileron, or rudder, designed to obtain reaction from the air through which it moves.

airplane. A mechanically driven fixed-wing aircraft, heavier than air, which is supported by the dynamic reaction of the air against its wings.

airworthiness. The quality of an aircraft denoting its fitness and safety for operation in the air under normal flying conditions.

altimeter. An instrument that measures the elevation of an aircraft above a given datum plane.

amphibian. An airplane designed to rise from and alight on either land or water.

artificial horizon. (1) A device that indicates the attitude of an aircraft with respect to the true horizon. (2) A substitute for a natural horizon, such as a liquid level, pendulum, or gyroscope, incorporated in a navigating instrument.

autogiro. A type of rotor plane whose support in the air is chiefly derived from airfoils rotated about an approximately vertical axis by aerodynamic forces and in which the lift on opposite sides of the plane of symmetry is equalized by the vertical oscillation of the blades.

automatic pilot. An automatic control mechanism for keeping an aircraft in level flight and on a set course. Sometimes called *gyro-pilot*, *mechanical pilot*, or *robot pilot*.

bank. The position of an airplane when its lateral axis is inclined to the horizontal. A right bank is the position with the lateral axis inclined downward to the right.

beaching gear. An arrangement of wheels to be attached to the hull of a seaplane to permit handling ashore.

biplane. An airplane with two main supporting surfaces placed one above the other.

cabane. An arrangement of struts used for bracing on an aircraft.

camber. The rise of the curve of an airfoil section, usually expressed as the ratio of the departure of the curve from a straight line joining the extremities of the curve to the length of this straight line. *Upper camber* refers to the upper surface; *lower camber* to the lower surface; and *mean camber* to the mean line of the section. Camber is positive when the departure is upward and negative when it is downward.

cap strip. A continuous member on the outer edge of a wing rib.

center of pressure of an airfoil. The point in the chord of an airfoil, prolonged if necessary, which is at the intersection of the chord and the line of action of the resultant air force.

center section. The central panel of a wing; in the case of a continuous wing or any wing having no central panel, the limits of the center section are arbitrarily defined by the location of points of attachment to the cabane struts or fuselage.

chord. An arbitrary datum line from which the ordinates and angles of an airfoil are measured. It is usually the straight line tangent to the lower surface at two points, the straight line joining the ends of the mean line, or the straight line between the leading and trailing edges.

compression ratio. The ratio of the volume of the gas in an engine cylinder at the beginning of the compression stroke to its volume at the end of the stroke.

control cable. The line of wire or stranded cable leading from the control levers to the control surfaces or interconnecting the control surfaces.

control column. A lever having a rotatable wheel mounted at its upper end for operating the longitudinal and lateral control surfaces of an airplane. This type of control is called *wheel control.*

control stick. The vertical lever by means of which the longitudinal and lateral control surfaces of an airplane are operated. The elevator is operated by a fore-and-aft movement of the stick; the ailerons, by a side-to-side movement.

control surface. A movable airfoil designed to be rotated or otherwise moved by the pilot in order to change the attitude of the aircraft.

controls. A general term applied to the means provided to enable the pilot to control the speed, direction of flight, attitude, power, etc., of an aircraft.

cowling. A removable covering, usually around an engine or cockpit.

dihedral angle. The acute angle between a line perpendicular to the plane of symmetry and the projection of the wing axis on a plane perpendicular to the longitudinal axis of the airplane. If the wing axis is not approximately a straight line, the angle is measured from the projection of a line joining the intersection of the wing axis with the plane of symmetry and the aerodynamic center of the half-wing on either side of the plane of symmetry.

directional gyro. A gyroscopic instrument for indicating direction, containing a free gyroscope which holds its position in azimuth and thus indicates angular deviation from the course.

displacement, engine. The total volume swept by the pistons of all the cylinders during one complete stroke of each piston.

dope, airplane. The liquid material applied to the fabric surfaces of airplanes to increase their strength, to produce tautness by shrinking, and to act as a filter for maintaining airtightness.

dope, fuel. Any material added to the fuel in small quantities for the purpose of preventing detonation.

drag. The component of the total air force on a body parallel to the relative wind.

induced drag. That part of the drag induced by the lift.

parasite drag. That portion of the drag of an aircraft exclusive of the induced drag of the wings.

profile drag. The difference between the total wing drag and the induced drag.

profile drag, effective. The difference between the total wing drag and the induced drag of a wing with the same geometric aspect ratio but elliptically loaded.

drag strut. A fore-and-aft compression member of the internal bracing system of an aircraft.

elevator. A movable auxiliary airfoil, the function of which is to impress a pitching moment on the aircraft. It is usually hinged to the stabilizer.

emergency flotation gear. A device attached to a landplane to provide buoyancy in case of an emergency landing on the water.

engine:

double-row radial engine. An engine having two rows of cylinders arranged radially around a common crankshaft. The corresponding front and rear cylinders may or may not be in line.

supercharged engine. An engine with a compressor for increasing the pressure of the air or mixture charge taken into the cylinder beyond that inducted normally at the existing atmospheric pressure.

exhaust-collector ring. A circular duct into which the exhaust gases from the cylinders of a radial engine are discharged.

fairing. An auxiliary member or structure whose primary function is to reduce the drag of the part to which it is fitted.

fin. A fixed or adjustable airfoil, attached to an aircraft approximately parallel to the plane of symmetry, to afford directional stability; for example, tail fin, skid fin, etc.

fitting. A generic term for any small part used in the structure of an airplane or airship. If without qualification, a metal part is usually understood. It may refer to other parts, such as fabric fittings.

flap. A hinged or pivoted airfoil forming the rear portion of an airfoil, used to vary the effective camber.

split flap. A hinged plate forming the rear upper or lower portion of an airfoil. The lower portion may be deflected downward to give increased lift and drag; the upper portion may be raised over a portion of the wing for the purpose of lateral control.

float. A completely enclosed, watertight structure attached to an aircraft to give it buoyancy and stability when in contact with water.

inboard stabilizing float. A stabilizing float placed relatively close to the main float or hull.

outboard (or wing-tip) stabilizing float. A stabilizing float placed relatively far out from the main float or hull, usually at or near the tip of the wing.

single float. A single central float fitted under a seaplane and usually requiring two stabilizing floats to give adequate stability and complete the float system.

stabilizing (or side) float. A float used in addition to a single float or hull and intended to provide lateral stability while the seaplane or flying boat is at rest on the water.

flutter. An oscillation of definite period but unstable character set up in any part of an aircraft by a momentary disturbance and maintained by a combination of the aerodynamic, inertial, and elastic characteristics of the member itself.

flying boat. A form of seaplane whose main body or hull provides flotation.

fuselage. The body, of approximately streamline form, to which the wings and tail unit of an airplane are attached.

monocoque fuselage. A fuselage construction that relies on the strength of the skin or shell to carry either the shear or the load due to bending moments. Monocoques may be divided into three classes (reinforced shell, semimonocoque, and monocoque), and different portions of the same fuselage may belong to any one of these classes. The reinforced shell has the skin reinforced by a complete framework of structural members. The semimonocoque has the skin reinforced by longerons and vertical bulkheads but has no diagonal web members. The monocoque has as its only reinforcement vertical bulkheads formed of structural members.

gap. The distance separating two adjacent wings of a multiplane.

glider. An aircraft heavier than air, similar to an airplane but without a power plant.

ground loop. An uncontrollable violent turn of an airplane while taxying or during the landing or take-off run.

gyro horizon. A gyroscopic instrument that indicates the lateral and longitudinal attitude of the airplane by simulating the natural horizon.

helicopter. A type of rotor plane whose support in the air is normally derived from airfoils mechanically rotated about an approximately vertical axis.

horn. A shorter lever attached to a control surface of an aircraft, to which the operating wire or rod is connected.

landplane. An airplane designed to rise from and alight on the land.

leading edge. The foremost edge of an airfoil or a propeller blade.

longeron. A principal longitudinal member of the framing of an airplane fuselage or nacelle, usually continuous across a number of points of support.

maneuverability. That quality in an aircraft which determines the rate at which its attitude and direction of flight can be changed.

mixture control, altitude. A device on the carburetor for regulating the weight proportions of air and fuel supplied to the engine at different altitudes.

nacelle. An enclosed shelter for personnel or for power plant. A nacelle is usually shorter than a fuselage and does not carry the tail unit.

oleo gear. A type of oil-damping device that depends on the flow of oil through an orifice for its shock-absorbing effect in a landing gear.

ornithopter. A form of aircraft heavier than air, deriving its chief support and propelling force from flapping wings.

overhang. (1) One-half the difference in span of any two main supporting surfaces of an airplane. The overhang is positive when the upper of the two main supporting surfaces has the larger span. (2) The distance from the outer strut attachment to the tip of a wing.

pitch of a propeller:

effective pitch. The distance an aircraft advances along its flight path for one revolution of the propeller.

geometrical pitch. The distance an element of a propeller would advance in one revolution if it were moving along a helix having an angle equal to its blade angle.

pitching. Angular motion about the lateral axis.

pitot tube. A cylindrical tube with an open end pointed upstream, used in measuring impact pressure.

pitot-static tube. A parallel or coaxial combination of a pitot and a static tube. The difference between the impact pressure and the static pressure is a function of the velocity of flow past the tube.

pitot-venturi tube. A combination of a pitot and a venturi tube.

propeller. Any device for propelling a craft through a fluid, such as water or air; especially a device having blades that, when mounted on a power-driven shaft, produce a thrust by their action on the fluid.

rate-of-climb indicator. An instrument that indicates the rate of ascent or descent of an aircraft.

roll. An angular displacement about an axis parallel to the longitudinal axis of an aircraft.

rudder. A hinged or movable auxiliary airfoil on an aircraft, the function of which is to impress a yawing moment on the aircraft.

rudder bar. The foot bar by means of which the control cables leading to the rudder are operated.

rudder pedals. The foot pedals by means of which the controls leading to the rudder are operated.

sailplane. A performance-type glider.

seaplane. An airplane designed to rise from and alight on the water.

servo control. A control devised to reinforce the pilot's effort by an aerodynamic or mechanical relay.

slot. The nozzle-shaped passage through a wing whose primary object is to improve the flow conditions at high angles of attack. It is usually near the leading edge and formed by a main and an auxiliary airfoil.

span. The maximum distance, measured parallel to the lateral axis, from tip to tip of an airfoil, of an airplane wing inclusive of ailerons, or of a stabilizer inclusive of elevator.

spinner. A fairing of approximately conical or paraboloidal shape, which is fitted coaxially with the propeller hub and revolves with the propeller.

sponson. A protuberance from a seaplane hull designed to increase the beam or give lateral stability at rest.

stability. That property of a body which causes it, when its equilibrium is disturbed, to develop forces or moments tending to restore the original condition.

automatic stability. Stability dependent upon movable control surfaces automatically operated by mechanical means.

directional stability. Stability with reference to disturbances about the normal axis of an aircraft, *i.e.*, disturbances that tend to cause yawing.

dynamic stability. That property of an aircraft which causes it, when its state of steady flight is disturbed, to damp the oscillations set up by the restoring forces and moments and gradually return to its original state.

inherent stability. Stability of an aircraft due solely to the disposition and arrangement of its fixed parts, *i.e.*, that property which causes it, when disturbed, to return to its normal attitude of flight without the use of the controls or the interposition of any mechanical device.

lateral stability. Stability with reference to disturbances about the longitudinal axis, *i.e.*, disturbances involving rolling or sideslipping. The term *lateral stability* is sometimes used to include both directional and lateral stability, since these cannot be entirely separated in flight.

longitudinal stability. Stability with reference to disturbances in the plane of symmetry, *i.e.*, disturbances involving pitching and variation of longitudinal and normal velocities.

static stability. That property of an aircraft which causes it, when its state of steady flight is disturbed, to develop forces and moments tending to restore its original condition.

stabilizer, airplane. Any airfoil whose primary function is to increase the stability of an aircraft. It usually refers to the fixed horizontal tail surface of an airplane, as distinguished from the fixed vertical surface.

stabilizer, stub-wing. A projection from the side of the central hull of a flying boat intended to increase the buoyancy and stability of a flying boat while the boat is at rest and to increase the hydrodynamic lift during the take-off. It is an integral part of the hull and usually takes the form of a stumpy airfoil or a stub wing.

stagger. A term referring to the longitudinal position of the axes of two wings of an airplane. Stagger of any section is measured by the acute angle between a line joining the wing axes and a line perpendicular to the upper wing chord, both lines lying in a plane parallel to the plane of symmetry. The stagger is positive when the upper wing is in advance of the lower.

static tube. A cylindrical tube with a closed end and a number of small openings normal to the axis, pointed upstream, used to measure static pressure.

step. A break in the form of the bottom of a float or hull, designed to diminish resistance, to lessen the suction effects, and to improve control over longitudinal attitude.

streamline. The path of a particle of a fluid, supposedly continuous, commonly taken relative to a solid body past which the fluid is moving; generally used only of such flows as are not eddying.

streamline form. The form of a body so shaped that the flow about it tends to be a streamline flow.

strut. A compression member of a truss frame.

oleo strut. A shock-absorbing telescopic strut in which an oleo gear is incorporated.

supercharge. To supply an engine with more air or mixture than would be inducted normally at the prevailing atmospheric pressure. The term *supercharged* is generally used to refer to conditions at altitudes where the pressure in the intake manifold is partly or completely restored to that existing under normal operation at sea level.

supercharger. A pump for supplying the engine with a greater weight of air or mixture than would normally be inducted at the prevailing atmospheric pressure.

sweepback. The acute angle between a line perpendicular to the plane of symmetry and the plan projection of a reference line in the wing.

tab. An auxiliary airfoil attached to a control surface for the purpose of reducing the control force or trimming the aircraft.

tachometer. An instrument that measures in revolutions per minute the rate at which the crankshaft of an engine turns.

tail, airplane. The rear part of an airplane, usually consisting of a group of stabilizing planes, or fins, to which are attached certain controlling surfaces such as elevators and rudders; also called *empennage.*

tail boom. A spar or outrigger connecting the tail surfaces and the main supporting surfaces.

tail-heavy. The condition of an airplane in which the tail tends to sink when the longitudinal control is released in any given attitude of normal flight.

tail skid. A skid for supporting the tail of an airplane on the ground.

tail surface. A stabilizing or control surface in the tail of an aircraft.

tank, service. A fixed fuel tank near each power unit, into which fuel from other tanks is pumped and from which the fuel supplying the engine is drawn.

trailing edge. The rearmost edge of an airfoil or of a propeller blade.

turn-and-bank indicator. An instrument combining in one case a turn indicator and a lateral inclinometer.

turn indicator. An instrument for indicating the existence and approximate magnitude of angular velocity about the normal axis of an aircraft.

venturi tube (or venturi). A short tube of varying cross section. The flow through the venturi causes a pressure drop in the smallest section, the amount of the drop being a function of the velocity of flow.

washin. A warp of an airplane wing giving an increase of the angle of attack toward the tip.

washout. A warp of an airplane wing giving a decrease of the angle of attack toward the tip.

weight, gross (airplane). The total weight of an airplane when fully loaded.

window, inspection. A small transparent window fitted in the envelope of a balloon or airship, or in the wing or fuselage of an airplane, to allow inspection of the interior.

wind tunnel. An apparatus producing an artificial wind or air stream, in which objects are placed for investigating the air flow about them and the aerodynamic forces exerted on them.

wing. A general term applied to the airfoil, or one of the airfoils, designed to develop a major part of the lift of a heavier-than-air craft.

wing-heavy, right or left. The condition of an airplane whose right or left wing tends to sink when the lateral control is released in any given attitude of normal flight.

wing rib. A chord-wise member of the wing structure of an airplane, used to give the wing section its form and to transmit the load from the fabric to the spars.

compression wing rib. A heavy rib designed to perform the function of an ordinary wing rib and also to act as a strut opposing the pull of the wires in the internal drag truss.

former (or false) wing rib. An incomplete rib, frequently consisting only of a strip of wood extending from the leading edge to the front spar, which is used to assist in maintaining the form of the wing where the curvature of the airfoil section is sharpest.

wing section. A cross section of a wing parallel to the plane of symmetry or to a specified reference plane.

wing spar. A principal span-wise member of the wing structure of an airplane.

wire:

antidrag wire. A wire intended primarily to resist the forces acting forward in the chord direction. It is generally enclosed in the wing.

drag wire. A wire intended primarily to resist the forces acting backward in the chord direction. It is generally enclosed in the wing.

landing wire. A wire or cable that braces the wing against the forces opposite to the normal direction of the lift.

lift wire. A wire or cable that braces the wings against the lift force; sometimes called *flying wire.*

stagger wire. A wire connecting the upper and lower wings of an airplane and lying in a plane substantially parallel to the plane of symmetry; also called *incidence wire.*

yaw. An angular displacement about an axis parallel to the normal axis of an aircraft.

APPENDIX II

TOOL REQUIREMENTS

In all aviation jobs, except those in the Army and Navy, a mechanic must have his own tools. The number of tools required for a beginner varies from factory to factory and from one airport to another. It also varies according to different departments within a plant or a repair station.

A mechanic applying for a job has a real advantage if he can claim a well-equipped toolbox. He has a still greater asset if he knows how to use his tools. It is suggested that mechanics who are now in training buy a toolbox and gradually acquire the tools that they will need at a later date.

The following lists are of tools required by the Lockheed Aircraft Co. of Burbank, Calif. Other factories may require more or less tools, but these lists for various departments are representative of most plants throughout the country.

FACTORY TOOLS

Tools Required for Elementary Sheetmetal Work

6 in. flexible scale (1/64 in. dimensions)
6 ft. flexible rule
12 in. scale (1/64 in. dimensions) and square head
Medium-sized screw driver
Ball-peen hammer, 6 oz.
Scribe
Diagonal cutters
Tin snips (3 in. combination)
3/32 straight-shank punch
Soft lead pencil
Toolbox

Tools Required for Cabinetmakers and Patternmakers

1 hammer, claw
1 plane, block
1 plane, jointer
1 set chisels, wood
1 combination square with protractor, 12 in.
1 shrink scale, 24 in.
1 standard scale, 24 in.
1 spoke shaver
1 pair dividers, small
1 set pinch dogs
1 set fillet nibbers
1 gage, radius
1 set gages
1 nail set
1 combination square, 6 in.
1 saw, cross-cut

1 pair trammel points
1 scriber
1 pair dividers, large
1 carpenter square, 2 ft.
1 set Russell Jennings wood bits

Tools Required by Drop-hammer Operators

1 pair snips, tin
1 micrometer, 1 in.
1 hammer, claw
1 mallet, rawhide
1 mallet, fiber
1 mallet, pyralin
1 wrench, crescent, 8 in.
1 pair dividers, 6 in.
1 pair pliers, 6 in.
6 chisels, cold, assorted
2 scrapers, bearing
1 combination square with protractor, 12 in.
2 scrapers, end
1 scale, 6 in.
1 flexible scale, 6 ft.
1 scriber
1 pair safety-toe shoes

Electricians—Airplane and Radio

1 pair diagonals
1 pair pliers, slip joint, 4 in.
2 screw drivers, small, 3 in.
1 screw driver, medium, 6 in.
1 screw driver, large, 12 in.
1 hack saw, midget
1 hack saw
1 hand drill, ¼ in.
1 set end wrenches, ¼ to ⅝ in.
1 screw driver, offset, 4 in.
1 set Spin-tight socket wrenches
1 pocket knife
1 pair pliers, long nose
1 pair snips, tin
1 hammer, ball-peen, small
1 hammer, ball-peen, medium
1 awl
1 scale, 6 in.
1 flexible scale, 6 ft.
1 center punch

Tools Required by Final Assemblers

1 set open-end wrenches, ⅜ to 1 in.
1 set sockets ⅜ in. shank, 7/16 to 1 in.
1 set box wrenches, ⅜ to ¾ in.
1 pair pliers, gas
1 pair pliers, long nose
1 pair diagonals, 4 in.
1 pair snips, tin, 10 in.
1 hack-saw frame
1 hand drill
1 hack saw, midget
1 hammer, ball-peen, 6 oz.
1 hammer, ball-peen, 8 oz.
2 screw drivers, 4 in. and 6 in.
1 scale, 6 in.
1 set drift punches, small
1 center punch
1 taper punch, long, ¼ in., at small end
1 steel tape, 72 in.

Tools Required by Skin Fitters and Frame Builders

1 chisel, cold
2 pair snips, Klenk airplane, right and left
1 hammer, ball-peen, 6 oz.
2 screw drivers, 4 and 8 in.
1 pair pliers, slip joint, 6 in.
1 pair pliers, diagonal, 7 in.
1 tape, steel, 72 in.
1 flexible scale, 6 in.
1 set Spin tight socket wrenches
1 set driftpins, 3/32, ⅛, 5/32, 3/16, ¼ in.

Tools Required by Machinists

1 flexible scale, 3 in.
1 flexible scale, 6 in.
1 scale, 12 in.
1 micrometer 1 in.
1 micrometer, 2 in.
1 set inside micrometers, 2 to 8 in.
1 set calipers, inside
1 set gage feelers
1 gage, drill grinding
1 screw driver, large, 10 in.
1 set calipers, outside
1 pair dividers, small
1 pair dividers, large
1 test indicator
1 combination square with protractor, 12 in.
1 gage, depth
1 gage, thread
1 screw driver, small, 4 in.
1 hammer, 8 oz.
1 prick punch

Tools Required by Metal Fitters

2 hammers, ball-peen, 8 and 32 oz.
1 pair pliers, slip-joint, 6 in.
1 screw driver, 8 in.
1 pair scribers
1 scale, 6 in.
1 scale, 12 in.
1 set combination square with protractor, 12 in.
1 protractor, bevel
1 pair dividers
1 micrometer, 1 in.

Tools Required by Riveters

1 each screw drivers, 4, 8, 12 in.
1 pair pliers, common
1 set Spin-tight socket wrenches
1 each hammers, ball-peen, 8 and 12 oz.
1 set driftpins, 3/32, 1/8, 5/32, 3/16, 1/4 in.
1 scale, 6 in.
1 chisel, cold, small
1 pair Klenk airplane snips, right and left
1 steel flexible scale, 6 ft.
1 pair snips, tin
1 pair pliers, diagonal cutters

Tools Required by Sheetmetal Workers

1 scriber
1 rule, 6 in.
1 rule, 6 ft.
1 mallet, as needed
1 combination square with protractor, 12 in.
2 pairs dividers, 6 and 10 in.
1 pair micrometers, 1 in.
1 pair pliers
1 each screw drivers, 3, 8, 14 in.
2 wrenches, crescent, 6 and 10 in.
1 pair Klenk airplane snips, right and left
1 pair snips, Wiss, 18 in.
1 hack-saw frame
1 set Spin-tight socket wrenches
Hammers and dollies (finishing), ball-peen, 8 and 16 oz.

Tools Required by Welders

1 pair welding goggles
1 hack saw
1 screw driver, 4 in.
1 screw driver, 10 in.
2 pairs pliers, slip-joint, 6 in.
1 chisel, cold
1 hammer, ball-peen, 8 oz.
1 scale, 6 in.
1 wrench, crescent, 10 in.

AIRLINE TOOLS

The following list is of tools required by American Airlines. It is presented here as an indication of the tools required by large lines. Preceding the list is a copy of a memorandum concerning tool requirements that was issued by the Supervisor of Apprentice Mechanics.

An excellent indication of the ability of an aircraft mechanic is his selection, use, and care of tools. A good mechanic understands the importance and value of good tools and realizes that by using inferior tools a high standard of workmanship cannot be obtained.

It is particularly important for all apprentice mechanics to start with and maintain a set of good tools purchased from reputable vendors. A good tool manufacturer is not ashamed of his product, nor does he hesitate to place his name on his tools. Most manufacturers of good tools also guarantee the majority of their products.

Attached hereto are two lists of tool requirements for apprentice mechanics.

List 1 covers the minimum tool requirements for *all* apprentice mechanics. Exceptions and special requirements for those apprentice mechanics who are continually assigned to Instrument and Radio Overhaul Shops are also indicated on List 1. It shall be a requirement that *all* apprentice mechanics who have completed 30 days of service with the company as apprentice mechanics shall possess *all* required tools, as outlined on List 1.

At the completion of 12 months service with the company all *General* Apprentice Mechanics shall be required to possess all tools as outlined on List 2.

List 2 does not pertain to those apprentice mechanics who are continually assigned to Radio Maintenance and Overhaul Shops, Instrument Overhaul Shop, or Engine Overhaul Shop, in lieu of which such apprentice mechanics shall obtain those tools recommended by the respective General Foremen of such shops (in addition to List 1). These shall also be secured at the completion of 12 months of service with the company as apprentice mechanics.

Apprentice mechanics on a temporary basis shall be required to possess those tools recommended by their respective Foremen.

A copy of this memorandum shall be kept in each apprentice mechanic's notebook file.

List 1

Minimum Tool Requirements for Apprentice Mechanics

(Required at completion of 30 days' service as apprentice mechanic)

1 screw driver, 4 in. blade, pyralin
1 screw driver, 6 in. blade, pyralin
1 screw driver, 10 in. blade, pyralin
1 screw driver, offset, medium size
1 hammer, ball-peen, 2 or 3 oz.
1 hammer, ball-peen, 12 oz.
1 mallet, pyralin or equivalent, medium size (radio-shop apprentices excepted)
1 scale, flexible, 6 in., steel
1 hack-saw frame, 8 to 12 in. blade capacity
1 pliers, regular
1 pliers, water pump, new type
1 pliers, diagonal cutting, 7 in.
1 pliers, long nose, 6 in.
1 snapper, machine screw
1 center punch, 4 in.
1 chisel, cold, 3/8 in.
1 set pin punches, small sizes
1 set open-end wrenches, 3/8 to 1 in., by sixteenths
1 box wrench, 5/16 by 3/8 in.
1 box wrench, 3/8 by 7/16 in. (radio-shop apprentices excepted)
1 box wrench, 7/16 by 1/2 in. (radio-shop apprentices excepted)
1 set socket wrenches, 3/8 in. drive, 3/8 to 7/8 in., by sixteenths, including speeder, ratchet universal, extensions, etc. (radio-shop apprentices excepted)
1 ratchet, 7 in. handle, 1/2 in. drive (radio- and instrument-shop apprentices excepted)
1 universal, 1/2 in. drive (radio- and instrument-shop apprentices excepted)
1 extension, 1/2 in. drive by 6 in. (radio- and instrument-shop apprentices excepted)
1 socket, deep 6 point, spark plug, applicable size (radio- and instrument-shop apprentices excepted)
1 set midget socket wrenches, 3/16 to 7/16 in., by sixteenths
1 file, 4 in., flat mill
1 file, 8 in., vixen
1 each drill Nos. 21, 30, and 40, high speed (radio-shop apprentices excepted)

1 flashlight, 2 cell vaporproof, A.A. standard
1 flashlight, pen type (optional)
1 hand drill, ¼ in., maximum chuck size
1 crescent wrench, 6 in.
1 pair straight tin snips, medium size (radio-shop apprentices excepted)
1 pair dutch snips, left (radio- and instrument-shop apprentices excepted), when assigned to airplane overhaul
1 pair dutch snips, right (radio- and instrument-shop apprentices excepted), when assigned to airplane overhaul
1 file handle
1 putty knife
1 jackknife
1 thickness gage, 0.0015 to 0.025 in.
1 thickness gage, 0.010 and 0.075 in., Wright Aero Corp. (radio- and instrument-shop apprentices excepted)
1 toolbox, adequate size
3 screw drivers, jewelers, A.B.D. (instrument-shop apprentices only)
1 pair tweezers, 3C (instrument-shop apprentices only)
1 pair tweezers, heavy-duty (instrument-shop apprentices only)
1 eye loop, 2 in. focus (instrument-shop apprentices only)
1 hand puller, shop-made (instrument-shop apprentices only)
1 staking tool, shop-made (instrument-shop apprentices only)
1 suction cup, 2 in. (instrument-shop apprentices only)
1 suction cup, 1 in. (instrument-shop apprentices only)
1 screw driver, midget, 2¼ in. blade, Pyralin (radio-shop apprentices only)
1 pliers, midget utility (radio-shop apprentices only)
1 open-end wrench, ¼ by 5/16 in. (radio-shop apprentices only)
1 box wrench, ¼ by 5/16 in. (radio-shop apprentices only)
1 set wrenches, spin type, ¼ to ½ in., by sixteenths (radio-shop apprentices only)
1 file, 6 in., round mill (radio-shop apprentices only)
1 file, 10 in. half-round bastard (radio-shop apprentices only)
1 set drills, Nos. 60 to 1, inclusive, high speed (radio-shop apprentices only)
1 soldering iron (radio-shop apprentices only)

List 2

Minimum General Apprentice Mechanic Tool Requirements

(Required at completion of 12 months as apprentice mechanic)

1 scale, 36 in., flexible steel
1 tap wrench, T handle
1 center punch, automatic (optional)
1 punch, aligning, ⅛ to ½ in. by 8 in.
2 taper drift punches, medium size
1 cold chisel, large
1 cape chisel, medium
1 diamond chisel, medium
1 set Allen wrenches
1 crescent wrench, 10 or 12 in.
1 box wrench, ½ by 9/16 in.
1 set combination square, 12 in. scale, level, protractor center head, and square head
1 scriber
1 pair inside calipers, medium size
1 pair outside calipers, medium size
1 micrometer, 0 to 1 in.

1 combination, fine and coarse India stone
1 tap and drill gage
1 dental mirror
1 pair dividers
1 cable-splicing vise
1 cable-splicing spike
1 screw-pitch gage (optional)
1 set socket wrenches, $3/8$ to 1 in., by sixteenths, $1/2$ in. drive complete with speeder, universal, and hinge handle
1 each $7/16$, $1/2$, $9/16$, and $5/8$ in. 12 point universal sockets, $3/8$ in. drive
1 each $5/16$, $3/8$, $7/16$, and $1/2$ in. deep sockets, $3/8$ in. drive, 12 point (optional)
1 each 6-32, 8-32, 10-24 taps (optional)
4 C clamps, 2 in. size
2 C clamps, 3 in. size

INDEX

S

T

W

Z